Actions & Travels

First published 2022
Auckland University Press
University of Auckland
Private Bag 92019
Auckland 1142
New Zealand
www.aucklanduniversitypress.co.nz

© Anna Jackson, 2022

ISBN 978 1 86940 918 0

Published with the assistance
of Creative New Zealand

A catalogue record for this book is available
from the National Library of New Zealand

This book is copyright. Apart from fair dealing
for the purpose of private study, research, criticism
or review, as permitted under the Copyright Act,
no part may be reproduced by any process without
prior permission of the publisher. The moral
rights of the author have been asserted.

Book design by Katie Kerr

Cover image: Richard McWhannell, *Pig Island
Postal Service*, 2016, oil on canvas on board,
760 x 600 mm. Private collection, photograph
by Stephen Goodenough.

This book was printed on FSC® certified paper
Printed in China by Everbest Printing
Investment Ltd

Actions & Travels

How Poetry Works   Anna Jackson

AUCKLAND
UNIVERSITY
PRESS

'I think a poem, when it works, is an action of the mind captured on a page, and the reader, when he engages it, has to enter into that action. His mind repeats that action and travels again through the action, but it is a movement of yourself through a thought, through an activity of thinking, so by the time you get to the end you're different than you were at the beginning and you feel that difference.'

Anne Carson

CONTENTS

Introduction	*Reading & writing poetry*	1
Chapter One	*Simplicity & resonance*	9
Chapter Two	*The ornate & the sumptuous*	25
Chapter Three	*Concision, composition & the image*	41
Chapter Four	*Sprawl*	59
Chapter Five	*Form*	77
Chapter Six	*Argument & conversation*	103
Chapter Seven	*Conversations with the past*	121
Chapter Eight	*Poetry in a house on fire*	145
Chapter Nine	*Letters & odes*	165
Chapter Ten	*Poetry & the afterlife*	183

Writing suggestions	210
The poets	222
Notes and references	244
Acknowledgements	279
Index	280

INTRODUCTION

Reading & writing poetry

> This living hand, now warm and capable
> Of earnest grasping, would, if it were cold
> And in the icy silence of the tomb,
> So haunt thy days and chill thy dreaming nights
> That thou would wish thine own heart dry of blood
> So in my veins red life might stream again,
> And thou be conscience-calm'd – see here it is –
> I hold it towards you.

This short poem by John Keats is the most haunting representation I know of the power of poetry to reach out to another person, even after death. Is it an icy hand, or a warm hand, that we grasp as readers? There is such a powerful warmth and urgency in the way the poet reaches out from this poem, it can feel as if it is the reader's own urgent responsibility to bring the poem, if not the poet himself, back to life. But there is also something a little chilling about being addressed like this from beyond the grave. All poetry collapses time, in the sense that we read now what was written then, as if the present tense of the moment in which the poem was written can be carried across to the present tense in which we are reading. But the warmth of the 'living hand' being held out from 'the icy silence of the tomb' makes the strangeness of this present tense particularly unnerving.

Actions & Travels is about both the uncanny pleasure of reading poetry by writers who are now long dead – poetry which I find just as alive, just as intimate and compelling as if it were written yesterday – and the pleasure of reading work that actually *was* written yesterday. Sometimes it can feel even more uncanny to be given access to the inner world of someone you have stood beside at a bookshop or a party, or to know someone intimately only through words you have read online. 'Irreducible Sociality', a poem about *not* going to a party by the Chinese-American poet Chen Chen, ends with the lines, 'Don't be a stranger, but be / strange. Come by often for a cup of tea, // in all your unbridled unknowability.'

For some readers, contemporary poetry can seem icier in its unknowability than the poetry of the past. Written without rhyme or metre, what even makes it poetry? The line break? For other readers, contemporary poetry is just another form of conversation between friends – including strangers befriending themselves to their readers through their poetry – while poetry of the past seems unapproachable without a knowledge of metrical scansion or historical context. Yet if you relish the ingenious and outrageous arguments of Luke Kennard's wolf psychiatrist in poems like 'Wolf on the Couch' and 'Wolf Nationalist', it would be a pity to miss out on John Donne's equally ingenious arguments in poems like 'The Flea'. If you like to luxuriate in the lush imagery and gorgeous vocabulary of Samuel Taylor Coleridge's 'Kubla Khan' or Keats's 'Ode to a Nightingale', you might find yourself equally taken with the queasy gorgeousness you'll find in the poetry of young New Zealand poet Rebecca Hawkes. Bill Manhire's

'Across Brooklyn' is as simple and mysterious as W. B. Yeats's 'Song of Wandering Aengus' or Robert Frost's 'Stopping by Woods'. Andrew Marvell's 'To His Coy Mistress' presents an argument that Annie Finch responds to, centuries later, with her own 'Coy Mistress', and Frost's horse, momentarily stopped in the woods, is set back in motion with Richard Wilbur's heady poem 'The Ride'.

No particular scholarly knowledge is needed to read any of the poems discussed in this book, and the discussions that I offer are not themselves very scholarly. I just write about poems I love and what it is I love about them – the simplicity and resonance of the poems in Chapter One, the sumptuousness of the poems in Chapter Two, the concision of the poems in Chapter Three, what a licence to sprawl allows in the poems of Chapter Four, the challenges and possibilities of form in Chapter Five. Chapter Six looks at poems centred around conversations and argument, while Chapter Seven looks at how poems can also be in conversation (or in an argument) with poetry from the past. Chapter Eight is about how contemporary poetry is being shaped by the ways it is shared on the internet, and looks at the urgent political and social work much contemporary poetry is doing. Chapter Nine considers the intimate address that is often transferred from the reader to some other dear person or object (from nightingales to tombs) in the odes and epistles that change form over time. Chapter Ten concludes the book by looking at poets who are writing to the intimate audience posterity offers, wondering about what it gives the reading of a poem to be read, now, in a present that when the poem was written used to be the distant future.

Every chapter includes a range of poems from canonical poets – from William Shakespeare to William Carlos Williams – as well as poems from contemporary poets such as Alice Oswald and Terrance Hayes. Most chapters also include some works by writers who may not be so well known, such as New Zealand poets Ash Davida Jane and

Helen Rickerby. Since I live in New Zealand, I am familiar not only with poets like James K. Baxter and Bill Manhire, well known locally and internationally, but also with the younger poets whose readings see audiences often spilling out onto the footpaths outside overcrowded bookshops or bars, who make their own zines and publish more often on the internet than in print – among them, Hera Lindsay Bird, whose poem 'Monica' went viral around the world in 2016, Rebecca Hawkes and Tayi Tibble. New Zealand readers may be interested in the connections I trace between these poets' work and the work of more established poets, while readers from outside New Zealand will, I hope, be pleased to be introduced to poets whose work they may not have heard of.

A list of poems is given at the start of each chapter for those who would like to read and think about them before reading the chapter, forming their own sense of the poems that can be compared with mine. Links to all the poems can be found on my website, www.annajackson.nz/actions-and-travels. If the book is read from cover to cover, you will have read or reread one hundred poems. There is no better preparation, I believe, for reading poetry than reading poetry. As Robert Frost rather dauntingly put it, 'A poem is best read in the light of all the other poems ever written. We read A the better to read B (we have to start somewhere; we may get very little out of A). We read B the better to read C, C the better to read D, D the better to go back and get something more out of A. Progress is not the aim, but circulation. The thing is to get among the poems where they hold each other apart in their places as the stars do.' If it is never possible to have read every poem ever written, it is always possible to expand our understanding of poetry with every additional poem we encounter.

At the end of this book is an appendix of writing suggestions for readers who write or might like to write poetry. Reading poetry often leads to writing poetry, as the American poet and essayist Brian

Blanchfield observes. Taking what has sometimes been seen as a problem – that poetry is mostly read only by other poets – Blanchfield points out that this suggests the act of reading poetry turns readers *into* poets and this is something we could celebrate. This is true, in a way, even when the reader *doesn't* go on to write their own poetry – to read poetry is to participate in the re-creation of the poem, its pattern of thought, its sensibility, its pacing, its tone. In poetry, more than in any other genre, Blanchfield writes, 'the sensations of reading are charged with the creative feeling of writing, and vice versa'.

If reading poetry is to become, in a sense, a poet, to go on and write new poetry can further transform our sense of the world around us, as well as our sense of self. I love the 2016 Jim Jarmusch film *Paterson* for its depiction of a poetry-writing bus driver who spends his days running lines of poetry through his head as he drives. His name, Paterson, and the town he lives in, pay homage to the poet William Carlos Williams, better known for his short, snapshot-like poems such as 'The Red Wheelbarrow' than for the book-length *Paterson*. The town as filmed by Jarmusch is full of the sorts of details that could belong in the poetry of Williams: the camera finds beauty in run-down buildings, small patches of decay, sunlight falling on streetscapes, people sitting on benches, suburban gardens and night rain. Paterson the character shows no interest himself in publishing his poetry, and while the poems we see him write (written for the film by poet Ron Padgett) are likeable enough he is not meant, I think, to be understood as an unrecognised genius, an Emily Dickinson figure. Yet like Dickinson, and like Williams, Paterson has an inner life lit up with aesthetic interest in the world's details.

The title of this book, *Actions & Travels*, comes from the description of poetry given by the Canadian poet Anne Carson in a *Paris Review* interview: 'I think a poem, when it works, is an action of the mind captured on a page, and the reader, when he engages it, has to enter into that action. And so his mind repeats that action and travels again through the action, but it is a movement of yourself through a thought, through an activity of thinking, so by the time you get to the end you're different than you were at the beginning and you feel that difference.' The actions and travels of the title belong, then, as much to the reader as to the poet, and this book, too, is simply structured around a series of travels as I read my way through one poem after another, following and finding connections and comparisons, and inviting you to compare your own discoveries with mine.

READING LIST

'Spellbound'
Emily Brontë

'Stopping by Woods on a Snowy Evening'
and 'After Apple-Picking'
Robert Frost

'Across Brooklyn'
Bill Manhire

'A Catalogue of What You Do Not Have'
Rebecca Gayle Howell

'Westron Wynde'
Anon.

'The Tides Run Up the Wairau'
Eileen Duggan

'The Song of Wandering Aengus'
William Butler Yeats

CHAPTER ONE

Simplicity
& resonance

'The Song of Wandering Aengus' by William Butler Yeats begins with the wandering singer going out into the woods 'Because a fire was in my head'. If the singer, or poet, composes with a fire in his head, the poem can be equally incandescent for the reader. Like wandering Aengus, the reader can be driven on, from poem to poem, never forgetting that first transformative encounter. This chapter looks at seven other powerfully resonant poems, before coming back round to 'The Song of Wandering Aengus' as its eighth, to consider the importance of simplicity in giving rise to this resonance.

Can resonance be discussed as a quality of poetry, or is it something that instead belongs to the reader of the poem? There can be all kinds of reasons a poem might resonate with a particular reader. In his book *How to Read a Poem and Fall in Love with Poetry*, Edward Hirsch introduces Emily Brontë's poem 'Spellbound' with a story about how he read it in an anthology as a young boy, believing it to have been written by his recently deceased grandfather. Its refrain, 'I will not, cannot go', spoke both to the child's own refusal to let go of his grandfather, and to his sense of his grandfather's attachment to him – his sense that his grandfather could not have wanted to go, in some sense *could not* have gone. Clearly this is a resonance that Hirsch himself brought to the poem, a resonance that the poem can't itself be said to contain. Yet in his discussion of how the poem came to have such a hold on him (so that, he writes, 'I felt as though the words of the poem, like the storm itself, had cast a "tyrant spell" on me. I couldn't move'), it is the form the poem takes that he emphasises: the simplicity of the three rhyming four-line stanzas, the simple and concrete vocabulary, the 'repetitive stresses' of the refrain, the vivid details of the storm it describes, the double meaning of the word 'move', the 'unremitting rhythm' of the lines, the poem's 'almost processional movement'. This is the poem:

> The night is darkening round me,
> The wild winds coldly blow;
> But a tyrant spell has bound me
> And I cannot, cannot go.
>
> The giant trees are bending
> Their bare boughs weighed with snow.
> And the storm is fast descending,
> And yet I cannot go.
>
> Clouds beyond clouds above me,
> Wastes beyond wastes below;
> But nothing drear can move me;
> I will not, cannot go.

Into these twelve lines, Hirsch writes, 'Brontë condenses . . . the feeling of exposure to the elements, to dangerous natural forces, that she enlarges into epic scope in *Wuthering Heights*'. The simplicity and compression of the poem, the absence of all the social, economic, cultural and narrative details that make up a novel, allow it to resonate beyond itself, making the poem paradoxically both smaller and larger than a novel.

Brontë's 'Spellbound' is not the only poem which seems to be *about* the way a poetic resonance holds a moment open, binding both the reader and the poem's speaker in time and space. Perhaps the best-known example would be Robert Frost's 'Stopping by Woods on a Snowy Evening', a poem, like Brontë's, distinguished by its simplicity and its concreteness. Just as 'Spellbound' gave the young Hirsch a way, as he puts it, of 'ritualising my grief' and thus 'giving me my childhood grieving', so has Frost's simple poem about riding past a wood, and stopping for a moment before continuing on, been read by many as a poem about mortality, the ultimate wood in which our lives will be stopped. But whatever symbolic resonance the moment holds, it is there in the poem quite simply as a moment in which the rider stops his horse and looks at the woods, and his horse, more conventional perhaps than he, less spiritually or aesthetically inclined, shakes his harness, impatient to move on:

> Whose woods these are I think I know.
> His house is in the village though;
> He will not see me stopping here
> To watch his woods fill up with snow.
>
> My little horse must think it queer
> To stop without a farmhouse near
> Between the woods and frozen lake
> The darkest evening of the year.

> He gives his harness bells a shake
> To ask if there is some mistake.
> The only other sound's the sweep
> Of easy wind and downy flake.
>
> The woods are lovely, dark and deep,
> But I have promises to keep,
> And miles to go before I sleep,
> And miles to go before I sleep.

There is something reassuring about the regular rhymes and metre of the poem. Every line is perfectly iambic, alternating an unstressed syllable with a stressed syllable, like the steady trot of the horse moving through the landscape. The rhymes are simple rhymes – 'know' and 'snow', 'deep' and 'sleep' – but the rhyme scheme is a little more complex than the conventional rhyming of the second and fourth lines of a stanza. Frost sets himself the challenge of rhyming the first, second and fourth lines of every stanza and carrying the rhyme of the third line into the next stanza, to make a chain of rhymes that could go on indefinitely. As the poetry critic John Ciardi observes, this creates a particular difficulty when Frost gets to the end of the poem: having left, in each stanza, 'a hook sticking out for the next stanza to catch', when Frost arrives at the fourth stanza and feels 'the poem rounding to its end', he has to decide what to do with this loose third-line rhyme. Ciardi suggests that a logical solution may have been to rhyme the third line of the last stanza with the rhymes of the first stanza, so that each rhyme would have been used four times. But this would have been a technical solution with little emotional impact, since 'a rhyme repeated after eleven lines is so far from its original rhyme sound that its feeling as rhyme must certainly be lost'. It is this problem that Frost solved with the poem's repeated two last lines: 'And miles to go before I sleep, / And miles to go before I sleep.' The result is the repetition that gives the poem such resonance. The simple fact of the distance that needs to be travelled is given, through its repetition, a symbolic weight that the whole poem as a consequence seems to share. If this distance comes to seem more than simply the distance between two geographical places, and the sleep at the end comes to seem more than an everyday sleep, then a deeper significance might also be felt in the mysterious appeal of the woods.

Frost's biographer Louis Mertins records a conversation with Frost in which the poet objected to Ciardi's interpretation of 'Stopping by Woods on a Snowy Evening' as a poem about mortality:

> I suppose people think I lie awake nights worrying about what people like [John] Ciardi of the *Saturday Review* write and publish about me . . . Now Ciardi is a nice fellow – one of those bold, brassy fellows who go ahead and say all sorts of things. He makes my 'Stopping By Woods' out a death poem. Well, it would be like this if it were. I'd say, 'This is all very lovely, but I must be getting on to heaven.'

And yet later in the same conversation, Frost himself emphasised the importance of not coming right out and saying a thing directly: 'If you feel it, let's just exchange glances and not say anything about it. There are a lot of things between best friends that're never said, and if you – if they're brought out, right out, too baldly, something's lost.'

The idea that interpretation can be a way of shutting down resonance does seem demonstrated by interpretations of Brontë's 'Spellbound' offered by student guides on the internet which map out a theology of heaven, hell and purgatory onto Brontë's imagery of moors and sky, and sum the poem up in terms of the moral advice it is said to offer its astute decoder. Frost resists any reading that will shut down the resonance of a work, even the poet's own reading. He advised his friend, the literary critic and scholar Sidney Cox, not to 'disillusion your admirers with the tale of your sources and processes', and went on to argue that the poet Tennyson had 'spoiled' his long poem 'The Idylls of the King' by revealing he had Prince Albert in mind when he was writing of King Arthur. By not bringing out, 'right out, . . . baldly', a precise correlation between the sleep at the end of 'Stopping by Woods' and the mortality we are all moving towards, other possibilities are also held open for the reader, who might think of other reasons for wanting to pause on an onwards journey, other situations which demand a person press on against their will. The possibility that the reader will think of mortality when reading about sleep will still, also, always be there.

In fact, Frost had more clearly made the same metaphorical association of sleep with death that he stops short of making in 'Stopping by Woods' in an earlier, longer poem (a poem which doesn't stop short at all), 'After Apple-Picking':

> My long two-pointed ladder's sticking through a tree
> Toward heaven still,
> And there's a barrel that I didn't fill
> Beside it, and there may be two or three
> Apples I didn't pick upon some bough.
> But I am done with apple-picking now.
> Essence of winter sleep is on the night,
> The scent of apples: I am drowsing off.
> I cannot rub the strangeness from my sight
> I got from looking through a pane of glass
> I skimmed this morning from the drinking trough
> And held against the world of hoary grass.

It melted, and I let it fall and break.
But I was well
Upon my way to sleep before it fell,
And I could tell
What form my dreaming was about to take.
Magnified apples appear and disappear,
Stem end and blossom end,
And every fleck of russet showing clear.
My instep arch not only keeps the ache,
It keeps the pressure of a ladder-round.
I feel the ladder sway as the boughs bend.
And I keep hearing from the cellar bin
The rumbling sound
Of load on load of apples coming in.
For I have had too much
Of apple-picking: I am overtired
Of the great harvest I myself desired.
There were ten thousand thousand fruit to touch,
Cherish in hand, lift down, and not let fall.
For all
That struck the earth,
No matter if not bruised or spiked with stubble,
Went surely to the cider-apple heap
As of no worth.
One can see what will trouble
This sleep of mine, whatever sleep it is.
Were he not gone,
The woodchuck could say whether it's like his
Long sleep, as I describe its coming on,
Or just some human sleep.

Like 'Stopping by Woods', this is a poem that gives resonance to a very particular, concrete experience, the experience of picking apples or, rather, of having picked apples. The vividness of the memories of the day spent apple-picking, embodied in the ache felt in the instep arch from standing too long on a ladder, gives them a resonance, a suggestiveness, so that even before the question about what kind of sleep the poet might be going to have, the apple-picking seems loaded with meaning. The separation of the apples, with all the fallen apples discarded 'as of no worth', is perfectly literal, as is the ladder 'pointing toward heaven', and yet its openness to symbolic interpretation is underlined with the suggestion that this process of apple-sorting 'will trouble / This sleep of mine, whatever sleep it is.' There is some strangeness about this sleep, this possible hibernation, this sleep which may be more than a human sleep, this sleep which hasn't happened yet. This is only an anticipated sleep, at the end of a day of labour that has left the apple-picker 'overtired', and yet he was already 'well upon my way to sleep' before the pane of ice that he skimmed from the water trough in the morning had fallen to the ground – a memory that is, perhaps, in the recalling of it becoming already the dream he will have when he falls asleep but seems to be already having. All through the poem, the words fall, fallen and fell recur, alongside the words tell, fill and all, suggesting a continual fall which nevertheless has already happened and has not happened yet – not an unprecedented way to think of the long harvest of our lives on Earth, but a particularly vivid representation of it, the more resonant because the poem both allows and withholds any such interpretation.

A sense of withheld interpretation is an essential element of Bill Manhire's elliptical 'Across Brooklyn'. That it is a poem about mortality is no mystery: the very first line places the speaker of the poem in 'the street where they still make coffins'. Again, we are presented with a vividly realised scene, with concrete details we can visualise and hear – planks and nails, darkening entrances, the sound of someone whistling. Yet, as with the other poems, the significance of these details doesn't seem quite limited to the literal meaning of them, though it is hard to point to any obvious symbolic meaning they might hold. The mystery of the poem is, perhaps, simply the mystery of our unease about our own mortality, here figured as a kind of uncanny tourism:

> This is the street where they still make coffins:
> the little workshops, side by side.
> I pass them with my daughter on our walk to the river.
>
> Are we seeking the bridge itself,
> or the famous, much-reported view?
>
> A few planks and nails lie around,
> and each of the entrances seems to darken.
> Far back, out of sight, someone is whistling.
>
> Yes, I suppose we do walk a little faster.
> There is a faint noise of hammering, too.

In the simplicity of its details and the particularity of the scene the poem is relatively straightforward, but there is much in it to prompt a sense of the uncanny. The first line introduces the coffins that the rest of the poem seems to try to run away from, passing them by on the way to the bridge. The bridge is well known for its view – these are tourists, looking for well-known sights – but the bridge is well known in poetry too, appearing in Walt Whitman's 'Crossing Brooklyn Ferry' (discussed in Chapter Four) and Hart Crane's 'To Brooklyn Bridge'.

Even in poetry we can be like tourists, wanting to keep revisiting the already familiar or famous. But in our search for the already famous, we might find something unexpected, something unsettling – though what could be more famous than death?

The coupling together of tourism and mortality also does something strange to the sense of audience that this poem evokes. Lyric poetry often involves a certain strangeness of address, so that reading a poem can be like eavesdropping on an improbable relationship as a poet addresses a rose, or talks to themselves, or addresses a lover whose replies can only be imagined. This poem seems to draw particular attention to the strangeness of lyric address, the last couplet in particular throwing a sense of address somehow off kilter. The ending, with the introduction of 'a faint noise of hammering, too', is curiously inconclusive, bringing in one more additional detail, as if in haste to get it in before the poem ends. It comes as the second line of a couplet that seems to have been already interrupted by its own first line, 'Yes, I suppose we do walk a little faster.' This seems to be a reply – but no one has asked a question. Yet there is a sense, perhaps, of someone else present, someone this anecdote is being reported to. It may be that this sense of someone else there but not there (are we, the readers, beginning to feel a little ghostly ourselves?) adds to the unease of the poem, a poem that seems to speed up as if hurrying past its own subject matter. The sounds from the workshop, the hammering, the whistling, are at once coming from somewhere else and are the sounds someone frightened might themselves be making – we whistle when we are frightened; a faint hammering might be the hammering of a pounding heart. This is no ordinary tourism anecdote, such as we might expect to be told in the past tense, perhaps with some pictures to accompany it. If this is a tourism anecdote, why is it being told in the present tense? Is it still happening? Are we ever even going to get to the bridge, let alone to the other side?

Resonance, then, which my chapter title suggests depends on simplicity, seems to depend as much on mystery, on a meaning just beyond the reach of the poem itself. Sometimes a poem can gain resonance in being lifted out of its original context and read in relation to a situation never imagined by the poet. Rebecca Gayle Howell's 'A Catalogue of What You Do Not Have' found a new audience during the Covid-19 pandemic when it was widely shared on Twitter. Its absolute simplicity spoke to how undefined but how vast the sense of loss, and lack, has been for so many people. This is the poem in full:

A Catalogue of What You Do Not Have

Enough

The poem was originally published in a collection, *Render: An Apocalypse*, which offers a kind of DIY guide to apocalyptic living, with poems such as 'How to Kill a Hen' and 'How to Cook the Head'. The poems are visceral and confronting, yet even in the most descriptive of them a sense of a metaphorical meaning hovers just out of reach. The title of the collection, *Render*, carries a biblical resonance with it, even as it is also the most realist of butchering terms, or cooking terms. The *Apocalypse* of the subtitle is no easier to pin down – is this a future apocalypse we will need to store this poetry away for, to bring out in that time of need, or the ongoing apocalypse that farming represents for farmed animals? Already the word 'Enough' shimmers with a sense of the incomplete narrative around it, but lifted out of the collection and set afloat in a global pandemic it carried not only our shared sense of loss but also the consolation of sharing.

The way a poem can seem to belong to a new time, the precise time the reader is living in, may feel like a mystery in itself, and almost uncanny in the case of a poem like Howell's 'Catalogue'. Yet the resonance of the anonymous sixteenth-century poem 'Westron Wynde' seems not so much uncanny as familiar and moving in its familiarity, despite the centuries separating the writer and the reader now. Preserved in a sixteenth-century songbook, the poem may have been composed even earlier, but it seems lifted out of time with all its immediacy lifted with it. Only one stanza long, the poem simply laments the distance between the poet, or singer, and the warm bed with his lover in it, without any suggestion there need be a second, transcendent interpretation of any of the details of the rain, the bed, the lover, the yearning that is expressed:

> Westron wynde, when wilt thou blow,
> The small raine down can raine.
> Cryst, if my love were in my armes
> And I in my bedde again!

For all the precision of the scene and the precision of the feeling expressed, there is a gap in our knowledge of what is keeping the lovers apart, of why the western wind, bringing its small rains, will allow them to be together again. But it is the gap in time between when the poem was first composed, and the time now when it still seems so fresh and so urgent, that becomes a part of the poem's resonance, part of what makes it so moving to read.

Another kind of resonance can be found in a twentieth-century poem by New Zealander Eileen Duggan. 'The Tides Run Up the Wairau' is another short poem with a regular rhythm, simple rhymes and vivid imagery:

> The tides run up the Wairau
> That fights against their flow.
> My heart and it together
> Are running salt and snow.
>
> For though I cannot love you,
> Yet, heavy, deep, and far,
> Your tide of love comes swinging,
> Too swift for me to bar.
>
> Some thought of you must linger,
> A salt of pain in me,
> For oh what running river
> Can stand against the sea?

Like 'Westron Wynde' and unlike Frost's 'Stopping by Woods', this poem rhymes in the simpler, more conventional way, with the second and fourth lines rhyming. But the theme is unconventional, the poem written not from the perspective of the lover wishing his love to be returned, but from the perspective of the loved one suffering from the love of someone she cannot love in return, a love which nevertheless causes 'a salt of pain'. The extended metaphor – the beloved as the river, the lover as the sea tide that runs up the river when it turns – is beautifully sustained, and completely contained within the poem. The resonance comes from how evocative it is to think of the heart 'running salt and snow', like a river touched by the tide, both hard to imagine and yet somehow very true to a feeling. The logic of the metaphor, as well as the demands of rhyme, seem, as in Brontë's 'Spellbound', to cast a kind of spell in which a troubling emotion is arranged into a form that recognises its inevitability, that transcends any individual personal circumstances giving rise to it. There is something at once spellbinding and liberating in this.

Perhaps what all of these poems have in common is a particular spellbound sense of time. This is vividly and strangely evoked in 'The Song of Wandering Aengus', the poem that set off the wandering route this chapter has taken:

> I went out to the hazel wood,
> Because a fire was in my head,
> And cut and peeled a hazel wand,
> And hooked a berry to a thread;
> And when white moths were on the wing,
> And moth-like stars were flickering out,
> I dropped the berry in a stream
> And caught a little silver trout.
>
> When I had laid it on the floor
> I went to blow the fire a-flame,
> But something rustled on the floor,
> And someone called me by my name:
> It had become a glimmering girl
> With apple blossom in her hair
> Who called me by my name and ran
> And faded through the brightening air.
>
> Though I am old with wandering
> Through hollow lands and hilly lands,
> I will find out where she has gone,
> And kiss her lips and take her hands;
> And walk among long dappled grass,

>   And pluck till time and times are done,
>   The silver apples of the moon,
>   The golden apples of the sun.

'The Song of Wandering Aengus' has the kind of symbolic resonance a fairy tale has, or a dream – everything in it seems shimmering with meaning. A trout fished for in the first stanza becomes a girl who appears and disappears in the second stanza, and by the third stanza the young man has become an old man while searching for her. Everything in this poem *must* mean something beyond its literal meaning: a trout that becomes a girl cannot just be a trout; silver apples of the moon and golden apples of the sun cannot just be apples. At the same time, any interpretation of the poem that defines a single meaning for each of the objects in it reduces and limits the poem's significance. It is a poem about yearning, clearly – the young man fishing, the old man still looking for the girl – yet it ends with a resolution, with the plucking of the apples. The poem shifts from the past tense into the future tense for this resolution, a resolution which hasn't happened yet, and we might read this future tense as being a *conditional* future – if, or when, he will find the girl, he will eat the apples. For a resolution, then, it is strangely unresolved. Yet the balance and beauty of the two lines and the obvious symbolism of the apples (even if what they symbolise remains open) makes them read as a very positive resolution to the poem, as conclusive as its final, spellbinding rhyme.

READING LIST

'Technicolour Dreamcake'
Rebecca Hawkes

Sonnet 30 ['When to the sessions
of sweet silent thought']
William Shakespeare

'Kubla Khan; or, a Vision in a Dream:
A Fragment'
Samuel Taylor Coleridge

'Ode to a Nightingale'
John Keats

'Helix'
Michele Leggott

'Lost Scrolls' and 'Monica'
Hera Lindsay Bird

CHAPTER TWO

The ornate
& the sumptuous

'I have been doing a little tapirising & reading Keats, you'll be sorry to hear,' Samuel Beckett wrote in a letter of 1930. 'I like the crouching brooding quality in Keats – squatting on the moss, crushing a petal, licking his lips & rubbing his hands, "counting the last oozings, hours by hours" . . . I like that awful sweetness and thick soft damp green richness.' This is a sorry confession indeed from the author of *Waiting for Godot*, whose work readers turn to when in the mood for the very bleakest modernism.

  The previous chapter looked at simplicity as a condition for resonance, in poems like Frost's 'Stopping by Woods' or Duggan's 'The Tides Run Up the Wairau'. The opposite of simplicity might be difficulty. Not all poets want to write poetry that is readily accessible. For some, the difficulty of poetry is part of how it works: meaning that is simple might seem simplistic; meaning that is easily grasped might not need the mode of *poetry* to be articulated at all. But difficulty isn't the only opposite of simplicity. A poem can be easily understood, simple in its meaning, but ornate in its manner, sumptuous in its language. This chapter looks at poems I love most of all for their surface pleasures, for how beautifully, richly, lyrically they are written.

There is plenty of crouching and brooding going on in the work of New Zealand poet Rebecca Hawkes, whose selection of poetry 'softcore coldsores', in the anthology *AUP New Poets 5*, is full of visceral accounts of milking cows sick with mastitis, eating pig skin still bristly with hair, falling in love like an insect surrendering to the syrup of a pitcher plant, paddling in the brackish shallows where mangroves grow, or descending into the cartilaginous depths of a cave. These are scenarios ripe with the potential for oozy descriptions, but as one of Hawkes's shorter poems, 'Technicolour Dreamcake', proclaims, sumptuousness depends too on the eye of the beholder. Many of her poems sprawl out over pages, often with spaces, slashes and other forms of punctuation adding to the sense of excess, and a number of them are also filled out with lists of the luscious names of things, unusual verbs and ambiguous syntax. But in 'Technicolour Dreamcake' her taste for the sumptuous is compressed into the ten lines of the poem, quoted here in full:

> well now I must admit to painting you
> in an unsayably saturated light
>
> pre-raphaelite nymphknave incendiary
> knelt among wildflowers
>
> bulging with significance
> souped up from the loam
>
> swaddled in kerosene fragrance
> I yield to pheromone and accident
>
> between our fluorescent camo and exposed roots
> we can only guess what moths might flock to us

Even the conversational opening of the poem suggests a richness of context beyond the scope of the poem, and the determined vision of the 'you' as a 'pre-raphaelite nymphknave' is wonderfully, ridiculously romantic. This might be a romance produced by not only the chemistry of pheromones but also the accidental significances of lovely-sounding word play – but aren't *all* romances concoctions of both will and desire, and as a reader, don't you, too, want to flock to this concoction like the moths?

Samuel Beckett may well have flocked like moths to the poetry of Rebecca Hawkes had she been writing when he was alive, just as he apologetically indulged in the oozy sweetness of Keats's poetry, but he could have turned to Shakespeare for some salutary bleakness. There is no bleaker line in poetry, surely, than the Beckettian 'Never never never never never' from *King Lear*. But Beckett also looked to Shakespeare for the same sweetness and richness he took from Keats. Into his journal Beckett copied lines from *A Midsummer Night's Dream*:

> And as imagination bodies forth
> The forms of things unknown, the poet's pen
> Turns them to shapes and gives to airy nothing
> A local habitation and a name.

Shakespeare's plays are rich indeed in names and habitations, characters and settings that a reader of the playscript might imagine as vividly as if they have seen them on the stage or on the screen, and they are rich as well in sumptuous language. A local habitation and a name are exactly what is *missing* from Shakespeare's sonnets – the identity of the young man addressed in the first 126 sonnets is a mystery, as is the identity of the dark mistress in the rest of them – and yet the sonnets, too, embody airy nothing with the most lyrical ornamentation. The first seventeen sonnets after all make the same essential argument over and over again, directing a young man to marry so as to reproduce his beauty in another generation. So many sonnets on a single theme suggests, I think, not so much conviction or a determination to persuade as an increasingly formal interest in what possibilities for variation might still remain after the first dozen, the thirteenth, the fourteenth variation on the theme. Each sonnet packs into its fourteen lines an argument with an elaboration of examples, a claim and counter-claim, a turn, a final summing up or a surprising refutation of all that has come before. Yet for all the neatness of the arguments, what makes the sonnets so memorable is the language.

Take Shakespeare's Sonnet 30, for instance, comparing the possibility of recalling old unhappinesses with the relief, or happiness, of thinking of the relationship with the young man who is the subject of the sonnet. Just as past unhappiness can be recalled in the present, so can present unhappiness be relieved by thinking of this friendship. Thoughts give rise to emotion. But thoughts can be chosen – and unhappy thoughts are perhaps chosen for the unhappiness they give rise to, the melancholy they allow in 'sessions of sweet silent thought'. For me, what makes this a beautiful poem is this phrase. The whole sonnet rests on the beauty of its two opening lines:

> When to the sessions of sweet silent thought
> I summon up remembrance of things past,
> I sigh the lack of many a thing I sought,
> And with old woes new wail my dear time's waste:
> Then can I drown an eye, unus'd to flow,
> For precious friends hid in death's dateless night,
> And weep afresh love's long since cancell'd woe,

> And moan th' expense of many a vanish'd sight;
> Then can I grieve at grievances foregone,
> And heavily from woe to woe tell o'er
> The sad account of fore-bemoanèd moan,
> Which I new pay as if not paid before.
> But if the while I think on thee, dear friend,
> All losses are restor'd, and sorrows end.

The language of accounting that increasingly directs the logic of this poem might seem rather strangely at odds with the lyricism of the opening lines. A line counting up sorrows owed, 'Which I new pay as if not paid before', has little lyrical beauty in itself, and while the 'fore-bemoanèd moan' of the previous line might *sound* poetic, can a line about having already moaned a moan, so therefore, in accounting terms, not owing another, be anything other than prosaic? How many tears are due to each grief is an oddly economic approach to sorrow, and this, of course, is the point the poem makes. But if every grief is endless, and can always be wept over again, so the happiness that love brings is beyond accounting. In the light of such present happiness, 'All losses are restor'd, and sorrows end' – yet it is in keeping with where the emotional and lyrical weight of the poem falls that loss, sorrow and ending should be its final notes. The poem holds open the possibility of finding beauty in sorrow from the beginning, with the phrase 'sessions of sweet silent thought' beautiful in its alliteration and its syncopated rhythm slowing down the pentameter line. The beauty of the phrase suggests the lure of the unhappiness that could be never-ending, never cancelled out, if it were not for the happiness the thought of the loved friend brings.

Many of the poems I have chosen to write about in this chapter for their lures, the beauty of their images and the language, have in common something missing at their heart – lost scrolls, a vanished dream of Xanadu, sweet silent thoughts of past unhappiness . . . It is as if the ornamentation makes up for the 'airy nothing' of what isn't there. Yet it is this absence that makes these poems so replete, full as they are of longing, and so full of beauty and the richness of the present moment and of sensory experience.

Samuel Taylor Coleridge's 'Kubla Khan; or, a Vision in a Dream: A Fragment' is, as the complicated subtitle suggests, both visionary, rich in ornamentation and vivid sensory detail, and constructed around absence – an account of a half-forgotten dream in fragmentary form. The poem was composed after Coleridge had been taking opium, and he seems to have been unsure whether this strange poem was a poem at all. He didn't publish it till 1816, nearly twenty years after he wrote it, and when he did he presented it as a curiosity, a fragment of a longer poem he would have completed had he not been interrupted by a visitor from Porlock. Yet it seems very complete as a poem about the wish to complete, or restore, a lost vision – the vision of the wondrous landscape created by Kubla Khan, a sunny, ordered, architectural wonder in a world of savage and tumultuous natural beauty, a place of peace in a world of empire-building and war.

As a poem made up of remembered and misremembered images and lines, 'Kubla Khan' makes an immediately powerful impression, and is full of lines and images that linger in the mind. When it was published, some of the first reviewers took Coleridge at his word, and criticised the publication of what was only a 'fragment', not a poem but a senseless reverie. Later nineteenth-century critics admired precisely its movement beyond sense, Coleridge's evocation of impressions 'vivid beyond common sight of common things, sweet beyond sound of things heard', and, above all, the musical rhythms of the poem, so that, as another critic, John Bowring, suggested, 'The effect could scarcely have been more satisfactory to the ear had every syllable been selected merely for the sake of its sound.'

The poem begins, indeed, with the exotic names of Xanadu and Kubla Khan, and the regular iambic metre of the first few lines involves, at the same time, a somewhat formal, somewhat archaic grammatical construction: Kubla Khan decreed a stately pleasure-dome (or decreed the building of a stately pleasure-dome) would be a far more prosaic opening.

> In Xanadu did Kubla Khan
> A stately pleasure-dome decree
> Where Alph, the sacred river, ran
> Through caverns measureless to man
>   Down to a sunless sea.

The iambic rhythms move us rapidly along with the running river, the enjambment as the river 'ran / Through caverns measureless to man' adding to the effect, until we are brought to a halt with the reversal of the rhythm in the final line of the stanza, opening with the strong stress on its first word, 'Down to a sunless sea.'

The pleasure of the rhythms is best heard reading the poem aloud, as the four stressed lines of the opening give way to the slower pace of the five stressed lines elaborating on the gardens, fragrant trees and sinuous rills, and then slowing down further with the exclamation 'oh!' introducing the 'deep romantic chasm' with a pause, the stress on 'Down' and the two stresses of 'green hill' giving a line of six stresses (as I hear it):

> So twice five miles of fertile ground
> With walls and towers were girdled round;
> And there were gardens bright with sinuous rills,
> Where blossomed many an incense-bearing tree;
> And here were forests ancient as the hills,
> Enfolding sunny spots of greenery.
>
> But oh! that deep romantic chasm which slanted
> Down the green hill athwart a cedarn cover!

Throughout the poem, the metre shifts between iambic tetrameter (the four-stressed line of nursery rhyme and song) and iambic pentameter (the five-stressed metre that contemporary poets still sometimes end a poem on to give it that resounding sense of lyric significance), till, by the end, the movement back into the four-stressed line seems to take on a magical force:

> Weave a circle round him thrice,
> And close your eyes with holy dread
> For he on honey-dew hath fed,
> And drunk the milk of Paradise.

To read those lines out loud to yourself is to feel yourself casting a spell, but whether you are casting a spell on the poet, the poem or your own self is not easy to determine. The effect of reciting the poem, whether alone or in company, is probably going to be even more powerful for the reader than for an audience, but it is worth listening to some of the memorable renditions of the poem available on YouTube. There is, for example, a striking contrast between Sir Ralph Richardson's dramatic, oratorical reading and Benedict Cumberbatch's reading of the poem as a dream-like reverie, a private musing. The poem, I think, has both qualities: it is dramatic and dream-like; about external, material accomplishment and about the interior, soul-building work of art, including poetry itself.

John Keats's 'Ode to a Nightingale' should *always* be read by Benedict Cumberbatch, or at least it is always a poem of reverie – 'Do I wake or sleep?' Addressed to the nightingale the poet hears, but beginning with the weight of physical sensation, a drowsy numbness, an aching heart, it is a poem about listening to pure lyric and being transported elsewhere without in reality leaving your own head. Like Coleridge's 'Kubla Khan', with its sinuous river, dark romantic chasm, incense-bearing trees and caves of ice, Keats's nightingale ode luxuriates in the sensuousness of the material world with its vintage wine, mossy ground and scented air. But it is also a poem about the beauty of language and the sensuous rhythms of poetry. It is only the poetry, after all, conjuring up all the details of the landscape that even in his imagination the poet cannot see in the imagined dark, in this fifth stanza of the eight-stanza poem:

> I cannot see what flowers are at my feet,
>   Nor what soft incense hangs upon the boughs,
> But, in embalmed darkness, guess each sweet
>   Wherewith the seasonable month endows
> The grass, the thicket, and the fruit-tree wild;
>   White hawthorn, and the pastoral eglantine;
>   Fast fading violets cover'd up in leaves;
>   And mid-May's eldest child,

> The coming musk-rose, full of dewy wine,
> The murmurous haunt of flies on summer eves.

Even the vivid realism of the third verse, conjuring up the 'weariness, the fever, and the fret' of the human condition in order to call for the escapism of poetry in response, is itself constructed out of the poetry of made-up or remembered details. When the poet wakes to follow the fading sound of the nightingale's song into the landscape he doesn't see and yet knows is there, what is the reality that the poet wakes into but one always made up from the memories, knowledge and imagination with which we organise our senses?

The poetry of Michele Leggott, New Zealand's Poet Laureate from 2007 and 2009, has always been language-driven, lyrical and rich in sensuous detail, even before she experienced the gradual loss of sight that is the loss at the centre of her fifth collection of poetry, *As Far as I Can See*. In the poem 'Helix', for instance, from the series 'Snake and Jewel', the final line repeats the words 'her helix' over and over until I hear the word 'elixir' in the line, just as in the poem 'all' she buries the name 'Sophia' between 'hys*sop*' and '*hia*tus', between 'calyp*so*' and '*phia*ls', and just as so much of her poetry is drenched with honeyed elixirs, sweet syrups and magical tastes (the poem 'Lebh' which follows 'Helix' begins 'and she's elixial elixirate'). 'Helix' is a poem of realist concerns – it includes 'tantrums in the real house of days' – but there is a lingering on the 'vicissitudes' that is pleasurable not just because of the beautiful sound of the word itself, repeated twice, and with the v sound picked up from the word 'lived' in the line before, and picked up again in the words 'devouring' and 'provender' that follow. There is, as the poet puts it, 'a tenderness taking the lyric and turning it inside / out'.

> what can you give me that begins with *hinna*?
> a vision twisting and twisting torch flame or genetic
> material from the island of the first morning
> a tenderness taking the lyric and turning it inside
> out because nothing will ever be the same
> a tantrum in the real house of days because some
> of them must be picked up and lived despite
> a vicissitude oh vicissitudes devouring
> the delicate provender of body and soul
> a patience on the ladder two steps short
> of the full house each keeps for the other
> a bed where text is getting around to being
> what they want to do today   helix a rich tissue
> helix her helix her helix her helix

Tenderness is not quite the word for what is going on with Hera Lindsay Bird's taking apart of the lyric in her dazzling and erotic first collection, titled *Hera Lindsay Bird*. Yet there is an equally interesting process of ornamentation at play in this collection, an ornamentation not so much of language but of imagery. This shift towards imagery as ornamentation can be found, too, in the contemporary American poets who are the most important influences on Bird's work and whose work, like hers, layers ornamentation over absence. Her extended sequence 'Lost Scrolls', for instance, borrows its form – and its suggestion of erasure – from Mark Leidner's 'Blackouts'. A blackout is a particularly physical kind of erasure, yet even Leidner's poem offers such a dazzling array of similes that rather than coming closer and closer to defining the experience of a blackout, the subject that 'it' is like (nearly every line begins 'it is like . . .') recedes further and further from us, and the blackouts multiply in possibility, figuring as nightfalls, gaps in poetry, art or interpretation, expressions of pain, distraction or orgasm, or as the blackouts at the end of films and TV shows.

The title of Bird's sequence foregrounds the textual nature of the loss for which the similes offer their compensation, yet at the same time the similes offer their own vivid array of losses, disappointments and inadequacies. These are the first six similes of a poem that goes on for nine pages:

> Like a passive aggressive gun that fires . . . . nothing instead of bullets
> Or Nostradamus predicting the invention of the Capri pant . . .
> Like a primeval tornado collecting nothing but air . . .
>
> Like accidentally wishing on a satellite and getting women's golf instead of happiness . . .
> Like your dad threatening to turn the planet around and keep driving . . .
> Like throwing your wedding bouquet backwards into a discount sporting goods store . . .

It is a poem made up of one-liners so funny that it hardly matters what exactly is being compared to your father threatening to turn the planet around and keep driving. We have examples of grotesque short-cuts that make no practical sense – 'Like freezing containers of vomit to reheat and throw down the toilet later' – and surreal difficulties only too easy to imagine – 'Like trying to find your way out of a door museum'. To be told, towards the end of the poem, 'That is what love is like', is a startling discovery that casts an even more bleakly comic light on the miserable situations we've been presented with, even as the poem does now take a more romantic turn. The poets Bird borrows from, however, keep their similes largely untethered to any referent, allowing them to float free as pure ornamentation over an airy nothing. 'This is like crying while trying on different outfits . . .' writes Chelsey Minnis in her collection *Poemland*. 'This is like crying because you can't open a jar . . . / This is like crying in a ditch . . .' What 'this' is, we are never told. The poem is all in the similes, and in the crying. As Minnis explains, 'When I try to write a poem it seems reasonable . . . / But it can never be reasonable . . .'

The sequence in *Hera Lindsay Bird* most closely modelled on Chelsey Minnis's *Poemland* is called 'Pain Imperatives', suggesting we might read this poem – and perhaps, by extension, the collection as a whole – as a pain imperative itself, writing that pain requires the writer to perform. Bird's most popular poem, 'Monica', begins as a rant about the inadequacies of the character Monica from the television show *F.R.I.E.N.D.S*. The poem, much shared over the internet, is a brilliant performance piece, reading even on the page like a comedy script. The pleasures are not the pleasures of lyrical ornamentation but of witty critical commentary. The poem begins:

> Monica
>
> Monica
>
> Monica
>
> Monica
>
> Monica Geller off popular sitcom F.R.I.E.N.D.S
>
> Is one of the worst characters in the history of television
>
> She makes me want to wash my hands with hand sanitizer
>
> She makes me want to stand in an abandoned Ukrainian parking lot
>
> And scream her name at a bunch of dead crows

> Nobody liked her, except for Chandler
> He married her, and that brings me to my second point
> What kind of a name for a show was F.R.I.E.N.D.S
> When two of them were related
> And the rest of them just fucked for ten seasons?

By the end of the poem, however, the poet's own vulnerabilities begin to be revealed, allowing all this witty irritation over Monica's failings to be read as ornamentation, covering over her displaced anxiety about entering a new relationship: 'I am falling in love and I don't know what to do about it / Throw me in a haunted wheelbarrow and set me on fire'. Just as Shakespeare plays logic off against sentiment in his Sonnet 30, so Bird uses rationality to set up the lyrical possibilities of irrational excess. While Shakespeare's sonnet essentially argues against the economic imagery it brings into play, the imagery still does have an anti-poetic effect, just as Bird's return to lyricism at the end of the poem takes nothing away from the comedy of the poem as a whole. But perhaps there is an effect that is resonant, lovely, beautiful in itself, in the playing of sentiment against logic. This is a form of beauty inherent in the sonnet form, which allows a poet precisely fourteen lines to outline an argument which is never really as much the point of any sonnet as is the uncontainable feeling the poem is really about.

Many contemporary poems by Bird and by the American poets she is reading gesture towards something large, abstract and essential – pain, love – that cannot be directly represented. The pyrotechnical imagery so gorgeously, extravagantly at play fills in for something lost, something that could be recovered perhaps only in lost scrolls. This is poetry that has moved on from the nightingales and incense-bearing trees of Keats and Coleridge. And yet, for all the bravado of a collection which includes a poem called 'Keats is dead so fuck me from behind', Bird's poems constantly refer to the great poets of the canon, Coleridge, Auden, Shelley, Wordsworth, Byron, Whitman, Wallace Stevens, along with contemporary canonical poets Bill Manhire, Billy Collins and Mary Oliver, if only to dismiss them – again and again and again. If a belief in poetry is the loss at the heart of these poems, can the poetry itself possibly compensate for such a loss? Perhaps it is the only thing that could?

— READING LIST —

'In a Station of the Metro'
Ezra Pound

'The Red Wheelbarrow'
William Carlos Williams

'Photograph', 'Being a Poet'
and 'In Memory'
Jenny Bornholdt

'Detail'
Ursula Bethell

'Why I Am Not a Painter'
Frank O'Hara

'Hotere'
Hone Tuwhare

'she cut her face shaving'
essa may ranapiri

'Linens'
Kay Ryan

Memorial
Alice Oswald

CHAPTER THREE

Concision, composition & the image

'No ideas but in things,' William Carlos Williams wrote. 'Use absolutely no word that does not contribute to the presentation,' wrote Ezra Pound. To revel today in the pleasures of the ornate and the sumptuous, to build poetry out of surface flourishes and words that are simply gorgeous words, is to turn away from the modernist principles that transformed poetry so dramatically at the start of the twentieth century.

We have already looked at the role simplicity can play in poetry, emphasising particularly the resonance that simplicity can give rise to, a resonance held by some of the chosen poems through a lengthy working out of narrative and dramatic details. This chapter focuses on the form of simplicity valued by the modernists, and the importance in their work of concision, formal unity and the visual image. With the modernists there was a shift in purpose, as English poet and essayist Stephen Spender put it, 'not to follow a story but discern a pattern'. Modernist works like Ezra Pound's *Cantos* could be monumental, but this chapter begins by looking at two of the shortest and simplest, and most famous, poems in the English language.

Ezra Pound was one of the most influential of modernist poets, as much for his role as an editor, anthologist and critic as for his poetry. The Imagist movement, which he arguably invented and certainly promoted, proclaimed the importance of the image as the central unit of poetry, and insisted on compression, concision and precision in the presentation of the 'thing itself'. Pound's 'In a Station of the Metro' is only two lines long, presenting two images, one a metaphor for the other:

> The apparition of these faces in the crowd;
> Petals on a wet, black bough.

It is a poem with the freshness and surprise of petals stuck to a bough after the rain, a poem which presents an image in order to capture an emotional response. The rhythm contributes to the effect: the relative rapidity of the first line, compared to the slowness of the second line beginning with a stressed syllable, and ending with the three stressed syllables in a row; the alternation between the more conventional rhythm of the first line, which can be read perfectly iambically, and the unexpected and beautiful rhythms of the second line, reflecting the way the poet transforms an ordinary experience of a crowded subway with his aesthetic response.

This is Pound's own account of writing the poem:

> Three years ago in Paris I got out of a 'metro' train at La Concorde, and saw suddenly a beautiful face, and then another and another, and then a beautiful child's face, and then another beautiful woman, and I tried all that day to find words for what this had meant to me, and I could not find any words that seemed to me worthy, or as lovely as that sudden emotion. And that evening, as I went home along the Rue Raynouard,

I was still trying and I found, suddenly, the expression. I do not mean that I found words, but there came an equation . . . not in speech, but in little splotches of colour . . .

I wrote a thirty-line poem, and destroyed it because it was what we call work 'of second intensity.' Six months later I made a poem half that length; a year later I made the following *hokku*-like sentence: –

> The apparition of these faces in the crowd:
> Petals, on a wet, black bough.

A year might seem a long time to write one sentence, but the work of modernism was in the editing. Concision was regarded as an essential aspect of a laborious approach to writing poetry.

Of all the poets influenced by Ezra Pound's ideas, William Carlos Williams was, in turn, the most influential as a poet himself. His work offered a model for how poetry might look on the page and sound to the ear, most famously in one of his shortest poems, 'The Red Wheelbarrow':

> so much depends
> upon
>
> a red wheel
> barrow
>
> glazed with rain
> water

> beside the white
>
> chickens

What depends on the red wheelbarrow, the rainwater and the chickens is the composition of the poem itself, which depends both on a composition of elements in the world, an *image*, and on the composition of words on a page.

Unlike Pound, Williams composed his poems relatively quickly, often between seeing patients when he was working as a doctor during the day. He, too, however, wrote and spoke often about the importance of editing, and his own editing focused on the line breaks and stanza forms, the arrangement of type. His alertness to the effects of the line break, the way a poem can have a visual rhythm, has been enormously influential, but so has his attention to the composition of elements in the world.

It is an influence that has reached around the globe, taking on national accents. Jenny Bornholdt, New Zealand's Poet Laureate from 2005 to 2007, takes the modernist attention to the composition of elements in the world, as well as to the composition of words on a page, and gives it a very local, very New Zealand, very domestic flavour. In the poem 'Photograph', Bornholdt acknowledges the closeness in practice of the poet and the photographer, except, paradoxically, in this poem it is the poet framing and capturing a found composition, as if taking a snapshot, while the photographer is pictured by the poet in the act of arranging and rearranging the material elements, the people being photographed, in the manner of a poet rearranging her line breaks:

A little to the left
Neil, that's nice, and
John, if you could come in
a bit, good, good,
now Neil, if you can turn
your body, this way,
yep, just a little, yep,
now turn your head
to me, yep, that's
good. Now Humphrey,
chin up a bit, up,
good, John, if you can
come in closer
to Michael, good,
more, yep, Neil back
a bit, one step, turn
just a little, yep,
now Humphrey,
chin up, turn to the side
a bit, bit more, yep
good, Neil, Neil, back
a bit, yep, Humphrey
chin, Neil, closer Michael,
John, in together, turn
and now, yep, good,
chin Humphrey, closer,
turn, closer, Neil
John, Humphrey, chin
Humphrey, John, Neil
closer, closer, turn,
yep, now

For William Carlos Williams, the only thing as important as 'the thing itself', the arrangement of objects in the world, in determining the design of the poem and the arrangement of the lines and the line breaks was the rhythms of American speech. He was tremendously alert to the cadences of ordinary, everyday speech, and worked to convey what he heard through the use of repetition, line breaks and vocabulary as he heard it spoken. In an interview he can be heard saying, again and again, 'Did you hear *that*?' with an irresistible relish for the spoken word, for language as it is used by people in their ordinary lives. Bornholdt's 'Photograph' shows how closely related this kind of modernist attention to language is to the attention to the visual image; how language, like the visual image, can be noticed in terms of its patterns and rhythms, and how it can be framed and arranged on the page. Her relish for the words ('yep') and the rhythms ('Humphrey, chin') of New Zealand speech is conveyed through the use of line breaks to suggest the syncopation of language as it is spoken, how speech falls into rhythms that have an artistry about them even as they are serving a functional purpose.

In another poem, 'Being a Poet', Bornholdt listens with wonder to the words she hears coming out of her own mouth, the surreal art of the everyday conversation that reveals the surreal art of domestic life:

> Yesterday I bought
> a blender – blue – from
> Briscoes, just like
> Marion's. Today
> we're dealing with the big
> issues, like: *How the World*
> *Began* and
> *Can We Have Fruit Loops*

For Breakfast?
Friends ask
what I'm reading.
By the bed is **Go, dog. Go.**
We looked at it this morning
just before our fight
over the nature of
Weetbix. *But it's soggy
every morning*, I hear myself say
*that's just what Weetbix does
that's just its way*.

What we read affects not only what we think about but also the rhythms in which we think, and the rhythms we hear in the language around us. Dr. Seuss can be as catchy as William Carlos Williams. The arrangement is not just of objects – the blender, the picture book – but of the incidents of a domestic life, and they too can form a sort of composition. And Bornholdt is alert to the beauty of more specialist words too, such as the evocative language of the gardening catalogue. She writes often about gardening, as an art form that is very unlike poetry, being so obviously material, grounded and physically laborious, and yet very like poetry in the way it depends on compositional arrangements of visual details. Like poetry, too, the art of gardening draws on associations and memories, as Bornholdt observes in her short poem, 'In Memory':

we planted one
Magnolia Stellata Waterlily
the word 'fragrant'

> convinced us.
> Something to do with fragrance
> and loss. Also 'Stellata', the way light
> keeps company
> with night.

'In Memory' looks back to Ursula Bethell, one of the first poets in New Zealand to write in the modernist strain of Pound and Williams. Bethell's first collection, *From a Garden in the Antipodes* (1929), was all about her garden – heroes of the collection include Omi-Kin-Kan, her mandarin tree, and Michael, the cat. When the early-twentieth-century English gardening revolutionary Gertrude Jekyll claimed that 'gardening is painting with living things', she clearly meant painting like a modernist painter, in terms of the arrangement of colour and form. But words, particularly the names of plants, as well as their arrangement take centre stage in Bethell's poetry. At a time when most poets in New Zealand were still writing in rhyme and metre, often about abstract topics, Ursula Bethell wrote about her garden in a series of poems that play with the composition of words and objects as they are presented on the page. The title of her poem 'Detail' itself suggests the attention to compositional detail that the poem celebrates and performs:

> My garage is a structure of excessive plainness,
> It springs from a dry bank in the back garden,
> It is made of corrugated iron,
> And painted all over with brick-red.
>
> But beside it I have planted a green Bay-tree,

– A sweet Bay, an Olive, a Turkey Fig,
– A Fig, an Olive, and a Bay.

The longing for something absent or lost, whether lost scrolls, a fading nightingale's song, a dream or a relationship, that is so often at the heart of ornate and sumptuous poetry stands in contrast to the presentation, in poems like 'The Red Wheelbarrow' or 'Detail', of material objects that are resolutely present. They have to be, the poems depend upon them!

The apparent solidity of the words composed on the page can, though, stand in place of a considerable amount of revising and erasure. Pound's story about the work involved in coming up with the perfect hokku-like sentence to capture an emotional response emphasises the conclusive success of this ultimate composition, permanently fixing a fleeting emotion about an ephemeral vision. Yet the story itself adds to the resonance of the poem, just as Coleridge's story about the person from Porlock's interruption of his work adds to the resonance of his 'Kubla Khan'. The work of 'second intensity' written, worked over and finally erased continues to exert a ghostly pressure on the work of first intensity that remains.

Frank O'Hara's poem 'Why I Am Not a Painter' paradoxically suggests that being a poet might not be very different from being a painter because of the way it involves exactly this kind of 'painting over', so that the finished composition is a palimpsest of revisions upon revisions, even if most of them will never be known. The first stanza of the poem (after an introductory three lines) describes a painting by his friend Mike Goldberg which has 'SARDINES' in it, because 'it needed something there'. In the same way that the red wheelbarrow can be seen as playing a primarily compositional role, it doesn't matter much what the word is in the painting; it becomes, as the composition changes, simply some letters. What matters is its placing within a frame:

> for instance, Mike Goldberg
> is starting a painting. I drop in.
> 'Sit down and have a drink' he
> says. I drink; we drink. I look
> up. 'You have SARDINES in it.'
> 'Yes, it needed something there.'
> 'Oh.' I go and the days go by
> and I drop in again. The painting
> is going on, and I go, and the days
> go by. I drop in. The painting is
> finished. 'Where's SARDINES?'
> All that's left is just
> letters, 'It was too much,' Mike says.

The second stanza of the poem, like a reflection of the first, tells a corresponding anecdote about the attempt to write about the colour orange, a subject that expands until it encompasses 'how terrible orange is / and life.' As the subject expands, so this imaginary poem expands to become twelve poems, which are finished before the word orange has even made an appearance. The series is called 'Oranges', and, O'Hara's poem concludes, 'one day in a gallery / I see Mike's painting, called SARDINES.'

Perhaps the best-known relationship between a poet and painter in New Zealand was the friendship between poet Hone Tuwhare and painter Ralph Hotere, both of them leading figures in their fields in the second half of the twentieth century. Tuwhare's work combines an interest in formal composition with a kind of aural impasto,

New Zealand speech rhythms and vocabulary applied in vigorous brushstrokes across a page. His poem 'Hotere' constructs an orderly arrangement of responses to Hotere's works, responding in turn to the painter's tactics of restraint, combination and composition – all tactics Tuwhare makes his own:

> When you offer only three
> vertical lines precisely drawn
> and set into a dark pool of lacquer
> it is a visual kind of starvation:
>
> and even though my eyeballs
> roll up and over to peer inside
> myself, when I reach the beginning
> of your eternity I say instead: hell
> let's have another feed of mussels
>
> *Like, I have to think about it, man*
>
> When you stack horizontal lines
> into vertical columns which appear
> to advance, recede, shimmer and wave
> like exploding packs of cards
> I merely grunt and say: well, if it
> is not a famine, it's a feast
>
> *I have to roll another smoke, man*
>
> But when you score a superb orange
> circle on a purple thought-base

> I shake my head and say: hell, what
> is this thing called aroha
>
> *Like, I'm euchred, man. I'm eclipsed?*

The power of restraint to take you inwards can be expressed as a hunger for mussels; the power of juxtapositions to create distance within a single space as a need to smoke; but the superb perfection of the orange on purple? It is this which brings into the poem the equally perfectly placed colloquialisms of the last line, the 'like', the 'man', and the question mark giving its rising inflection not just to this last line but to the whole poem. This rising inflection is often dismissed as the expression of a tentativeness that girls, in particular, are encouraged not to demonstrate, and perhaps there is a humility expressed here, as well, in Tuwhare's respect for Hotere's work. What *would* be enough to say? But there is a power, too, to this rising inflection, a confidence in his own vernacular, a pleasure in conversation that the conversational rhythm reflects, an invitation to further conversation and an opening out of the poem onto the ineffable, perhaps the beginning of the eternity that Tuwhare first glimpsed back in the poem's first stanza.

Conversations involve a composition of remark and reply, observation and response, even when they are not conversations *about* compositions. The conversation between Tuwhare and Hotere in this poem takes place on two levels at once, but the most essential arrangement is taking place within the poet himself as the self is eclipsed, examined and re-inscribed.

In 'she cut her face shaving', essa may ranapiri observes the process of self-composition as it is manifest externally – as a process of preparing an appearance with which to face the world – from the detached perspective of a third-person narration.

>   the smeared blood / flat down caught
>   over creases in the neck / the base
>   of the chin / the pencil skirt / the
>   short / cut / the hair / the straight
>   lines of the jaw / that testosterone
>   bought her / the droplets glistening / about
>   her adam's apple / quivering to the beat
>   of her / lateness / twenty years
>   late to work in / the morning

The presentation of self, in terms of a chosen gender identity, is described in terms of a series of visual details composed on the page not entirely unlike petals on a wet, black bough, or a wheelbarrow glazed with rainwater and set beside white chickens, but there is an urgency and movement to this scene that is quite different. The slashes within the lines – like line breaks within line breaks – add to the compositional energy, emphasising the placement of one detail after another. At the same time, they also suggest rupture and allow ambiguity – does the 'short / cut' refer to the hair, even though it is placed before the hair is mentioned, or the skirt, or both? Is the 'cut' even a noun, or might it be read as a verb? When you are twenty years late, might you need to employ such short cuts? Is the tension – the 'beat / of her / lateness' to which she quivers – positive as well as negative? In an interview about the collection *ransack*, from which this poem comes, ranapiri talks about their disruption of form and use of layout as a response not only to the complications of gender identity – they themself identify as non-binary – but also to the gaps, ruptures and violence of colonial history. It is a creative disruption that attempts, ranapiri explains, 'to stretch over breaks and if not necessarily healing them, finding healing in the breaks'.

It is not only the layout of a poem on the page that can 'stretch over breaks'. A life itself can do this, too. In the tightly constructed poem 'Linens', with its rhymes and off-rhymes – bristles, stasis, creases, places – neatly tucked into its sixteen lines, American poet Kay Ryan suggests that attention to the arrangement of material detail and a moment in time might be about what is lost as much as what is present, or about what must not be thought. In contrast to the sumptuous poem glutting itself on loss, the poem of concision and composition places the material and present object centre stage where it can block *out* loss, or whatever it is that is not allowed to enter the poem:

> There are charms
> that forestall harm.
> The house bristles
> with opportunities
> for stasis: refolding
> the linens along
> their creases, keeping
> the spoons and chairs
> in their right places.
> Nobody needs to
> witness one's exquisite
> care with the napkins
> for the napkins
> to have been the act
> that made the fact
> unhappen.

Yet while attending to composition and the material object can, for Ryan, be a way of avoiding narrative or action, making 'the fact / unhappen', Alice Oswald's *Memorial* demonstrates the power of composition and the image to make happened facts *felt*. *Memorial* is a radically concise translation of Homer's *Iliad* – Oswald confesses to a 'reckless dismissal of seven-eighths of the poem' – but whereas earlier translators aimed for narrative pace by cutting out much of the metaphorical imagery and the biographical details of minor characters, Oswald cuts out the main narrative thread, removing the plot 'as', she writes, 'you might lift the roof off a church in order to remember what you're worshipping'. The poem begins with a roll-call of all the fallen soldiers whose deaths will be the focus of the rest of the collection. The long list of capitalised names has the appearance of a contemporary war memorial. Each soldier is then given his narrative moment in turn, a description of how each death occurred, followed by a metaphorical image giving another way of imagining the death, another way of feeling it again. Each time the image that follows the narrative is repeated, and while repetition might seem to be the opposite of concision, it works like the radical concision of the text as a whole by demanding an even more focused attention and a deepening of the empathy already evoked. This is the death of Democoon, following straight on from the death of Leukos:

> And someone's face pierced like a piece of fruit
> That was Priam's son unlucky man
> Who made his living in the horse country
> North of Troy he was stepping backwards
> When the darkness hit him with a dull clang
> His name was DEMOCOON

> Like a man steps back
> Seeing a snake almost under his foot
> In a heathery hollow
> The fear flutters his knees it
> Sucks him white he steps back
>
> Like a man steps back
> Seeing a snake almost under his foot
> In a heathery hollow
> The fear flutters his knees it
> Sucks him white he steps back

The vivid jolt of fear that makes someone step back on seeing a snake is felt by the reader all the more powerfully and poignantly since the stepping back that saves a man from death is here a simile for the stepping back of Democoon into a death that cannot be avoided. Again and again through *Memorial* the reader is given these vivid jolts of perception, as the deaths are kept as the focus of attention through narrative followed by simile followed by repetition. The elements of ritual, and the awareness of composition – the repeated stanzas, the shapeliness of a stanza circling around the words 'steps back' in the first and last lines – heighten the effect of what Oswald tells us ancient critics found in Homer's *Iliad*: its 'energeia' or 'bright unbearable reality'. *Memorial* gives us concision, composition and the image as epic effects.

— READING LIST —

'Song of Myself' and
'Crossing Brooklyn Ferry'
Walt Whitman

'A Supermarket in California'
and 'America'
Allen Ginsberg

'Before Completion'
and 'The Chance'
Arthur Sze

'After Modernism' and
'Letter to Anne Kennedy'
Paula Green

CHAPTER FOUR

Sprawl

In a long poem called 'Confessional', Jenny Bornholdt writes: 'when people talk about poetry they often mention *compression* – yes, it can / be that, but it can also be a great sprawling / thing.' This chapter looks at what sprawl allows, what poetry can do when the lines are allowed to reach further towards the margins, when lines are allowed to continue mounting up to the end of the page and beyond, sometimes over pages and pages. Sprawl is not epic. The reader wanting the vast vistas and metaphysical reach of poems such as Homer's *Odyssey* or *Iliad*, or Milton's *Paradise Lost*, is more likely today to turn to novelist Philip Pullman's *His Dark Materials* trilogy than to poetry. Sprawl lacks the architecture and ambition of epic. It is easy to disapprove of sprawl. Kay Ryan writes:

> I guess I could say I don't read Whitman because I don't need Whitman's big stride, his wide, encompassing arms, his hug. The poets I go back to are not at all welcoming. I don't apparently like to be welcomed. My poets are a dryish people. Lonely, and what of it. They do not gather around the campfire. My poets don't cherish even

the illusion of ease and camaraderie; they do not laze and invite
their souls . . . What their souls need is a little discipline, thank you.

When I think of Whitman, I think of bulk. Page after page of the
SAME POEM, rectangle after rectangle of self-delighted self-
examination, undulating in the hot wholesome American breeze
like sections of Kansas wheat . . .

Encompassing is a good word to describe Walt Whitman's poetry. From 1856 to 1892, Whitman published nine different editions of his book *Leaves of Grass*, every time not only including more poems but also increasing the length of existing poems with new lines and stanzas. He was less interested in composition than in connection. In writing about himself, he invited his readers to read the poems as a song, also, of themselves:

> I celebrate myself, and sing myself,
> And what I assume you shall assume,
> For every atom belonging to me as good belongs to you.
>
> I loafe and invite my soul,
> I lean and loafe at my ease observing a spear of summer grass.

Readers in the nineteenth century may not have expected the discipline, dryness and interiority that Kay Ryan demands of poetry today, but the formlessness of such sprawling lines set Whitman's poetry apart when it was written. With its absence of metre or rhyme, readers wondered whether it was poetry at all, or, as one contemporary reviewer described it, 'a sort of excited prose broken into lines without any attempt at measure or regularity'. What excites the prose into poetry? There are rhythms, even if the rhythms are not strictly metrical but are closer to the rhythms of the Bible or oratory. Much of the poetry is built around different forms of repetition: the repetition of anaphora, with passages in which line after line begins with the same word or phrase; chiasmus and reflection, where a phrase is turned around or reversed ('what I assume you shall assume'; 'I loafe and invite my soul / I leane and loafe at my ease'); returns to phrases used earlier in the poem or the collection. There is a constant movement from the general to the specific, from the concrete to the abstract, and from 'I' to 'you', and back again.

The movement allows the long poems to include anything and everything in a way that is curiously untethered. 'Crossing Brooklyn Ferry' is one of the more precisely situated poems, and begins with the poet's view of the water below and the sunset to the west, situating the poem both in location and in time:

> Flood-tide below me! I see you face to face!
> Clouds of the west – sun there half an hour high – I see you
>   also face to face.
>
> Crowds of men and women attired in the usual costumes,
>   how curious you are to me!
> On the ferry-boats the hundreds and hundreds that cross,
> returning home, are more curious to me than you suppose,
> And you that shall cross from shore to shore years hence
> are more to me, and more in my meditations, than you
> might suppose.

For all the specificity of the place and time, however, and for all the poet's professed curiosity about the hundreds and hundreds of people crossing on the ferry, this face-to-face encounter between the poet and the world, and between the poet and the reader – the supposing 'you' – is open to the point of abstraction, and open to a future that unfolds without limits. For Whitman, what sustains the poet sustains the poem, and the other way around; the 'scheme', perhaps another word for composition (the composition of both the poem and the world), doesn't require concision or compression to be 'well-join'd' (though he does surprisingly call it 'compact'):

> The impalpable sustenance of me from all things at all hours
>   of the day,
> The simple, compact, well-join'd scheme, myself disintegrated,
>   every one disintegrated yet part of the scheme,
> The similitudes of the past and those of the future,
> The glories strung like beads on my smallest sights and hearings,
>   on the walk in the street and the passage over the river,
> The current rushing so swiftly and swimming with me far away,
> The others that are to follow me, the ties between me and them,
> The certainty of others, the life, love, sight, hearing of others.

Here, as throughout Whitman's poetry, the self is insistently, repeatedly present, yet it is the disintegrated self of American transcendentalism, a self that fits Ralph Waldo Emerson's description of an ideal writer existing like a 'transparent eyeball' seeing all and being nothing, allowing the 'Universal Being' to circulate through a self that is 'part and particle of God'. For poets writing in the wake of modernism and in the wake of the New Criticism that understood poetry in modernist terms (compression, concision and the image), Whitman's openness to the world and to all that might sustain a poem has proved a liberating example.

In the liner notes for a 1959 LP recording of the long poem 'Howl', Beat poet Allen Ginsberg explains how leaving behind the short lines William Carlos Williams had popularised released him from a constraining idea of what it meant to write *poetry*:

> By 1955 I wrote poetry adapted from prose seeds, journals, scratchings, arranged by phrasing or breath groups into little short-line patterns according to the ideas of measure of American speech I'd picked up from W. C. Williams's imagist preoccupations. I suddenly turned aside in San Francisco . . . to follow my romantic inspiration – Hebraic-Melvillian bardic breath, I thought I wouldn't write a *poem*, but just write what I wanted to without fear . . .

Williams himself – despite the encompassing nature of his own sprawling, book-length poem *Paterson* – was regretful when the young writers he knew turned away from the influence of his short lines to try a more expansive way of writing. Having championed the work of the young Ginsberg ('he had something to say and I wanted him to say it. And I wanted to befriend him'), he found himself, as he told Ginsberg, 'disgusted with him and his long lines'. But for Ginsberg, the longer line allowed not just a different aesthetic but also a different kind of content. Writing 'without fear' and without a sense of audience, except for 'my own soul's ear' and the golden ears of his closest friends, Ginsberg found that with 'Howl' he had composed a performance piece that became an anthem for a generation.

'A Supermarket in California', written the same year, suggests the importance of Whitman to the young Ginsberg, who begins the poem marvelling at 'What thoughts I have of you tonight, Walt

Whitman,' before walking into a supermarket 'shopping for images' and eventually following Whitman himself around the lit-up corridors with their brilliant stacks of cans:

> Where are we going, Walt Whitman? The doors close in an hour. Which way does your beard point tonight?
> (I touch your book and dream of our odyssey in the supermarket and feel absurd.)
> Will we walk all night through solitary streets? The trees add shade to shade, lights out in the houses, we'll both be lonely.
> Will we stroll dreaming of the lost America of love past blue automobiles in driveways, home to our silent cottage?
> Ah, dear father, graybeard, lonely old courage-teacher, what America did you have when Charon quit poling his ferry and you got out on a smoking bank and stood watching the boat disappear on the black waters of Lethe?

In 'America', which Ginsberg wrote a year after 'A Supermarket in California', we can recognise in the warmth and charge of the poem's address to America the same paradoxical intimacy we find in Whitman's poetry between the poet and an abstract and all-encompassing 'you'. When Ginsberg begins the poem 'America I've given you all and now I'm nothing', the disintegration of the poet's self that allows the radical transcendentalism of a vast and democratic vision becomes not simply a state of mind but a part of the drama that plays out in the poem between the poet and America itself. The poet is 'sick of your insane demands', but makes his own demands on America, questioning American politics, demanding answers, offering confessions, moving between personal anecdote, politics and metaphysics ('America after all it is you and I who are perfect not the next world'):

> America I've given you all and now I'm nothing.
> America two dollars and twentyseven cents January 17, 1956.
> I can't stand my own mind.
> America when will we end the human war?
> Go fuck yourself with your atom bomb.
> I don't feel good don't bother me.
> I won't write my poem till I'm in my right mind.
> America when will you be angelic?
> When will you take off your clothes?
> When will you look at yourself through the grave?
> When will you be worthy of your million Trotskyites?
> America why are your libraries full of tears?
> America when will you send your eggs to India?
> I'm sick of your insane demands.
> When can I go into the supermarket and buy what I need
>   with my good looks?

Twenty-two lines into the seventy-four-line poem we come to the words, 'I'm trying to come to the point.' But the point is being made, in part, by the juxtapositions and associations the sprawling structure allows, the way the political is presented as painfully personal. The poet's homosexuality, his marijuana smoking, his communist sympathies place him in an antagonistic relationship with the America he is nevertheless a part of, and which the sprawling structure of the poem presents as full of contradictions, open to more than the America he addresses might have supposed or imagined. The poem creates and enlarges the imagination of 'America'.

For contemporary Chinese-American poet Arthur Sze, Whitman's influence has been similarly liberating. In a commentary he gives on a reading of Whitman's 'Crossing Brooklyn Ferry', he explains: 'Walt Whitman's poetry has been important to my evolution as a poet . . . I wanted to break apart the conception of a poem as a well-wrought urn, so that more of the world could enter into my poetry.' For him there was potential in a more open, less linear poetry to accommodate Asian as well as Western aesthetics. With William Carlos Williams as an early influence, Sze's poetry continues to focus on precise images of material objects in the world, but has increasingly expanded to follow stanza on from stanza, idea on from idea. Many of his poems take very expansive viewpoints, often, as in 'Before Completion', looking beyond this world into the skies. But the essential expansiveness of the poems lies between the lines and between the details, between (in this case) the image of the vast vista the telescope offers to view, and the images the poem jumps to – a baby placed in a dumpster, deer munching apple blossoms – in a series of scenes that seem untethered to the poet's experience gazing through the telescope:

> I gaze through a telescope at the Orion Nebula,
> a blue vapor with a cluster of white stars,
> gaze at the globular cluster in Hercules,
> needle and pinpoint lights stream into my eyes.
> A woman puts a baby in a plastic bag
> and places it in a dumpster; someone
> parking a car hears it cry and rescues it.
> Is this the little o, the earth?
> Deer at dusk are munching apple blossoms;
> a green snake glides down flowing acequia water.
> The night is rich with floating pollen;

> in the morning, we break up the soil
> to prepare for corn. Fossilized cotton pollen
> has been discovered at a site above six thousand feet.
> As the character *yi*, change, is derived
> from the skin of a chameleon, we are
> living the briefest hues on the skin
> of the world. I gaze at the Sombrero Galaxy
> between Corvus and Spica: on a night with no moon,
> I notice my shadow by starlight.

How do we get from the view through the telescope to the image of the child in a dumpster? Is this a news report, a remembered anecdote, a scene from another work of literature or a film? What is the relation between this image and the images following in such quick succession of the deer, the green snake, the floating pollen, and the facts that are recorded about the fossilised cotton pollen, and the derivation of the character *yi*, for change? The stanza begins in the first person, but this 'I' who might offer a viewpoint from which we could get our bearings is almost completely missing throughout most of the stanza, returning only in the last lines, back at the telescope again, gazing now 'at the Sombrero Galaxy / between Coverus and Spica', and noticing his own shadow.

'Before Completion' is made up of six separate numbered sections, of which this is the first. Just as the first section of the poem juxtaposes images that seem to come from different contexts, only to circle back around to the observing self, so the poem as a whole juxtaposes the coordinating ideas and images of each section. The looping first section is followed by a section which opens with a question – 'Where does matter end and space begin?' – that is answered, or followed, by a series of images set out as an extended list. The third section uses the second-person 'you' to recount blunders and recollections – 'You recollect watching a yellow- / and-black-banded caterpillar' – with images like shots from a film, and snatches of apparently unrelated conversations. The fourth section follows the story of 'a poet' who 'axes his wife and hangs himself' with a return to the first-person narrative, as the 'I' of the poem lies listening to a 'you' breathing, and then the scene shifts again to an outdoor scene. With sections five and six, we move back and forth again from a list format to a personal narrative in which the personal soon gives way to the visual image.

In an interview with Ayleen Perry for the online journal *Terrain*, Sze said, 'I find that when I'm writing, I write lots of fragments and lots of phrases. I almost think of them as charged phrases and, though I may not understand them completely, there could be a sharp visual image or rhythm – a musicality to the phrase.' The idea of the charged phrase is, again, a modernist idea, and both the idea of the charge and the emphasis on the musicality of the phrasing recall the ideas of Ezra Pound even more than Williams. Pound's *Cantos* might seem an obvious model for a poetry made up of charged phrases, sharp visual images and phrases founded on a musicality, a rhythm. But there is something more essayistic, more sprawling about the way Sze puts together his poems. Possibly influenced by the journal in which the interview was going to appear, Sze talks in terms of 'terrain': 'I need to spread out and give myself room to discover what's really there. In letting the poem expand and discover where its terrain is, it goes into a lot of different arenas – and I'm using arenas as equivalent to muses.'

The poem that sprawls works in the opposite mode from the aphorism. As aphorist Sarah Manguso writes, the aphorism is not a fragment, but a complete stand-alone text, a piece of writing that cannot be condensed. The aphorism goes nowhere, relates to nothing, but, poet and essayist John McGhee suggests, 'the aphorism when memorised may not change minds but may accelerate action'. The sprawling poem is unlikely to accelerate action, but may change minds, in the way Anne Carson describes the mind being changed by poetry in the passage from which the title of this book is taken: the poem being 'an action of the mind captured on the page', the reader by the end of the poem is transformed, as well as transported, through having travelled the action of thinking. Unlike the aphorism, and unlike the modernist epic, the sprawling poem involves movement.

Some method of propulsion is necessary. Whitman and Ginsberg use the propulsion of anaphora, repetition and the list. In Sze's poetry, too, the list serves this propulsive function, as in the second stanza of 'Before Completion', with its list of apparently random images and events in the continuous present: 'blue jays eating suet' is one, 'sobbing' another, the drawing of equations on butcher paper, the folding of paper cranes. They are connected not only through the movement of the mind as the poet, and the reader, bring them together, but also through a shared, implied connection with the question at the start of the stanza – 'Where does matter end and space begin?' – and with the throw of the I Ching at the end, 'Before Completion'. The list takes us from question to answer. Stanzas three and four feature a psychic offering advice about a missing ring, the 'changing lines of divination', the poet lying in bed in the dark guessing at the freckles on his partner's arms, a daikon picker giving directions, 'point[ing] the way with a daikon'. The relationship between all these images and events is not obvious, and yet it seems resonant, with the particular resonance allowed by imagery of chance, absence, loss, divination and direction-taking.

Sze's poem makes me think of a favourite aphorism of mine, generated by an aphorism-generating program designed to demonstrate the rigidity of the aphorism's syntactic structure. It reads, 'When fate sleeps, it dreams of chance.' If aphorisms seem inevitable, the sprawling poem seems full of possibility. Section five of 'Before Completion' introduces another one of Sze's lists with another throw of the I Ching

– this time 'He threw Duration' – and concludes with a repetition of the line that opened stanza two: 'Where does matter end and space begin?' In the *Terrain* interview, developing the idea of 'charged moments, or revelatory moments', Sze explains:

> George Zweig, a contemporary physicist, once said to me, 'The great question of 20th century particle physics is, "Where does matter end and space begin?"' I'll never forget that line. Eventually, it found a place in an elegy for Gu Cheng, a Chinese poet who killed himself.

Although there is nothing in 'Before Completion' that presents it as an elegy, it is a poem charged with absence and loss. Perhaps always when a poem gestures towards a still-deferred completion, it is this ultimate distance that is brought to mind. In a very different poem, 'The Chance', a well-turned exposition of an idea almost sonnet-like in its construction, Sze cautions against the risk of becoming trapped by your own passions, like 'the ex-musician, insurance salesman, / who sells himself a policy on his own life; / or the magician who has himself locked / in a chest and thrown into the sea, / only to discover he is caught in his own chains.' The solution is to make sure your passions can keep growing, defined by 'your actions, thoughts, feelings'. Perhaps this is what sprawl allows, 'Before Completion' ending with the first person again, stopping and gazing, grief dissolving and the mind clearing, as a series of visual images of things in the world are placed in the stanza before it comes to its close. This is the whole of the final sixth stanza of the poem:

> Mushroom hunting at the ski basin, I spot
> a blood-red amanita pushing up under fir,
> find a white-gilled Man On Horseback,

> notice dirt breaking and carefully unearth
> a cluster of gold chanterelles. I stop
> and gaze at yellow light in a clearing.
> As grief dissolves and the mind begins to clear,
> an s twist begins to loosen the z twisted fiber.
> A spider asleep under a geranium leaf
> may rest a leg on the radial string of a web,
> but cool nights are pushing nasturtiums to bloom.
> An eggplant deepens in hue and drops to the ground.
> Yellow specks of dust float in the clearing;
> in memory, a series of synchronous spaces.
> As a cotton fiber burns in an s twist
> and unravels the z twist of its existence,
> the mind unravels and ravels a wave of light,
> persimmons ripening on leafless trees.

The relation between the movement allowed by the longer length of a poem in terms of the poem's own composition, and a movement across geographical or temporal spaces and subjects, is foregrounded from the start of New Zealand poet Paula Green's long poem to a fellow writer, 'Letter to Anne Kennedy'. Green's first collection of poetry, *Cookhouse* (1997), was full of very short poems, several no longer than two lines and a title, mostly fitting several to a page. Where Imagist poets like Ezra Pound juxtaposed two images, these poems more often juxtapose sensual details (frequently of food – one poem was included as a recipe in the cooking pages of the *New Zealand Listener*) with obliquely related, more abstract lines. A typical example is the poem titled 'freshly picked blueberries' which continues: 'the cook re-dresses / the abstract / any sort of building / stitching or paste.'

In the collection in which 'Letter to Anne Kennedy' appears, *Making Lists for Frances Hodgkins* (2007), the poet situates herself as writing after modernism, most explicitly in the poem which takes 'After Modernism' as its title:

> After Modernism I walked to the shops
> to buy a loaf of bread and a bottle of milk
> with the leaffrocked wind in my hair
> and the waterlogged tyre in my ear
> and the backblock road in my eye
> and the woebegone fog in my nose
> and the forgetmenot paper in my hand
> and the slipknot word on my cheek
> and the crisscrossed sign on my thigh
> and the defrosted pronoun on my brow.
>
> I saw a flowerpot that looked a lot like gorse
> gorse that looked a lot like barleycorn
> barleycorn that looked a lot like a harpsichord
> a harpsichord that looked a lot like a hobbyhorse.

This poem is characteristic of Green's work in how patterned it is, in the importance of the image and the detail, and in its apparent simplicity. But it is also characteristic in the work it requires of the reader to make the connections between the claim she makes for the poem as coming 'After Modernism' and the significance of the imagery – particularly the imagery of the last few lines, in which simile is recast as descriptions that are hard to picture. Where Pound's 'In a Station of the Metro' casts the bustling crowd of people as petals on a wet black bough, replacing movement with stasis, positioning the viewer beyond the scene, here the poet herself moves through a landscape with a very domestic purpose, and the world, both its images and its words, becomes a part of the poet's embodied self.

In 'Letter to Anne Kennedy', however, the poet is removed from the domestic rhythms so important in much of her poetry, as she gives herself to the art and monuments of Rome, the windows of Florence and the frescoes of Padua, and 'tries to think the thoughts of others', following in the footsteps of literary characters. The poem begins airborne, 'Flying above Rome in the summer heat', the city seen from above fitting 'in the palm // of your hand like a book.' The story of the journey is written in the second person, and the 'you' is easily read, at the beginning of the poem, as the letter's addressee. This offers the disconcerting possibility of a letter that, instead of recounting the details of the writer's life for a distant reader, presents the reader with an intimate account of their own movements and experiences: 'you read // the rust-coloured walls and the fountain's music, the lines of acquaintances / and the loss of freedom, you reach the crowded trattoria in the half-dark street.' As the experiences accumulate, however, the second-person 'you' becomes more and more readily understood as the poet sharing her own experiences, with the second-person pronoun an invitation to the reader – in the place of the addressee – to imaginatively share the experiences as the poem spools out in long-lined couplets over several pages:

> . . . For a whole day you hear the clanking of bells,
>
> the goats clambering about the cottage, and you fool yourself
>   into thinking the wolves

>   are still there with the timid moon and that the people are
>   disguised as something else,
>
> patron saints are disguised as bleating cows and twisted bundles
>   of rags are babies
> or babies are unburdened of secrets in the lament for the living.
>   You are calling
>
> out to someone who is far away, as though you will find poetry
>   in the distant people.
> It isn't quite clear how the private lives have such a miraculous
>   power as you sit
>
> on the Spanish steps or circle the points of the Four Rivers
>   Fountain. Presently,
> with Italy ahead of you like the symptoms of love, you begin
>   to count the storms at
>
> sea. It is not as though you are lost . . .

The reference near the end of the poem to a long illness spent lying in bed, staring at the paintings of Frances Hodgkins and making lists, confirms the autobiographical nature of a poem. It references both the title of the collection and the endnote on the page opposite which describes the collection as 'an autobiography in the light of art' that the poet decided to write during her illness. The poem concludes with a description of reading Anne Kennedy's own verse novel, *The Time of the Giants*, and letting 'the immense beautiful spaces become a refuge', and at last it becomes apparent how this poem is a letter to Anne Kennedy.

The significance of this moment of reading is enlarged, however, by all the references to reading that fill the poem.

Like an essay, the long poem can develop themes across time, with one scene following another, and actual experiences of reading alternating with more metaphorical instances of reading a culture, a landscape, art, customs, signs, 'the symptoms of love'. The theme of reading is richer for sitting alongside other themes that also develop across a range of scenes and images – politics, empathy, hunger, what can be spoken and what remains unsaid, what can be understood and what can only be witnessed, freedom and imprisonment, solitude and what it gives and what it withholds. Reading has a significance in relation to all these other themes. For all the rich material and connections the longer poem allows Green to offer, still the reader is left to do the work of thinking through what all this amounts to. Or the reader may be content simply to luxuriate in not understanding, in seeing the beauty of a meaning just beyond their reach.

READING LIST

'The fish'
Marianne Moore

'What lips my lips have kissed,
and where, and why'
Edna St Vincent Millay

'sonnet'
sam sax

'American Sonnet for my Past
and Future Assassin' ['I lock
you in an American sonnet
that is part prison']
Terrance Hayes

'Duplex'
Jericho Brown

'One Art'
Elizabeth Bishop

'Five Limericks on Grief'
Nick Ascroft

'My Brother at 3 A.M.'
Natalie Diaz

'Sextina'
Erin Scudder

'Like, the Sestina'
A. E. Stallings

CHAPTER FIVE

Form

All poets are concerned with form, including the form of poems that sprawl out across pages, built on patterns of repetition, return and removal, set out with consideration for the white spaces between and around lines and stanzas. This chapter is concerned with a stricter definition of form – form that involves constraint. A poem can be set into couplets, even couplets with a count of ten stresses for every line, without the layout determining the poet's choice of words or narrative direction. It is a different matter to write in the form of a villanelle, with its repeated lines and limited number of rhymes, or a sestina with its rearrangement of words from stanza to stanza. To write towards a rhyme at the end of a line, or to fit an argument into fourteen lines of iambic pentameter, can be challenging and even limiting, but it can also be paradoxically liberating – as the poet A. E. Stallings explains: 'I like to say that form is not about having control, but giving up control, allowing other forces into the poem.'

To write in established forms is also to evoke a tradition. A sonnet might look nothing like one of Shakespeare's sonnets, yet to write a sonnet sets up a relationship with poets writing sonnets in the past, and sets up expectations, whether met or resisted, for what the sonnet might be about and the way it might play out. William Carlos Williams, intent on writing a new and American poetry, 'to set American poetry on its proper tracks', as he said, *hated* the sonnet. 'Forcing twentieth-century America into a sonnet – gosh, how I hate sonnets – is like putting a crab into a square box,' he said. 'You've got to cut his legs off to make him fit. When you get through you don't have a crab anymore.' Williams wanted his poetry to fit the things in the world as he encountered them – 'no ideas but in things'.

To find an American, modernist crab, we'll need to turn away from the sonnet and look to the work of Marianne Moore, a poet contemporary with Williams. Like Williams, she found ideas in things – she was fascinated by material objects and by all living creatures – and, like Williams, she rejected traditional forms and developed her own idiosyncratic ways of patterning her poetry. But far from resisting constraint, she revelled in the most complex, difficult restrictions that she set entirely for herself. The crabs in this poem hardly seem to need legs as they slide, like the starfish and jellyfish, underwater, but the poem's complicated formal patterning does constantly seem to require 'the physical features of // ac- / cident – lack' that Moore attributes to the 'defiant edifice' described, but never quite defined, in the poem.

This 'defiant edifice' is the subject of the poem titled 'The fish', in which fish are just the first of the ornamental creatures decorating the underwater landscape. It has become more common now than it was in the early twentieth century when Moore was writing to give a poem part of its first sentence for its title, but usually this adds to the poem's informality and a sense of fluidity, the title flowing into the poem without distinction. Here, the break between the title and the poem has the opposite effect. Set up to read a poem about a fish, we are first caught up by the verb 'wade' that continues what we realise only then is the start of a sentence, a sentence not about a fish but fish, plural, perhaps a school of fish. The word 'wade' is itself an odd word to describe the movement of fish, more usually describing a person walking through deep water, but it rather beautifully suggests the slow pace of these fish. It suggests, too, a sense of the water as somehow more solid than we would ordinarily imagine it, and this is fitting in a poem in which the sea itself is both the landscape and the main player. With each line of the poem, we adjust our reading of the line before, gradually finding ourselves moving away from the fish to focus on other sea creatures, which themselves are only the ornamentation on the underwater edifice that becomes the 'it' of the poem's last line:

The fish

wade
through black jade.
    Of the crow-blue mussel-shells, one keeps
    adjusting the ash-heaps;
        opening and shutting itself like

an
injured fan.
    The barnacles which encrust the side
    of the wave, cannot hide
        there for the submerged shafts of the

sun,
split like spun
    glass, move themselves with spotlight swiftness
    into the crevices –
        in and out, illuminating

the
turquoise sea
>of bodies. The water drives a wedge
>of iron through the iron edge
>>of the cliff; whereupon the stars,

pink
rice-grains, ink-
>bespattered jelly fish, crabs like green
>lilies, and submarine
>>toadstools, slide each on the other.

All
external
>marks of abuse are present on this
>defiant edifice –
>>all the physical features of

ac-
cident – lack
>of cornice, dynamite grooves, burns, and
>hatchet strokes, these things stand
>>out on it; the chasm-side is

dead.
Repeated
>evidence has proved that it can live
>on what can not revive
>>its youth. The sea grows old in it.

In Chapter One, on simplicity and resonance, we looked at how poems like Emily Brontë's 'Spellbound', Robert Frost's 'Stopping by Woods on a Snowy Evening' or William Butler Yeats's 'Song of Wandering Aengus' use rhyme to cast a kind of spell, giving a dream-like resonance and sense of inevitability to the rhyming lines. It is as if the poet found the lines as much as invented them, surrendering to 'the other forces' that A. E. Stallings allows into her poetry through the use of form. But there is nothing lyric or spellbinding about the rhymes in 'The fish', which instead emphasise the way the poem has been constructed, drawing attention to the patterning of each stanza according to an apparently arbitrary, but repeated, arrangement of a one-syllable line followed by one of three syllables, then one of nine, one of six and finally one of eight. Given that the sentences run across the stanzas, and even a word can be broken if necessary, and given there are no other constraints of metre or length, without the rhyme the patterning would be only a pattern on the page. The rhymes, though, force the poet's hand, allowing some of those accidents of outside forces in, like the word 'ac- / cident' itself, with its rhyme of 'lack'. While the rhythms remain relentlessly prosaic, more the rhythm of a non-fiction article even than the rhythm of conversation, the rhymes and layout on the page add an estranging element that makes prose itself sound strange, full of awkward echoes, with sound rubbing up against and across sense. Yet I find the poem beautiful, not only because of the beautiful imagery, with the sea lit up by shafts of sunlight 'split like spun / glass', but because of the awkward, fractured, intricate prose rhythms set against the poem's layout on the page.

We can see how differently this reads from the iambic pentameter of a conventionally formed sonnet if we follow it with a sonnet written not many years later by Edna St Vincent Millay.

What lips my lips have kissed, and where, and why,
I have forgotten, and what arms have lain
Under my head till morning; but the rain
Is full of ghosts tonight, that tap and sigh
Upon the glass and listen for reply,
And in my heart there stirs a quiet pain
For unremembered lads that not again
Will turn to me at midnight with a cry.

Thus in the winter stands the lonely tree,
Nor knows what birds have vanished one by one,
Yet knows its boughs more silent than before:
I cannot say what loves have come and gone,
I only know that summer sang in me
A little while, that in me sings no more.

The poem itself is as lyrical as a half-forgotten song, with the lines of perfect iambic pentameter flowing in the first eight-line stanza across one sentence, now running a phrase over a line break, now pausing in the middle of a line, and returning again and again to the quiet rhymes of 'why' with 'sigh', 'rain' with 'pain'. A further formality is added in the second stanza as the clauses of another single sentence end with the line ends, until in the last two lines once again the remembrance of the summer is allowed to run over into the last line, before we are brought back to the present season. The image of the lover growing older as a tree losing its leaves is a traditional one, borrowed even by Shakespeare from earlier poets when he began his Sonnet 73 with these lines:

> That time of year thou mayst in me behold
> When yellow leaves, or none, or few, do hang
> Upon those boughs which shake against the cold,
> Bare ruined choirs, where late the sweet birds sang.

Four lines to Millay's six, this includes the additional image of the boughs as 'bare ruined choirs', as if from an abandoned church where the choirboys once sang. But where Shakespeare begins with this image, and continues on to argue for the urgency of love in the face of time's relentless progress, Millay writes when love is already consigned to an almost forgotten past, and allows the lovely image of the bare tree to stand as the poem's conclusion. The use of the Petrarchan sonnet form, ending not with the rhyming couplet that concludes a Shakespeare sonnet but with the six-line stanza with its more subtle rhyme scheme c-d-e-c-d-e, works beautifully with the more backwards-looking ending. Yet the poem was originally published in 1920 in *Vanity Fair*, a fashionable high-society magazine then as now, contributing to an early version of celebrity culture with its glossy photographs and profiles of Interesting People. It is a Jazz Age poem, written when the Flapper was shocking society with a new note of frivolity we might hear in the poet's claim to have kissed so many lovers that she can't remember any of them – a strikingly bold claim then for a woman.

Poets continue to make the sonnet new, and to make it American. The Imagist poetry of William Carlos Williams would have been well suited for Twitter (and his poem 'This Is Just to Say' is a Twitter staple, in the form of parodies and variations), but sam sax may have written the most perfect Twitter sonnet:

sonnet

funny
how
spring
always
makes
me
feel
as
tho
we're
not
already
almost
dead

The title of the poem, 'sonnet', does a tremendous amount of work, largely fulfilling, even before it is made, the poem's opening promise of comedy: it's funny how a tweet can be presented as a sonnet, evoking a tradition that the poem brilliantly upholds. The changing of seasons is traditionally linked to thoughts of mortality – Edna St Vincent Millay contrasts a summer of youth with a present winter, Shakespeare's season of aging is the late autumn when 'yellow leaves, or none, or few' hang on the trees – and spring offers the sharpest contrast of all between the eternal renewal of the seasons and the reminder, with every falling blossom or hasty daffodil, of our own mortality in the face of time. The movement of sax's 'sonnet' from the opening word 'funny' to the closing word 'dead' is like a sped-up repetition of the movement of the Millay sonnet, going even further, faster. Yet it is the belief that we are *not* already almost dead that gives the poem its energy and its charm, even if it is only a conditional belief, more to do with feeling than logic.

Where sam sax speeds up the sonnet by paring it back to one word a line, another contemporary American poet, Terrance Hayes, packs more than the conventional ten syllables into each of the fourteen lines of his dense sonnets. But they are no more lacking in velocity for that. His 2016 collection, *American Sonnets for my Past and Future Assassin*, is made up of seventy sonnets all with the same title, 'American Sonnet for my Past and Future Assassin', suggesting the sense of menace that pervades the collection, as well as the sense of tradition it also draws on, referencing in particular the one hundred American sonnets (all with the title 'American Sonnet') written by Wanda Coleman in the 1990s. Many of his sonnets are about the sonnet form itself, represented in one as 'part prison, / Part panic closet':

> I lock you in an American sonnet that is part prison,
> Part panic closet, a little room in a house set aflame.
> I lock you in a form that is part music box, part meat
> Grinder to separate the song of the bird from the bone.
> I lock your persona in a dream-inducing sleeper hold
> While your better selves watch from the bleachers.
> I make you both gym & crow here. As the crow
> You undergo a beautiful catharsis trapped one night
> In the shadows of the gym. As the gym, the feel of crow-
> Shit dropping to your floors is not unlike the stars
> Falling from the pep rally posters on your walls.
> I make you a box of darkness with a bird in its heart.

> Voltas of acoustics, instinct & metaphor. It is not enough
> To love you. It is not enough to want you destroyed.

The inadequacy of love and destruction can be extended beyond the relationship with the poet's 'past and future assassin' to the sonnet form itself, which is both celebrated and re-imagined with the composition of this sonnet, as well as in the images with which it describes the form. It is prison and panic closet, representing both confinement and safety, but it is also music box and meat grinder, and a container for both darkness and song. The 'you' addressed in the poem is also doubled and doubled again: an assassin of an assassination that has already taken place as well as a future threat, someone at the same time 'made' by the poet into both gym and crow, actor and spectator, agent and addressee of the poetry. The gym and crow indirectly reference the Jim Crow laws and the whole history of racial injustice and violence that frames every sonnet in the collection, while each word gives rise to its own extended metaphor as 'you' become the crow trapped in the gym even while you are the gym itself with crow-shit dropping to your floors. The imagery in which you are figured is both your prison and a box given to you as a gift. Part of the gift is the possibilities it opens up of reading both this and other sonnets in the light of these metaphors: as boxes of darkness we can open up into song as we read them; as panic closets we might take refuge in; as gyms for our interpretative play; as prisons in which we might find ourselves trapped, longed for, loved and destroyed, separated from our physical selves, caught up in the flames of poetry.

Poets can invent entirely new forms, and can rework old forms to new ends. Jericho Brown does both at once in his invention of the duplex, a new form of the sonnet. Like Hayes, Brown writes with a complicated sense of his place within an inherited tradition – his five duplexes, each titled 'Duplex', are part of a collection called *The Tradition*. The form they take – fourteen lines, with the first line echoed in the last line, the second line echoed, becoming the third line, the fourth line echoed and becoming the fifth line, and so on until the penultimate line becomes the first line of the couplet that leads to the final (and first) line – answers the question Brown put to himself about writing in the sonnet form: how to make it his own:

> What does a sonnet have to do with anybody's content? And if the presumed content of a sonnet is that it's a love poem, how do I – a believer in love – subvert that. What is a Jericho Brown sonnet? . . . So I wanted a form that in my head was black and queer and Southern. Since I am carrying these truths in this body as one, how do I get a form that is many forms?

And so he built into the sonnet form the repetition of the blues, and fills his duplex poems with stories of love, loss and trauma. Where the sonnet builds towards a final resolution, the duplex begins with the line it will end on, opening as it ends with a larger idea framing the details given as the poem goes on. This is the first duplex in the collection:

> A poem is a gesture toward home.
> It makes dark demands I call my own.
>
> Memory makes demands darker than my own:
> My last love drove a burgundy car.
>
> My first love drove a burgundy car.
> He was fast and awful, tall as my father.

>   Steadfast and awful, my tall father
>   Hit hard as a hailstorm. He'd leave marks.
>
> Light rain hits easy but leaves its own mark
> Like the sound of a mother weeping again.
>
>   Like the sound of my mother weeping again,
>   No sound beating ends where it began.
>
> None of the beaten end up how we began.
> A poem is a gesture toward home.

The shifting pattern of repetition and variation is a pattern that this poem presents as the form life takes after trauma. Every beating ends up other than it began, but the beatings are repeated, and the line 'None of the beaten end up how we began' seems to be contradicted by the concluding line that is, after all, a return to the beginning. Yet the line that, at the beginning, introduced a poem about home might be heard, at the end of the poem, as a confession that a poem can only 'gesture' towards home. The sense of home, too, perhaps has shifted – perhaps it is poetry itself that offers a sense of home to the poet now, even as poetry makes its own 'dark demands'.

Forms patterned on repetition, like the villanelle, the sestina and the pantoum, have been taken up increasingly over the last century to write about trauma and grief. The repetition of lines reflects the return of difficult emotions, even as the demands of form offer a way of managing – at least in print – emotions which have no bounds. Elizabeth Bishop, who usually wrote in free verse, perfecting a digressive, descriptive, conversational style of poetry, turned to the villanelle form partway through the long drafting process that eventually led to perhaps her best-known poem, 'One Art'. An early draft plays with the idea of 'mislaying', playing it up as a psychological defence against accepting unbearable loss in such a way that, even though the draft material itself doesn't get past this false start, it is easy enough to see that the completed poem was always going to be a poem about the loss its opening lines were seeking to deny. By the second draft she has already introduced the rhyme of 'master' and 'disaster' that the final villanelle is built around, the two poles of mastery and loss so important to the villanelle form. It is only in the eighth draft, however, that she begins to map out the form in terms of where the rhymes will have to fall, and begins collecting the rhymes that will eventually find their place in the finished poem. Beginning with the loss of a pen, the poem progresses in an almost stately manner through a series of increasing losses, from her mother's watch, to houses, continents and, finally, the ultimate loss, the loss of 'you':

> The art of losing isn't hard to master;
> so many things seem filled with the intent
> to be lost that their loss is no disaster.
>
> Lose something every day. Accept the fluster
> of lost door keys, the hour badly spent.
> The art of losing isn't hard to master.
>
> Then practice losing farther, losing faster:
> places, and names, and where it was you meant
> to travel. None of these will bring disaster.
>
> I lost my mother's watch. And look! my last, or
> next-to-last, of three loved houses went.

> The art of losing isn't hard to master.
>
> I lost two cities, lovely ones. And, vaster,
> some realms I owned, two rivers, a continent.
> I miss them, but it wasn't a disaster.
>
> – Even losing you (the joking voice, a gesture
> I love) I shan't have lied. It's evident
> the art of losing's not too hard to master
> though it may look like (*Write* it!) like disaster.

I think perhaps I love most of all the first exclamation mark after the 'look!' inviting the reader to share in the astonishment of what can be lost without disaster. Even keeping perfectly to the villanelle's strict form, keeping not only to the pattern of repetition and rhyme but also to the iambic metre, Bishop maintains a conversational tone as if she just happens to be talking a villanelle. It might feel as if she is talking directly to us, until in the last stanza she addresses the poem to 'you', the person whose loss is, for all her denials, evidently a disaster – and by the final line, with the italicised '*Write* it!' in parentheses, it is clear she is talking, as she surely was all along, to herself.

Although the villanelle now seems so evidently a form suited to writing about grief and loss, when it began to be taken up early in the twentieth century it was regarded as a form suitable only for light verse. With its origins thought to be in song, its repetitions gave it a beauty but also an artificiality that could be heard as essentially frivolous, if not comic. Associations with forms can shift over time, but the limerick might be the least likely form to give rise to an ongoing tradition of writing about grief. New Zealand poet Nick Ascroft has pulled off this apparently impossible feat – though the only way to pull off the feat is *not* to pull it off as a feat so much as to write about grief in the limerick form because it has somehow, strangely but certainly, become the *necessary* form for the poem:

> When I see a young boy and his dad,
> I'm brought back to the one that I had.
> They seem charged, holographic.
> Then I lose them in traffic,
> and it leaves me reflective and sad.
>
> There was an old man with dementia
> whose passing, I'm willing to venture,
> was, they said, for the best,
> and at last he could rest,
> and they spoke unexpecting of censure.
>
> There was an old man they embalmed
> And he lay there so clean and becalmed.
> The work loving, unrushed –
> his eyebrows were brushed –
> and I wasn't emotionally armed.
>
> Like a walnut resistant to shelling,
> my feelings are screened, but it's telling
> that I ask am I grieving
> or just self-deceiving,
> that I'm silent and suddenly yelling.
>
> There's an image I chose for my profile:
> I'm three, on his knee, looking docile.

> Now a couple months on
> I feel weird it's not gone.
> But I stare at the picture immobile.

Part of the enjoyment of a limerick is often in the ingenuity of the rhymes. Ascroft – a Scrabble champion known, as a poet, for his formal virtuosity – begins with the simplest of rhymes, but the more surprising rhymes that follow don't take away from the sobriety of the poem even as they add a charged, holographic awareness of the poet's art. The reader is left at the end of the poem sharing the sense of how impossible it is to move on from the grief that has been expressed, staring immobile at the words on the page.

The more ingenuity a form demands, the greater the challenge to make the form seem necessary, inevitable: it becomes both harder and more essential for the formal arrangement not to seem an end in itself, a technical exercise before it is a poem. Like the villanelle, the pantoum is a form with origins in song (the Malaysian pantun), adapted for poetry on the page in the nineteenth century and increasingly taken up by poets writing in English over the twentieth century. The pattern of repetition is even stricter than in the villanelle, with the second and fourth lines of every stanza repeated as the first and third lines of the next stanza. This means every line has to work in relation to the lines before and after it – a serious constraint on the working through of a situation, thought or narrative. A joke can be made of its repetitiveness, as in 'Cashpoint: A Pantoum' by James Brown, made up of the instructions from an ATM machine comically getting absolutely nowhere, or it can offer a more serious take on the helpless submission to relentless forces, as in Donald Justice's 'Pantoum of the Great Depression' (see Notes and references, p. 259). 'But it is by blind chance that we escape tragedy', reads the second to last line of 'Pantoum of the Great Depression', returning to a variation on its starting line, 'Our lives avoided tragedy'. Then an extra line is added to the pantoum, a line that stands alone outside a stanza: 'And there is no plot in that; it is devoid of poetry.' The impossibility of narrative, if not of poetry, could be thought inherent in the pantoum form.

Natalie Diaz demonstrates how powerful the pantoum form can be, however, in the fast-paced, dramatic story she tells in 'My Brother at 3 A.M.':

> He sat cross-legged, weeping on the steps
> when Mom unlocked and opened the front door.
> > *O God*, he said. *O God.*
> > > *He wants to kill me, Mom.*
>
> When Mom unlocked and opened the front door
> at 3 a.m., she was in her nightgown, Dad was asleep.
> > *He wants to kill me*, he told her,
> > > looking over his shoulder.
>
> 3 a.m. and in her nightgown, Dad asleep,
> *What's going on?* she asked. *Who wants to kill you?*
> > He looked over his shoulder.
> > > *The devil does. Look at him, over there.*
>
> She asked, *What are you on? Who wants to kill you?*
> The sky wasn't black or blue but the green of a dying night.
> > *The devil, look at him, over there.*
> > > He pointed to the corner house.

> The sky wasn't black or blue but the dying green of night.
> Stars had closed their eyes or sheathed their knives.
>> My brother pointed to the corner house.
>>> His lips flickered with sores.
>
> Stars had closed their eyes or sheathed their knives.
> *O God, I can see the tail*, he said. *O God, look.*
>> Mom winced at the sores on his lips.
>>> *It's sticking out from behind the house.*
>
> *O God, see the tail*, he said. *Look at the goddamned tail.*
> He sat cross-legged, weeping on the front steps.
>> Mom finally saw it, a hellish vision, my brother.
>>> *O God, O God*, she said.

The repetitions which usually seem to stall movement here add to the sense that the drama is building up, and the doubling pattern of call and response that the form creates seems particularly fitting to a poem in dialogue, a conversation between two people. Remembering the poem before I read it again, I thought, in fact, that the mother repeated some of the lines of the brother, but in fact it is only in the last line that her exclamation, '*O God, O God*,' picks up her son's words, and, even so, this is not a line in his own dialogue. But the repetitions and echoes between them do reflect the disjunction between the son's vision and the mother's, until she finally comes to share his own horror, a vision of hell. Most of the lines are repeated exactly, or nearly, with a shift in the syntax being enough to adjust the relation of one line to the next (from 'looking over his shoulder' to 'He looked over his shoulder', for instance). Where the lines are altered more, it is often an alteration of perspective – 'His lips flickered with sores' becomes, in the next line, 'Mom winced at the sores on his lips.' The effect is to maintain the momentum and almost cinematic sense of drama as we switch perspective from the son's vision to the mother's, and back. But there is a third perspective too, of course: this is a story told by the sister, an onlooker, who has, perhaps, understood sooner than the mother how hellish a story it is they are caught up in.

The sestina is another form that can act like a net, catching up its protagonists in a cycle of repetition. Unlike the pantoum or the villanelle (or the duplex), individual lines are not repeated, but the six end words of the first stanza are repeated as the end words of every subsequent stanza in an alternating pattern, so that the last word of the first stanza becomes the first word of the second, then the first word of the first stanza the second word, and so on, like shuffling a pack of cards. The effect can be claustrophobic or at least tightly confined: the six words of Elizabeth Bishop's 'Sestina' – house, grandmother, child, stove, almanac and tears – construct a very small stage for its minimalist play of emotional undercurrents. Erin Scudder's 'Sextina', more unusually, emphasises the variation in order over the repetition of words to question the ways narratives are constructed, and the different ways a story can be told and imagined. The first stanza begins with the word 'See', addressed to the reader, suggesting the past can be objectively viewed:

> See Sextus slip
> into Lucretia.
> She didn't want to let him but he told
> her he'd kill her and wreck her repute too. Do
> you see how grittingly, today,
> she wills herself away.

Even in this first stanza, however, we move from actions that can be seen to emotions that are told to us, and from being told to see to being asked, 'Do / you see'. After this stanza, all the following stanzas begin with the word 'Or', and each presents a variation on the same story, with a different interpretation:

> Or: In spite of herself Lucretia feels her guard slipping away. Slip
> into me, whispers she. Today
> with a sigh she side-steps enmity. See Lucretia
> cheating on her husband. The adulteress Lucretia will not do as she is told.
>
> Or: *I told*
> *you to go away*,
> says Lucretia to herself all day. *Do*
> *promise to avenge me!* she says to her family and then *slip*
> goes the blade into her belly as – crazy all the while, see – Lucretia kills Lucretia
> today.
>
> Or: Today
> someone told
> me that there was no way Lucretia
> could get away
> with murder. Hell-bound Lucretia is tried posthumously. Slip
> into the back of the court-room to watch. *See what a woman like that can do.*

Or: *What was she to do?*
is what I thought today.
I am sure Lucretia gave Sextus the slip
just like I myself told
you to go away.
I'm like Lucretia.

Or: See Sextus slip into Lucretia.
Do
you think they'll put him away
today?
It depends on how we read her mind. Truth be told,
he's not the one on trial. This wasn't *his* slip.

What are we to make of you, Lucretia?
Today, and today, however the story is told,
away you slip quietly, into the fold.

Unlike a conventional sestina, the lines are unmetred and the radical variations in length add to the sense of contingency and to the amount of variation possible in how this story is told. The rape of Lucretia by Sextus Tarquinius is a story that is known only through its retellings, the earliest version written almost five hundred years after the events. The poem tells the story in the present tense, yet the word 'today' reads a little strangely here. It is one of the ways poetry works, to hold open the present tense of a moment in time (like Keats holding out his living hand), but writing 'today' almost seems to date the action to an immediate present. As one of the six repeating words of the sestina, the word 'today' plays an interesting role in interrogating the relationship between the past and the present, history and story: in the fourth and fifth stanzas, for instance, the poet herself enters the poem, thinking 'today' about what someone told her in the 'today' of the previous stanza (which feels, by the following stanza, as if it must now be today's yesterday). If in the first three stanzas the story took place in a past imagined as if still present, and in stanzas four and five we switch to a present-tense perspective looking back on a past now distant, how do we read the ongoing court case discussed in the fifth and sixth stanzas? Is this a trial taking place two-and-a-half thousand years ago, or the ongoing trial of Lucretia's reputation that continues to be carried out in art and literature?

When we read, 'Truth be told, / he's not the one on trial', this might seem to reflect on contemporary rape cases as much as on the original story (in which not only Sextus but his entire family was driven out of Rome after what could be called a trial, though not a court case). Perhaps it also reflects on this sestina itself, which might be expected to have 'Sextus' as one of its six words but doesn't even include his name in half of the stanzas. His name isn't in the final refrain either. Another word, too, is missing from the refrain, which by convention ought to include all the six end words of the sestina, but in this case has missed the word 'do'. 'What are we to make of you' has perhaps replaced 'What do we make of you', shifting the problem into a future tense and suggesting work still be done 'Today, and today'. Or perhaps it replaces 'What are we to do with you', but the lines that follow suggest nothing will be done either with or to Lucretia, who has slipped 'into the fold' – an odd word to end on. There is no formal necessity to account for it – a sestina doesn't usually end on a rhyme. What kind of a fold is it: a fold in time, a narrative fold, turning one event up against another? It seems, all the same, a comforting word – a lost sheep might return to the fold. And it seems to fold up the sestina itself into some kind of quiet closure.

Where Erin Scudder allows her 'Sextina' its own quiet variations on the rules, 'Like, the Sestina' by A. E. Stallings at once obeys all the rules of a sestina while being defiantly, ridiculously transgressive. Every line is in regular iambic pentameter, but every line ends with the same end word, 'like'. Is this a further, ridiculous challenge Stallings has set herself, or has she found a way to get around the complicated rules of return for the sestina's six end words? And is the 'like' at the end of each of the poem's lines even the same word each time? The question that the form raises is the cultural question at the heart of the poem. Is to 'like' a post on social media the same as liking a person? Does it indicate emotion, or affinity? Does it serve or replace relationships? Are we liking the person who posted what we 'like', or are we liking the product? Does a culture of 'liking' bring everything, and everyone, to the same level? The sestina doesn't have the same association with love as its subject as the sonnet does. Though the obsessive cycling around of a few key words could well lend itself to the representation of romantic love, it works as well to evoke ordinary domestic unhappiness, as in Bishop's sestina, or to interrogate sexual and gender politics, as Scudder does. 'Like, a Sestina' begins by lamenting the loss of Love as a defining value for a culture now defined by liking:

> Now we're all 'friends,' there is no love but Like,
> A semi-demi-goddess, something like
> A reality-TV-star look-alike,
> Named Simile or Me Two. So we like
> In order to be liked. It isn't like
> There's Love or hate now. Even plain 'dislike'
>
> Is frowned on: there's no button for it.

This is in fact a sestina that is itself consumed with disliking, rather than liking, liking. The second stanza rails against the 'virtual support' for political causes the 'like' offers in place of any genuine action; the third stanza introduces a dislike of the way the word 'like' has come to infiltrate ordinary conversation: '"I'm like, / So OVER him," I overhear. "But, like, / He doesn't get it. Like, you know?"' The fourth and fifth stanzas elaborate on the meaningless way the word is used, and on its invasive proliferation, which is compared in the sixth stanza to the equally disliked proliferation of 'Redundant fast food franchises, each like / (More like) the next.' This stanza ends on a challenge – 'I'd like / us just to admit that's what real speech is like' – before the final refrain of the sestina gives way to defeat, and conceding to the culture of liking:

> But as you like, my friend. Yes, we're alike
> How we pronounce, say, 'lichen,' and dislike
> Cancer and war. So like this page. Click *Like*.

Poetry now circulates on the internet as much as, if not more than, it circulates in print. Does this change the relationship between the poet and the reader? Is the experience of reading a poem reduced to the clicking of a 'like' button? Like posts on social media, conversations between a poet and a reader take place in a virtual space. Yet while social media is often framed, as in Stalling's sestina, as essentially shallow, a space in which all is alike, poetry can be seen as offering depth to the space of social media. Poetry itself, whatever platform it is shared on, can be seen as a space, both more interior and more otherworldly, *beyond* the marketplace of franchises and 'likes'. The following three chapters each look at some of the deeper forms of conversation that poetry both allows and represents. Some of the poems are written in conventional forms, some in free verse. Some find their ideas in things, some in words, some in relationships, but all of them, one way or another, allow the drama of outside forces into the poetry.

READING LIST

'Odi et amo'
Catullus

'The Flea'
John Donne

'To His Coy Mistress' and 'A Dialogue
Between the Soul and the Body'
Andrew Marvell

'The Eolian Harp'
Samuel Taylor Coleridge

'Conversation with a Stone'
Wisława Szymborska

'Wolf on the Couch' and 'Wolf Nationalist'
Luke Kennard

'Coy Mistress'
Annie Finch

CHAPTER SIX

Argument
& conversation

Frank O'Hara wondered whether he might be able to initiate 'the death of all literature as we know it' with a proposal that, instead of writing a poem, the aspiring poet might do better to pick up the telephone: 'The poem is at last between two persons rather than two pages.' His declaration of the death of literature in his two-page 'Personism: A Manifesto' didn't slow his own rate of poetry writing, but his observation that he could use the telephone instead does point to the strangeness of a form of communication that is not a conversation in any ordinary sense. 'Odi et amo' – I love and I hate – wrote Catullus more than two thousand years ago, and today these words continue to be repeated and reprinted on tee-shirts, posters and tote bags, and in books about poetry. 'You ask why?' Catullus continues, but if the reader is invited here to take up the position of the 'you', addressed across the years by the poet with his still-incomprehensible emotions, surely the enduring attachment readers have felt for this poem comes from their taking up for themselves the position of the tortured lover, a position they perhaps already feel is their own: 'I do not know why, but this is what I feel, and it is an agony.' Perhaps poems could be thought of as conversations that poets have with their own feelings, arguments that poets have with themselves, opening up a space of dialogue and ambiguity for the reader to inhabit as well. But some poems more than others centre on conversation and argument, and the reader may not always find the place of the second person inviting.

John Donne's 'The Flea' constructs a very private space in which the speaker addresses his argument to an audience of one. He almost certainly ought not to be alone with her, and yet he would hardly welcome company as he puts forth his elaborate arguments to persuade her she need not wait for marriage to consummate their relationship. From the very first line, the reader is in the middle of a drama already unfolding – if not as much in the middle of it as the flea, perhaps in the position of a fly on the wall. 'Mark but this flea, and mark in this, / How little that which thou deniest me is', the poem begins. The argument is launched, with all three characters already present in the scene – the arguing suitor, the resisting girl, and the flea which has bitten them both. If this *flea* can enjoy the commingling of their blood before marriage, runs the argument, what a pity *they* should wait! Throughout the three stanzas of the poem we are given only the words of the suitor, as if we were listening to only one side of a telephone conversation, and yet these words are enough to let us know the girl is holding her own. For all his artistry in building the flea up to be a cloister for their intermingled blood, built of 'living walls of jet', and for all his arguments against her killing it, which take up the whole of the second stanza ('Oh stay, three lives in one flea spare,' it begins), the third stanza opens with her fingernail 'purpled', the flea already squashed:

> Cruel and sudden, hast thou since
> Purpled thy nail, in blood of innocence?

> Wherein could this flea guilty be,
> Except in that drop which it sucked from thee?
> Yet thou triumph'st, and say'st that thou
> Find'st not thy self, nor me the weaker now;
>> 'Tis true; then learn how false, fears be:
>> Just so much honor, when thou yield'st to me,
>> Will waste, as this flea's death took life from thee.

Yet if he allows her to have 'triumph'st' in killing the flea and finding neither of them weakened by the act he has called murder, self-murder and sacrilege, it has to be admitted that she has allowed the argument to entertain her over three whole stanzas. The detail revealed in the middle stanza, that it is their parents who 'grudge' the marriage, might perhaps account for the space she allows him – the literal space in the room, as well as the space of those three stanzas in which to mount such an elaborate argument. Having granted her the triumph of proving the death of the flea an inconsequential matter after all, the poem ends in a dazzling about-turn, almost as if the whole argument were a set-up for the reversal it will now take, declaring if the death of the flea could be so little a sacrilege, just so little a loss of honour would it be 'when thou yield'st to me'. After all, the concepts of sacrilege, of honour, of chastity are themselves only elaborate conceits made out of words – as, of course, the whole poem has been, along with what I called 'the literal space' of the room it takes place in, a room entirely imaginary. Complete in its walls of rhyme and metre, the poem will never reveal whether the yielding confidently predicted ('when' not 'if') will ever take place. That the last lines so brilliantly win the argument, however, we have seen means little in a conversation between two well-matched characters whose battle of wills has played out in actions as much as in words.

The 'mistress' addressed in Andrew Marvell's 'To His Coy Mistress' is given no such dramatic presence, and yet the title – his, not my, coy mistress – suggests we read the elaboration of the argument in this poem much as we do the elaboration of the argument in 'The Flea' – as a drama played out for the reader rather than the characters in it who are, after all, elaborations themselves. The argument is as absurd a confection of sophistry as the argument of 'The Flea'. Rather than rely on logic to support its claim – that there simply isn't *time* to worry about honour before getting on with the act (implying without quite making the argument that there isn't time to *marry*, which perhaps was never really on the cards) – the poem works by way of contrast. The following lines, from the middle of the much longer poem, build up such an exaggerated idea of how much time should ideally be allotted a worthy courtship that any actual amount of time does, indeed, seem so minuscule that, in the face of eternity, it might as well be skipped over:

> My vegetable love should grow
> Vaster than empires and more slow;
> An hundred years should go to praise
> Thine eyes, and on thy forehead gaze;
> Two hundred to adore each breast,
> But thirty thousand to the rest;
> An age at least to every part,
> And the last age should show your heart.
> For, lady, you deserve this state,
> Nor would I love at lower rate.
>   But at my back I always hear
> Time's wingèd chariot hurrying near;
> And yonder all before us lie
> Deserts of vast eternity.

'To His Coy Mistress' could have been placed in the chapter on sumptuousness and the ornate, with its gorgeous elaboration of the quantities of time that should be spent on courtship, its lovely rhyming iambic lines with the four stresses instead of five able to offer both speed and delay as the sentences running over the ends of the lines so often extend the sense beyond the rhymes. And of course it is a paradoxical argument to make in a poem: as in 'The Flea', here too 'Time's wingèd chariot' never will arrive. This is a poem with all the time in the world for courtship; already, it has lasted centuries.

Samuel Taylor Coleridge's 'The Eolian Harp' is one of several odes collectively called his 'conversation odes'. In this poem, as in 'The Flea' and 'To His Coy Mistress', only one side of the conversation is given, addressed to his 'pensive Sara', whose cheek reclines on his arm as he speaks, but it is her argument that in this poem prevails – or at least gives the poem its conclusion if not its substance. This is a poem full of autobiographical details – the description of the cottage, with its white-flowered jasmine, the scents on the air from the nearby bean-field, the 'stilly murmur of the distant sea' – exactly locating a conversation which we might imagine the poem as a kind of recording of, recollected in tranquillity (all the more tranquil, perhaps, without the pensive Sara's presence) but written in the present tense as a still-unfolding drama. The wind harp itself, the only sound to interrupt the silence that the sea's stilly murmur speaks of, responds to the breeze that plays on it as if it is the silent addressee of a poem by Marvell or Donne: 'Like some coy maid half yielding to her lover, / It pours such sweet upbraiding, as must needs / Tempt to repeat the wrong!' The central conceit of the poem arises naturally out of the extended description of the harp and its music: the Romantic idea of poetry as inspiration that plays on the passive instrument of the poet, and the further idea of a spirituality that might resonate like poetry throughout all the world:

> And thus, my Love! as on the midway slope
> Of yonder hill I stretch my limbs at noon,
> Whilst through my half-closed eyelids I behold
> The sunbeams dance, like diamonds, on the main,
> And tranquil muse upon tranquillity:
> Full many a thought uncalled and undetained,
> And many idle flitting phantasies,
> Traverse my indolent and passive brain,
> As wild and various as the random gales
> That swell and flutter on this subject Lute!
>
> And what if all of animated nature
> Be but organic Harps diversely framed,
> That tremble into thought, as o'er them sweeps
> Plastic and vast, one intellectual breeze,
> At once the Soul of each, and God of all?

But with this more metaphysical conjecture, he earns himself 'a mild reproof' from his 'beloved Woman'. He uses then a curiously double-negative construction to tell her what she has just told him, this practice of telling the addressee what they already know being one of the stranger conventions of lyric poetry: 'nor such thoughts / Dim and unhallowed dost thou not reject, / And biddest me walk humbly with my God.' The remaining dozen lines of the poem offer her his willing assent, dismissing all the ideas that have played out so far in the poem as 'Bubbles that glitter as they rise and break / on vain Philosophy's aye-babbling spring', and expressing gratitude to God for the 'Peace, and this Cot, and thee, heart-honored Maid' with which the poem concludes.

 Even if her speech is heard only as it is reported back to her, still she changes the course of the argument in this poem more effectively even than the unheard addressee of 'The Flea'. And nothing was going to change the course of the argument in 'To His Coy Mistress', certainly not the woman the argument is addressed to, each of whose breasts alone are worth two hundred years of gazing but who isn't given a voice or even an action in the poem. Yet while the arguments of those poems 'glitter as they rise' and have their value only *in* their rising and glittering within the works themselves, the image at the heart of 'The Eolian Harp' is persuasive beyond even the bounds of the poem.

Another form of conversation poem gives equal space to both sides of an argument, though the two speakers in these poems are as often as not inanimate objects or metaphysical ideas, rather than a poet and partner – which, it occurs to me, may be more than a coincidence. William Blake's 'The Clod and the Pebble' attributes to the clod and pebble two opposing ideas about love; Adrienne Jansen's 'The Rain and the Spade' is subtitled 'a poem about love and ambiguity?'; and Marvell himself, whose 'To His Coy Mistress' left the coy mistress so entirely out of the conversation, wrote many conversation poems in which both sides of an argument are explored, including more than one poem in which the soul argues against the pleasures – or miseries – of the body. As the character Thestylis argues, in Marvell's mock-pastoral 'Ametas and Thestylis Making Hay-Ropes', 'Think'st thou that this rope would twine / If we both should turn one way? / Where both parties so combine / Neither love will twist nor hay.'

The idea that opened this chapter, that the conversation poem is particularly close to drama, is borne out by the way Marvell sets out many of his conversation poems like play scripts, with each stanza headed up with the name of the speaker of the lines that follow. This is how, for instance, 'A Dialogue between the Soul and the Body' is set out, with each stanza headed 'SOUL' or 'BODY' as the characters of each take turns setting out their argument against the other.

SOUL

O who shall, from this dungeon, raise
A soul enslav'd so many ways?
With bolts of bones, that fetter'd stands
In feet, and manacled in hands;
Here blinded with an eye, and there
Deaf with the drumming of an ear;
A soul hung up, as 'twere, in chains
Of nerves, and arteries, and veins;
Tortur'd, besides each other part,
In a vain head, and double heart.

BODY

O who shall me deliver whole
From bonds of this tyrannic soul?
Which, stretch'd upright, impales me so
That mine own precipice I go;
And warms and moves this needless frame,
(A fever could but do the same)
And, wanting where its spite to try,
Has made me live to let me die.
A body that could never rest,
Since this ill spirit it possest.

Marvell writes beautifully about both the pleasures of the body and the freedom of the imagination in poems like 'To His Coy Mistress', with its dream of endless, languid worship of the body's charms, and 'The Garden', which offers a gorgeous vision of the sensuous pleasures the garden can offer: grapes crush their wine into the poet's mouth; the 'curious peach' reaches itself into the poet's hands, till, stumbling on melons, he falls, 'insnared with flowers' onto the grass – only to move on to the still greater pleasures offered by the mind's withdrawal into its own happiness, 'annihilating all that's made / To a green thought in a green shade', as the soul glides into the boughs of a fruit tree to sing like a bird 'till prepar'd for longer flight'. Lovely though that longer flight may be, Marvell presents this temporary mortal life as a paradise in which both body and soul have their pleasures. From beginning to end of 'A Dialogue between the Soul and the Body', however, neither body nor soul has a good word for each other. In contrast to Coleridge's image of the 'organic Harps diversly framed, / That tremble into thought,' Marvell has his soul picture the body as 'chains / Of nerves, and arteries, and veins' in which the soul is 'hung up', enslaved 'with bolts of bones'. The body, in turn, regards itself as impaled upon the soul which, like a fever, warms it and moves it, making it live only to let it die. From the soul's point of view, it is the body making it live, with the cures even worse than the diseases the body makes it endure: 'ready oft the port to gain, / Am shipwreck'd into health again.' As the body points out, the worst diseases are not physical, but the cramps of hope, and the palsies of fear, knowledge, memory and sin; and sin itself, the body concludes, is what the soul builds up the body for, as 'architects do square and hew / Green trees that in the forest grew.' The soul's response to this isn't given; the opposite idea, that it is the body that leads the *soul* into sin is, after all, a commonplace that this poem has moved far beyond.

    Perhaps it is not surprising for a conversation between a soul and a body to reach towards the metaphysical, but it might be surprising to find a conversation with a stone becoming metaphysical just as readily. In the Polish poet Wisława Szymborska's 'Conversation with a Stone', the first-person speaker is herself engaged in an argument that might, from the start, seem destined to be frustrated, but which proves resonant all the same. This is a poem with a narrative, but a narrative mostly made up of a conversation, a series of refusals to a persistent request, with the dialogue given in speech marks. In a sense, the request – 'let me come in' – has been made before the conversation even begins, in the action of knocking on the door that takes place in the first line:

> I knock at the stone's front door
> 'It's only me, let me come in.
> I want to enter your insides,
> have a look around,
> breathe my fill of you.'
> 'Go away,' says the stone.
> 'I'm shut tight . . .
> Even if you break me to pieces,
> we'll all still be closed.
> You can grind us to sand,
> we still won't let you in.'

As the poem continues, its speaker tries out any number of persuasive arguments – they only want to look around, they haven't much time (that problem of mortality again), the stone's interior beauty needs witnessing:

> I knock at the stone's front door.
> 'It's only me, let me come in.
> I hear you have great empty halls inside you,
> unseen, their beauty in vain,

> soundless, not echoing anyone's steps.
> Admit you don't know them well yourself.'

But the stone, being a stone, remains adamant:

> 'I'm made of stone,' says the stone,
> 'and must therefore keep a straight face.
> Go away.
> I don't have the muscles to laugh.'

In all the stone's replies, it beautifully expresses the fact of its being a stone: it will remain closed even if broken to pieces or ground to sand; it doesn't have the muscles to laugh at that old argument about mortality; it has no room inside it; its whole surface is turned outwards, its insides turned away; witnessing is not a taking part. These are all good arguments, but the final statement which ends the argument, and thus the poem, is conclusive: '"I don't have a door," says the stone.'

The stone could hardly be more stone-like, yet part of the pleasure of the poem is the sense that it could stand for something more. If put in the place of the stone, almost any abstraction – God, art, love, faith – seems to become comprehensible in new ways. It would be a reduction to read 'Conversations with a Stone' *simply* as a poem about poetry, when it is such a perfect poem about the inaccessibility of a stone, and yet this reading, too, offers insights that feel both new and familiar: it is true that breaking a poem to pieces doesn't necessarily open it up; it is true we have all the time we need for poetry; it is true a poem can be 'Great and empty, true enough . . . but there isn't any room', since the insides are turned away: 'You may get to know me but you will never know me through.' Perhaps it is a poem about the very poem we are reading. And perhaps the stone, in having the last word, doesn't win the argument – perhaps the poem itself wins the argument. Door or no door, here we all are, inside poetry's vast spaces!

Misunderstandings, refusals, closed doors and persistent requests can all be full of meaning: ask any psychoanalyst. Psychoanalysis, like poetry, offers a setting in which, as psychoanalyst Adam Phillips puts it, the self can be overheard. According to Phillips, the 'productive shocks' such overhearing allows 'are only made possible by the presence of the other person'. Luke Kennard's collections of poetry are full of the disagreeable, nonsensical, unimportant, irrelevant and startling ideas that Freud listed as being 'of particular value' in the psychoanalytic setting. In his extended sequence 'Wolf on the Couch', he makes full use of the psychoanalytic method the wolf has learned about through a correspondence course to bring forth a disorienting and dazzling series of the shocks that produce poetry. When the poem's speaker, the 'patient' whom the wolf has lured into his office on the pretext of 'a nice drink', finally caves in to his hectoring demand to disclose who it is who lives in his head, we think we can guess who the description refers to:

> 'There is one thing,' I say, trying to stop the points of light pitching and rolling. 'I have created an alter-ego through whom I voice opinions I am not brave enough to voice myself and whom I also use for self-censure and masochism.'
>
> 'Hmm,' says the wolf, his pen scratching across his Psychologist's Jotter. 'Sounds more like an alter-*super*ego. Describe him.'

The first poem in the sequence ends on that cliff-hanger; the second begins with the announcement, 'He's an owl.' Like the wolf, we may feel this is a preposterous suggestion. If the owl is the alter-ego, who then is the wolf? If the owl is made up, as the speaker goes on to explain, of 'a network of tiny cities', he might require close reading – the speaker suggests using a microscope – but how do we analyse the wolf, who blusters, blanches, tries 'very hard to compose himself' before finally tearing the owl to pieces, discovering him to be made of nothing more than bits of fluff and a tape-recorder? The phrases he settles on – phrases such as 'ORALLY FIXATED' – only contribute another layer of the disagreeable, nonsensical and irrelevant. And the disagreeable, nonsensical and irrelevant proves just as resonant in Kennard's poetry as it does for a Freudian analysis.

Another sequence, 'Wolf Nationalist', plays up the absurdity of British forms of nationalism as the wolf dedicates different days of the week to different parts of his heritage, being a Welsh Nationalist on Monday, Northern Irish on Tuesday, and so on. Every day allows for further inventive digs against the English, except Thursday when he is an English Nationalist himself. His arguments have an absurd logic as enjoyable as that of Donne's 'The Flea'. When our hapless speaker defends his English ancestors as equally oppressed, the wolf responds:

> 'Your ancestors should have found out what was going on
> and seized power in a humourless coup.'
>
> 'Bloodless coup,' I say.
>
> 'Blood is one of the humours,' says the wolf.

There can be no satisfactory arguing with Kennard's wolf, except for the satisfaction that can be found in being frustrated so surprisingly, again and again. As Adam Phillips points out, the maddening aspect of frustration is also what gives it its power to change the direction of a desire, a narrative, a relationship, or an idea of the self: 'The frustration scene,' Phillips writes, 'is the scene of transformation.' In place of argument, poetry can offer a change of direction or a change of perspective, a transformation of identity.

If frustrated argument is always going to generate an excess of argument, perhaps it is not surprising that some poets have gone beyond reading (and being transformed by) the arguments within these poems, and have argued back. Given how little Marvell allowed the coy mistress of his poem to say, it was only a matter of time (and what's three-and-a-half centuries?) before a poet like Annie Finch would write back. Refusing to 'seize the day' like 'a bird of prey', the speaker of Finch's poem 'Coy Mistress' offers instead imagery that might suggest a form of housekeeping: 'I trust that brief Time will unfold / our youth, before he makes us old.' The argument she develops, that there is plenty of time not only for love-making but also for writing verses, perhaps hardly needs to be made, given that 'To His Coy Mistress' is, after all, a piece of poetry in place of an act of love. But just as Marvell's argument for seizing the moment becomes a poem about more than its argument, so Finch's argument in favour of delay allows her to take on other matters:

> Sir, I am not a bird of prey:
> a Lady does not seize the day.
> I trust that brief Time will unfold
> our youth, before he makes us old.
> How could we two write lines of rhyme

> were we not fond of numbered Time
> and grateful to the vast and sweet
> trials his days will make us meet?
> The Grave's not just the body's curse;
> no skeleton can pen a verse!
> So while this numbered World we see,
> Let's sweeten Time with poetry,
> and Time, in turn, may sweeten Love
> and give us time our love to prove.
> You've praised my eyes, forehead, breast:
> You've all our lives to praise the rest.

The poem's concluding couplet makes the obvious feminist point that for all the lavish praise the poet imagines he could pour out had he only enough time, even in his imagination he hasn't gone beyond the surface. But subtler points have been made along the way. Finch is well aware of both the patriarchal tradition and the liberating possibilities that metre evokes: in an article she has written, she describes Emily Dickinson as '[choosing] to gnaw at iambic pentameter'. In 'Coy Mistress', the argument of the poem in favour of time's slow unfolding becomes an argument for a mathematical, and therefore proportionate, approach to living in what she describes as 'this numbered world', suggesting a feminist appropriation of both mathematics and metre. But the poem also evokes more traditionally feminine housekeeping imagery. When she suggests it will take time 'our love to prove', for instance, the suggestion that proof may need to be more than rhetorical, more than a question of logic, takes on further resonance if we think of 'to prove' in terms of its meaning as a baking term for allowing dough the time to ferment that will give rise to a good loaf of bread.

No argument with Marvell, however, can contain the resonance of the poem, or keep lines and phrases – 'vaster than Empires, and more slow', 'Time's wingèd chariot', 'world enough and time', the 'fine and private place' of the grave – from making new, transformed appearances in later poems and other texts. Arguments and conversations take place within poems and between poems. 'To write is to want to rewrite,' Roland Barthes has said, and the next chapter looks at poems in conversation with other poems, and at the many forms of rewriting this might involve.

— READING LIST —

'The Ride'
Richard Wilbur

Fragment 31
Sappho
(translated by Anne Carson)

poem 51
Catullus

'Lovely   I have none'
Diana Harris

'After Sappho'
Janet Charman

poems 5 and 7
Catullus

'Song to Celia' ['Come my
Celia'] and 'To the Same'
['Kiss me sweet']
Ben Jonson

poems 4 and 5
from 'The Clodian Songbook'
C. K. Stead

'Catulla' and 'Basia Mille'
from *Catulla et al*
Tiffany Atkinson

'Viewless Wings'
Mark Ford

CHAPTER SEVEN

Conversations with the past

Poems can contain conversations, they can present arguments, they can take the place of letters or phone calls, they can continue a night's entertainment, as when Catullus, fired up from the exchange of witticisms, one-liners and improvised versifying with his friend Licinius, went home and, unable to wait to talk again the next day, composed another poem. Whether addressed to someone in particular, or, as Emily Dickinson said of her poetry, written as a letter to the world, all poetry is conversation of a kind, if a rather strange – and estranging – kind. All poetry, too, is written after other poetry; all poets enter a tradition. Some poems, like Annie Finch's 'Coy Mistress' discussed in the previous chapter, respond directly to earlier poems; other poems, like Richard Wilbur's 'The Ride', are more indirectly in conversation with the past. Wilbur has described, in an interview, what it means to him to feel 'a member of the congress in the republic of letters, not debating, but discussing'. It is a discussion carried out by allusion, response, imitation and transformation in the composition of new and original poetry. 'In the poems I like best,' Wilbur says, 'there is – often by the subtlest signs – that discussing of things with other poets of the past.'

That this conversation with the past doesn't take the poet backwards, or stall poetry's forward momentum, is suggested by the heady pace and originality of Wilbur's 'The Ride'. From the third line of the poem we know this is a ride taking place in a dream, not reality, yet the details of the snow, the wind, the 'veils' of the horse's 'patient breath' and 'the mist of sweat from his flank' make this a very vivid and realistic dream:

> The horse beneath me seemed
> To know what course to steer
> Through the horror of snow I dreamed,
> And so I had no fear,
>
> Nor was I chilled to death
> By the wind's white shudders, thanks
> To the veils of his patient breath
> And the mist of sweat from his flanks.

Richard Wilbur has called himself 'a continuator of Robert Frost', and while this poem is complete in itself, there is a resonance too in its echoes of Frost's 'Stopping by Woods', discussed in Chapter One. But while Frost's poem is centred around stillness, the entire poem in fact taking place during the halt in the ride 'between the woods and frozen lake', Wilbur's seven-stanza poem has a relentless trajectory towards the end of the ride, the arrival at the inn and the wakening from the dream. With its rhyming four-line stanzas of steady three-stressed lines, the poem seems to share the 'magic ease' of the ride and the horse's 'quick, unstumbling trot'. The movement 'through shattering vacancies / On into what was not' might be describing the act of writing poetry as much as riding through a storm, with the danger coming not from the snow and the chill but from the difficulty of sustaining the act of imagination. Sure enough, it is not long

> Till the weave of the storm grew thin,
> With a threading of cedar-smoke,
> And the ice-blind pane of an inn
> Shimmered, and I awoke.

We never learn what promises the rider of Frost's little horse had to keep, or where the miles still to go were taking him; in contrast, the destination here of the inn with its cedar-smoke is very specific, if only a dream. The 'ice-blind pane' of the inn which shimmers as the dreamer wakes might recall the 'pane of glass' that drops and melts in another Frost poem discussed in Chapter One, 'After Apple-Picking', as the speaker of that poem is 'well upon my way to sleep'. It is a mirroring with curious reversals: in place of a 'pane of glass' skimmed from a water trough, Wilbur gives us an 'ice-blind' window pane that wakes the speaker as it dissolves instead of shifting the poem into the dream state in which 'After Apple-Picking' ends. Dreaming in both 'Stopping by Woods' and 'After Apple-Picking' has its dangers: the promises that must be kept keep the rider going through a snowy landscape it would be fatal to stall in for too long; the sleeping looked forward to in 'After Apple-Picking' may be 'just some human sleep' but brings to mind other kinds of 'long sleep' to come. But the speaker of 'The Ride' feels a responsibility to the dream itself, and his promises are very specific promises he must keep for the sake of the dream horse that, waking, he has left behind:

> How shall I now get back
> To the inn-yard where he stands,
> Burdened with every lack,
> And waken the stable-hands
>
> To give him, before I think
> That there was no horse at all,
> Some hay, some water to drink,
> A blanket and a stall?

It is hard for the reader not to feel haunted by Wilbur's dream horse, left stranded in a dream without a dreamer. This same sense of urgency drives many poets back to the dreams of other poets besides themselves. A poem like Sappho's Fragment 31 has been circulated, copied, translated and reworked for thousands of years now, and still it demands new forms of attention. It is, in fact, a poem *about* attention, and perhaps it particularly lends itself to appropriation because it is a poem that places the poet speaker in the position the reader of a poem is so often in, watching and overhearing a romance between two others:

> He seems to me equal to the gods that man
> whoever he is who opposite you
> sits and listens close
> > to your sweet speaking
>
> and lovely laughing – oh it
> puts the heart in my chest on wings
> for when I look at you, even a moment, no speaking
> > is left in me

> no tongue breaks and thin
> fire is racing under skin
> and in eyes no sight and drumming
> > fills ears
>
> and cold sweat holds me and shaking
> grips me all, greener than grass
> I am and dead – or almost
> > I seem to me.
>
> But all is to be dared, because even a person of poverty . . .

This translation by Anne Carson includes the final fragmentary last line that most translations leave off since, after all, the three existing stanzas seem complete in themselves and any further stanzas are impossible to construct from the one remaining line. Very little of Sappho's poetry has survived the more than two-and-a-half thousand years since she wrote it. Out of a collection that once took up nine volumes, only a few relatively complete poems remain, and this one has been translated, rewritten and returned to far more than any of the others. Apart from this, there are just fragments, stanzas without poems, lines without stanzas, sometimes single words. Carson's edition of Sappho's poetry, *If Not, Winter*, includes every fragment 'of which at least one word is legible', and includes, too, brackets to indicate 'missing matter', whether destroyed papyrus or illegible words. As Carson says, '[b]rackets are exciting', and she sees no reason why the reader of translations 'should miss the drama of trying to read a papyrus torn in half or riddled with holes or smaller than a postage stamp – brackets imply a free space of imaginal adventure'. Perhaps it is with this sense of adventure that Catullus, when he made his own translation (poem 51) of the Sappho poem half a millennium after Sappho composed it, followed her four complete stanzas with his own entirely original final stanza (my translation):

> Leisure, Catullus, is bringing you down,
> it's too much leisure that accounts for these extravagant gestures,
> leisure, that has already brought down kings and
> prosperous cities.

These lines seem such a radical departure from a translation that is otherwise quite close to the original that many scholars have questioned whether the stanza was originally intended as part of the same poem. Given that the Catullus poems are known only through one manuscript, it is quite possible that it was a transcription error, and this stanza happened to be copied below the others either because it was mistakenly thought to be part of the poem or because it was grouped alongside it as another poem with a matching metre. To add a new stanza is entirely in keeping with the approach Catullus took to translation, however, at a time when Roman literature was understood to be founded on the translation and appropriation of Greek models. The ideal of translation was not to convey the original as faithfully as possible but to take over the original and make it the poet's own. The innovation Catullus and his circle brought to a Roman literature founded on the appropriation of the Greek epic was to turn instead to the Greek lyric, bringing into play the lyric's concentrated, emotional, personal voice. The connection Catullus makes in his final stanza between the epic destruction of kings and cities and his own love-sick misery is absolutely central to this project. At the same time, it is itself the sort of extravagant gesture the poet castigates himself for in these lines.

Catullus makes changes within the first three translated stanzas as well as adding on the fourth. In the second stanza, for instance, he includes a direct address to Lesbia, the subject of so many of his love lyrics: 'From the very first instant, each time that I see you, Lesbia, nothing is on the tip of my tongue.' Given how many of his poems are addressed to, or about, his love affair with Lesbia, naming her in this translation is as much a signature move as the inclusion of his own name in the final stanza. It is typical of a Catullus poem, too, to circle around from an address to Lesbia to an exhortation to himself, or the other way around. His poem number 8, for instance, in which he exhorts himself to give up longing for a girl who no longer wants him, suddenly turns on the girl herself, telling her how sorry she will be, warning her she will have to find her pleasures elsewhere, and dwelling on what those pleasures might be to the point where he is almost ready to succumb once more and must exhort himself yet again to hold firm. And it is typical of Catullus, when alluding to another literary work, to take a part for himself that in the original text was a female part: in other poems, he reworks the role of Medea or pictures himself as Ariadne.

In translating Sappho's poem of a love triangle, he adds in the names of Lesbia and himself, but leaves unnamed the other man who sits opposite her. He does, however, add in other details. Where to Sappho the other man seems like a god, Catullus suggests he is *more* than god-like. Not only does he sit, watching and listening to her laughter, he does so repeatedly:

> he who sits across from you repeatedly
>   watching you, listening

or, in the Latin:

> qui sedens adversus identidem te
> spectat et audit

Classics scholar and translator Daniel Mendelsohn observes that the Latin word for 'repeatedly', *identidem*, is derived from the repetition of the word *idem*, or 'same', and in turn gives us the concept of identity. We are known through the repetition of ourselves, our repeated actions and gestures, our signature notes. But we are known, too, through our differences from others; our identity is formed through what we imitate and through what we oppose. As Mendelsohn puts it:

> There is another way to know yourself, and that is not by identification with the thing you love, by collapsing into the other, but by differentiating yourself from it. Catullus is aware of this and wants to remind us of this . . . In ordering the words out of which he creates his own version of Sappho, he puts the adverb adversus, 'opposite,' immediately next to identidem, so that one of the effects of this climactic line is to make you hear the words opposite and same one after the other: otherness, alterity, and sameness, identity, are exquisitely contraposed.

The translator, and the reader of poetry, similarly identifies with the speaker of a poem – or, perhaps, with another character in the poem – while necessarily conscious of difference, whether the difference of language or differences of identity and time. The Catullus translation of the Sappho poem brings out its play of difference and identity, as the love-sick poet differentiates himself both from the loved one and from the rival, as unlike the loved one with her sweet laughter as he is unlike the rival who can listen unaffected.

This way of establishing the poet's identity through difference is brought out through the sonnet-like translation by New Zealand poet Diana Harris, 'Lovely   I have none', published in a small-press edition of translations by various Auckland poets in 1998:

> There you sit man-god
> you the one that I adore sit there
> he listens to love laughter
> spill/flowing from your lips
> I from this small distance can
> no longer distinguish sound
> from sense from heartbeat
> my ears my eyes burn my
> hot breath is stopped
> frozen in my mouth
>
> still as sweat/tears swell
> and flame and flood and fall
> he listens to your language
> lovely   I have none

But even as, circling around to its own title, the poem emphasises the difference between the self and the beloved, with the gap opening up between the loveliness of the beloved's language and the silence of the poet, it finds, too, resemblances, repetitions and the blurring of boundaries. The second person shifts from the 'man-god' to 'you the one that I adore', as the opening 'There you sit' is mirrored in 'you . . .

sit there', and it is only a 'small distance' between this symmetrical arrangement and the poet's confusion of senses, the running on of phrases and sentences over unpunctuated lines, the multiple possibilities for words that could be offered as laughter spills and flows. Like a translator, the speaker is awash with the possibilities of language, even as the language comes from elsewhere and she herself has none; and in this description of the impossibility, in love, of either attending to the loveliness of language or finding any words of her own, she has of course spilled out her own lovely lyric.

In Harris's version of the poem, both the 'man-god' opposite the lovely beloved and the speaker are silent listeners to the laughter and language that fills the poem. In another remarkable New Zealand translation, the radically pared down 'After Sappho' by Janet Charman, the emphasis is on how alike they are in how they *look*:

> love him
> if
> you will
>
> he looks
> like me

In Charman's version, the geometry of the love triangle is not only emphasised but is all that is left when the disruption of the senses and the dissolution of self are no longer the focus of the poem. 'After Sappho' is part of a longer sequence, 'Mrs Harry Kember, Remember', which was published in Charman's 1999 collection *Rapunzel, Rapunzel*. As the titles of the poem, sequence and collection all suggest, this version of the Sappho poems comes out of a sustained interest in writing back, retelling stories from different perspectives. Mrs Harry Kember is a minor character in Katherine Mansfield's long story 'At the Bay', a married woman who is joined, briefly, in one scene, by the unmarried Beryl. Something makes Beryl uncomfortable about Mrs Harry Kember's attentions, so that Beryl flinches away as Mrs Kember touches her waist, and says 'Don't' when she calls her a little beauty, and yet she does feel like a little beauty when she is with Mrs Kember. Mrs Kember is described as oddly androgynous, while her husband is 'at least ten years younger than she was, and so incredibly handsome that he looked like a mask or a most perfect illustration'.

In seeing the love triangle of Sappho's poem as structuring the relationship between the Kembers and Beryl, the implicit anxiety of Sappho's speaker, that the beloved may be falling in love with the rival sitting opposite her, is made the subject of the first stanza, even as it is coolly dismissed: the invitation to love him, if you will, is made as if the speaker couldn't care less. It is, after all, merely an act of will – if such an act of will were even possible, the placement of the word 'if' on its own line rather suggesting it probably isn't. In any case, the following stanza suggests, to love him is the same as loving her, a substitution that is no substitution at all, since 'he looks / like me', a phrase beautifully open to interpretation. For the translator, too, identification with an original text can be thought of in terms of likeness, so that the translated text looks like the original, retaining the format and retaining, perhaps, elements of form such as metre and rhyme, and with a vocabulary offering the closest literal match to the original. Or it might be thought of in terms of a similar quality of attention, looking 'at' the subject of the poem as if the translator were able to make it their own to identify with the feelings evoked and evoke them in turn. The reader of a poem, too, makes it their own through a similar act of shared attention and shared desire.

How this shared attention and shared desire might account for very different versions of the same poem being written by different poets in different contexts is shown not only in the versions of the Sappho poem first translated by Catullus but also in the various translations, versions and responses to the poems of Catullus that poets have written over the centuries. Those most returned to are the two poems listing the hundreds and thousands of kisses he would like to give his Lesbia: poems number 5 and 7 in the Catullus manuscript. This translation of 5 is my own but draws on the translations of others and is fairly literal:

> Let us live, my Lesbia, and let us love,
> counting all the gossip of old men
> as worth no more than one cent.
> The sun can set and rise again;
> for us, when our brief light has set,
> we have only the long sleep of one perpetual night.
> Give me a thousand kisses, then a hundred,
> then another thousand, then a second hundred,
> then we will have made so many thousands
> that we confuse ourselves, and neither ourselves
> nor anyone who might want to talk behind our backs
> will even know how many kisses they are talking about.

The follow-up poem 7 answers Lesbia's quite reasonable question, given the complicated mathematics of poem 5, of how many kisses it would take to satisfy the poet: as many as the sands of Libya, he writes, or as many as there are stars in a silent night watching secret lovers.

Ben Jonson's seventeenth-century version replaces the judgemental old men of Roman society with the 'household spies' whom lovers in a large English household might have to watch out for, and extends the accounting language Catullus applies to the gossip of old men to the spending of time's goods during our brief time alive:

> Come, my Celia, let us prove,
> While we may, the sports of love.
> Time will not be ours forever;
> He, at length, our good will sever.
> Spend not then his gifts in vain.
> Suns that set may rise again,
> But if once we lose this light,
> 'Tis with us perpetual night.
> Why should we defer our joys?
> Fame and rumour are but toys.
> Cannot we delude the eyes
> Of a few, poor, household spies?
> Or his easier ears beguile,
> Thus removèd by our wile?
> 'Tis no sin love's fruit to steal,
> But the sweet theft to reveal.
> To be taken, to be seen,
> These have crimes accounted been.

Jonson leaves out the hundreds and thousands of kisses in this version which, like Janet Charman's 'After Sappho', originally took on additional layers of meaning as part of a longer narrative – in this case a play, *Volpone*, satirising the materialism and greed of a culture in which gold is declared 'the world's soul' and more welcome than the sun. The kisses are restored in a follow-up poem 'To the Same', placed after the first

Celia poem in a small collection of lyrics, inviting Celia to 'First give a hundred / Then a thousand' until 'the store' of kisses should equal:

> All the grass that Rumney yields,
> Or the sands in Chelsea fields,
> Or the drops in silver Thames,
> Or the stars that gild his streams,
> In the silent Summer-nights,
> When youths ply their stolen delights . . .

And if the lyrics of Catullus can be so at home by the silver Thames, set to a Renaissance metre and English rhymes, perhaps it is no more surprising that they could be found at home on the other side of the world, reworked again in the twentieth century for 'The Clodian Songbook' by New Zealand poet C. K. Stead. Metre and rhyme are replaced by a liberal use of the tab key, and the household spies have become simply the frowning 'old old':

> Clodia
>   do you care
>   does it chip at you
>   that the old old
>   should frown?

This love affair plays out in a distinctly realised New Zealand landscape in which the setting sun of the Catullus poem is marked by a 'bush-spike burned black on it / on the red flush', and in a modernity distinguished not only by the relative freedom of the young lovers to kiss and argue on the black sands of Auckland's beaches or 'numb with cold' on their backs on a golf course, but also by the ways in which earlier poems have already established the conventions that these poems dismiss. Stead's poem 5 from 'The Songbook', his version of Catullus 7, for instance, begins:

> 'Countless' as they say also of
> > stars / sandgrains –
> ask a conventional question
> Clodia . . .

But now we are in a new millennium, and the modernism of 'The Clodian Songbook' might itself look 'old old' to poets more interested in tildes and asterisks than the tab key, more interested in the bisexuality and constantly shifting erotic focus of the Catullus poems than in the romance with Lesbia (and Stead's choice of the name Clodia over Lesbia could read as an insistence on the heterosexuality of the characters in his songbook). A collection like *Catulla et al.* by Tiffany Atkinson captures the sense of the wide-ranging but interconnected social group important in the Catullus poems for providing both characters and an audience for the poetry: her poems are addressed to, or are about, variously, Rufus, Clodia, Rufus's dog, Kate, Egnatius, Aurelius, Sestius, Iuventius, and 'Rufus's youngest, ASBO-boy, / whose hot-wire skills are known through / seven counties'. Perhaps this generation is more comfortable, too, with the exploration of female sexual desire that Atkinson's gender reversal allows – her Catulla is attracted to both Rufus and Clodia, among others, and is both predatory and preyed upon.

Stead's Catullus silences Clodia with his kisses:

> Lose count Clodia
> lip and tongue tell
> but not
> number
> nor mumble anything
> but these kisses
> and this
> and these.

Atkinson's Catulla keeps her own silences:

> May you never know
> how slow unlovely women burn,
> nor how we keep our heads down.
> Sod you. All the books say I must
> break this at the stem. Live long,
> die happy. Take these petals as they come –
> for kisses, curses, kisses.

These lines are from 'Catulla', drawing on Catullus 8 and 11. Her version of Catullus 5, 'Basia Mille', has echoes also of Renaissance love lyrics like Ben Jonson's. Its opening 'Then live with me, Rufus,' recalls the opening to Christopher Marlowe's 'The Passionate Shepherd to his Love' – 'Come live with me, and be my love' – and her offering of 'four fine rooms / and an excellent kitchen' is perhaps no more realistic than

Marlowe's offerings of fields of madrigal-singing birds, gowns made of wool pulled from pretty lambs, and straw belts with coral clasps. The future is a dream, but present desires are urgent, whatever the context, and in Atkinson's version of the scenario supermarket tellers take the place of the 'old old' or 'household spies':

> Meanwhile
> kiss me in the checkout queue
> and let the tight mouths clatter –
>
> scandal's for neurotics and they live
> on small change. Kiss me then, as
> daylight follows to the power of

Here the poem breaks off, the mathematics beyond calculating, and the poet presumably silenced by the kisses that follow.

These poems are all versions of canonical poems, rewriting – if not quite translating – them to make them into new works, a Sappho poem becoming a Catullus poem, a Catullus poem becoming a poem by Tiffany Atkinson. As Atkinson's 'Basia Mille' shows, though, a poem doesn't have to be a translation or even a version of another poem to recall lines or conventions from other poems. It depends on the reader, too, of course, whether they think of Frost's 'Stopping by Woods' when they read 'The Ride', or of Marlowe's 'The Passionate Shepherd' when they read 'Basia Mille', and neither poem depends on the reader's knowledge of the earlier poems to make complete sense. But the sense of a poem is never precisely complete; it always depends on what the reader brings to it, and the more poems a reader knows, the more resonances they will find in poems which include lines, images or phrases that call up other works. As in new translations or new versions of well-known poems, poems looking back to earlier poems can offer new perspectives that change or sharpen our readings.

If Richard Wilbur's 'The Ride' gives us one set of images for how a poem can take off from another poem, for the obligations a poet might have towards images even in their dreams or from their reading, and for the exhilaration of travelling with these visions into new territory, Mark Ford's 'Viewless Wings' offers another sort of imagery altogether for this same relationship. 'I (gulp) had / to have a certain operation,' the poem begins, and the anaesthesia proves even more effective than the 'drowsy numbness' that launches Keats's 'Ode to a Nightingale' at bringing on a kind of waking dream. Almost immediately the speaker is assailed by birds, and as the poem goes on, the birds continue to increase in number and activity as swallows, wrens, magpies, a cormorant, as if from every conceivable poem, join the attack. The solution he comes up with is a strange one: to plunge a cormorant quill into a nightingale's breast, while chanting 'the poor / bird's ode', surely Keats's ode, which works with the same kind of power we feel with the chanting lines at the end of Coleridge's 'Kubla Khan', enthralling the birds, to the dreamer's own surprise:

> I (gulp) had
> to have a certain operation, and as
> I went under, found
> myself assailed by a flock
> of hostile pigeons, by a whole
> parliament of fowls, cooing
> hysterically – blackbirds
> and ospreys
> and screaming gulls. *How daft*

> *are you!* mocked
> a jackdaw, jabbing
> its beak at my groin. Vile droppings
> filled my mouth
> and throat, while swallows and wrens
> and magpies settled
> on my midriff . . . aghast, barely
> able to breathe, I stretched
> forth a hand and seized
> a cormorant's quill
> that I plunged
> deep into the breast
> of a hapless nightingale, all
> the while chanting aloud the poor
> bird's ode; which, to my surprise, worked.

The birds under control, the speaker feels like Orpheus, the singer who can charm animals. But Orpheus is also the singer who descends to the underworld, and so by this logic our speaker is now 'surrounded / by the dead', with the insistent bird imagery of the poem transforming the encounter with Eurydice:

> I was Orpheus in the underworld, surrounded
> by the dead, and my long-sought
> Eurydice was a moulting eagle
> shrieking at me to turn
> around, to let
> her be. Twisting,
> sliding, I flapped

> my leaden wrists and arms and tried
> to look ahead, but heard
> as my own requiem an owl
> hooting mournfully to its mate – *who – who – who –*
> *killed Cock Robin?*

As the classicist Shane Butler has described it, the Orpheus story, as written by Vergil and by Ovid, is a story about looking back, and the language used by both poets suggests it can be read as a metaphor for the ways poets look back to the past, recovering lost voices and lost images, but losing in turn the originals that any translation can only gesture towards. Butler suggests, too, that the image of the singer looking backwards might suggest the poet's own backwards glance at the lines they have just written, as their own work becomes, on completion, another text they are no longer writing but can only read. This attempt at holding on to the long-sought becomes in Ford's poem an act of violence, and there is violence on both sides, beginning with the birds assailing the patient going under. As he struggles to hold on to his eagle-Eurydice, all the while struggling, too, to keep from looking backwards, he hears 'as my own requiem an owl / hooting mournfully to its mate'. The last third of the poem – twenty-seven lines – is given over to the owl's haunting, hooting musings on the dreamer's failure to recognise his own peril, until the poem concludes with the owl wondering, 'does he wake / or sleep?'

'Do I wake or sleep?' is the line that ends Keats's 'Ode to a Nightingale', and it is from this ode, too, that Ford has taken his title, 'Viewless Wings'. If not the word 'gulp' in Ford's first line, it might be the title I love most about the poem – the way it so brilliantly captures the complicated tensions between vision and blindness, looking back and looking onwards, waking and dreaming, struggling and soaring, and for the way it brings the phrase 'viewless wings' into a new focus, bringing out the strangeness of this line in the Keats ode. Listening to the nightingale singing 'in full-throated ease', the poet has yearned first for wine as a way to fade away with the nightingale into the forest, but poetry offers another release into the same dream-like state:

> . . . for I will fly to thee,
> Not charioted by Bacchus and his pards,
> But on the viewless wings of Poesy,
> Though the dull brain perplexes and retards . . .

Why *are* the wings of poesy viewless? The expected word might be 'peerless' – nothing compares to poetry, not even wine. Peerless is a word Keats uses often, as when, in his 'Ode on Melancholy', he advises, 'if thy mistress some rich anger shows', to revel in it and 'feed deep, deep upon her peerless eyes.' It is almost as if there has been a strange transposition, as if the word 'peerless' has somehow suggested 'peering', and in this way 'peerless' has transformed into 'viewless'. Perhaps, in contrast to the visual extravaganza of a flight charioted by Bacchus and his pards (or even a more literal display of drunkenness), to travel by way of poetry might seem more discreet, an inward journey that is outwardly invisible. 'Viewless' wouldn't usually mean 'invisible', however, but would refer to something that offers no view outwards, and this seems a very strange way of describing poetry. Poems like 'Ode to a Nightingale' or Ford's 'Viewless Wings' are full of vivid imagery. When we travel through the lines of Keats's ode we see what isn't there as clearly as we see what is – the imagined wine vividly realised 'with beaded bubbles winking at the brim' – and we see, even, what is only known to be there in the dark forest, the 'White hawthorn, and the pastoral eglantine; / Fast fading violets cover'd up in leaves.' Perhaps this is exactly why the wings of poesy are viewless, because the views can only be imagined. Two months before writing 'Ode to a Nightingale', Keats had decided, 'I will not spoil my love of gloom by writing an ode to darkness.' 'Ode to a Nightingale', written one sunny May morning outside in the garden, under a plum tree, is very much an ode to darkness, as 'in embalmed darkness' the poet can only imagine the imagery the poem describes, and listens, 'darkling', 'half in love with easeful death'.

A further resonance is given to this reading of the word 'viewless' for readers familiar with (or curious enough to look up) the source of the epigram Ford gives his poem, 'What aileth thee now, that thou art wholly gone up to the housetops?' For the reader who knows nothing about its context, it reads as a wonderful image for the speaker's panicky loss of consciousness, in which 'going under' might feel more like a rising upwards, thoughts taking off like panicked birds seeking higher ground. Such is, indeed, almost exactly the situation of the people who have gone wholly up to the housetops in Isaiah 22.1, surrounded by an encroaching army, except rather than prepare for battle they are on the rooftops distracting themselves with feasts – 'let us eat and drink, for tomorrow we will die.' It is the carpe diem song all over again. The moral of the story – 'the burden of the Valley of Vision' – is that rather than panic too soon, or feast when it is too late, the people should have placed their trust in God. The speaker in 'Viewless Wings' has presumably placed trust if not in God, then in the surgeon, and yet the panic, like a flock of birds, has its own momentum. If the panicking becomes a kind of poetry, indistinguishable from revelry and song, so much the better. This is a poem that makes visible, and tangible, the work – whether conscious or unconscious – of making poetry, a poetry that is inevitably in contact with the poetry of the past, however hard it is to grasp hold of it.

As readers and as writers of poetry, we both wake and sleep, and if the view is inwards it is a view rich in imagery. But *should* the view be inwards? If we think of readers and writers of poetry as wholly gone up to the housetops, is revelry all the work to be done, or can the work of poetry be directed outwards, not only serving poetry as an art or a tradition, but also taking part in politics, ethics and community building?

── READING LIST ──

'Good Bones'
Maggie Smith

'Good People'
Ash Davida Jane

'Love Poems in a Time of Climate Change:
Sonnet XVII'
Craig Santos Perez

'Identity Politics' and 'Assimilation'
Tayi Tibble

'Rape Joke'
Patricia Lockwood

'Notes on the Unsilent Woman'
Helen Rickerby

CHAPTER EIGHT

Poetry in a house on fire

Poetry opens up the possibility of conversations that can extend into the past, and into an unknown future, but for many poets writing today the urgent conversations are taking place in the present, with readers distanced not by time but by space. If for Catullus writing poetry was an extension of conversations with a circle of friends, and for Frank O'Hara writing poetry was a droll alternative to the possibility of picking up the telephone, today poetry is just one kind of writing that can be posted on social media along with, and often indistinguishable from, aphorisms, quips, status updates, life hacks, images, links and tweets. According to James Baldwin, talking in 1973 from his self-imposed exile in France, the poet is needed to begin a disturbance and bring to attention the need for change, and if the people might not recognise the poet's work till after the poet is dead, 'that's all right, the point is to get your work done, and your work is to change the world.' Poetry is a social medium and always has been, but it makes a difference when readers – your twenty followers, a few hundred or, in the case of some Insta-poets like Rupi Kaur, millions – like, comment on and re-post your poems within seconds of their publication. But is this poetry revelry or panicking?

Maggie Smith, who was named the 2016 Ohio Poet of the Year and whose poem 'Good Bones' was declared the 'Official Poem of 2016' by Public Radio International, has commented on how strange it is for a poem of hers to play the public role 'Good Bones' has played: 'when my mentions start blowing up on social media, I know something bad has happened somewhere in the world,' she said. 'That's when people start sharing "Good Bones" again.' The poem was first published in a small literary journal, *Waxwing*, three days after a gunman shot down forty-nine people at a nightclub in Orlando, Florida, on 12 June 2016. A reader posted a screenshot on Facebook, which was then tweeted on Twitter, and the retweets and shares soon saw it shared hundreds of thousands of times within a couple of months. It was shared in Britain as well as the US in response to the murder of politician Jo Cox on 16 June. Later that year, the poem was shared again in response to the unexpected election victory of Donald Trump, and in July 2017 the Manchester bombing saw the poem once again shared by a grieving community.

It is a poem neither of panic nor revelry, but it is in a way an unlikely poem to have taken on this role of public consolation, being a poem as much about the ways in which the world is 'fifty percent terrible' as it is about hope and the possibility of renovation:

> Life is short, though I keep this from my children.
> Life is short, and I've shortened mine
> in a thousand delicious, ill-advised ways,
> a thousand deliciously ill-advised ways
> I'll keep from my children. The world is at least
> fifty percent terrible, and that's a conservative
> estimate, though I keep this from my children.
> For every bird there is a stone thrown at a bird.

> For every loved child, a child broken, bagged,
> sunk in a lake. Life is short and the world
> is at least half terrible, and for every kind
> stranger, there is one who would break you,
> though I keep this from my children. I am trying
> to sell them the world. Any decent realtor,
> walking you through a real shithole, chirps on
> about good bones: This place could be beautiful,
> right? You could make this place beautiful.

As a poem about the possibility of making something beautiful out of this 'at least half terrible' world, it remains ambiguous. The poet tries to sell the world to her children, but the comparison with the real-estate agent suggests the 'good bones' might be dubious. Whose doubt is expressed in the rising inflection of the claim, 'This place could be beautiful, right?' The real-estate agent's pitch depends on the willingness of the prospective buyer to enter into the visionary space in which this place could be made beautiful. For readers looking for solace in the face of tragedy, perhaps it is only this ambiguity and this acknowledgement of the darkness we keep from our children that makes it possible still to accept the poem's invitation to share a willed belief in the possibility of change.

As novelist Kazuo Ishiguro has said, 'To some extent at least you have to shield children from what you know and drip-feed information to them . . . When you become a parent, or a teacher, you turn into a manager of this whole system. You become the person controlling the bubble of innocence around a child, regulating it.' He made these remarks after he had just published his 2005 novel *Never Let Me Go*, in which the gradual revelation that the child characters are clones being raised for their body parts is only as shocking as their acceptance of the limitations of their short lives – a passivity that shocks because of how familiar, how ordinary it is. As Ishiguro has pointed out, we are *all* mortal, and he claims to have written this wrenching novel believing it to be his most cheerful work: 'Unless you have a real sense of precious things under threat there would be nothing sad about time being limited.' At the same time, along with the inevitable threat of mortality, we accept many threats to precious things we could be doing more to panic about. The teenaged climate activist Greta Thunberg explains that the generation not yet old enough to vote *want* the adults to panic: 'Adults keep saying we owe it to the young people, to give them hope. But I don't want your hope. I don't want you to be hopeful. I want you to panic. I want you to feel the fear I feel every day. I want you to act. I want you to act as you would in a crisis. I want you to act as if the house is on fire, because it is.'

Twenty-one-year-old Ash Davida Jane's poem 'Good People' begins with her wish to be able to recycle her soy milk cartons (unrecyclable as cardboard because of their inner linings) and builds to an increasingly panicked sense of the gap between the concerns of her generation and the complacency she sees in the generation still in charge of the world. She dreams 'of drowning in a sea of bubble wrap and single-use plastic bags / while around me people lounge on cruise chips drinking / pina coladas and saying   But I Use Them For Bin Liners.' The combination of panic and wry comedy is as much a marker of the poetry of her generation as the long lines, the use of the tab key in place of quotation marks, and the capital letters that turn a common argument in favour of plastic bags (much repeated in the letter pages of New Zealand daily papers) into a hilarious slogan. The poem continues:

> I have dreams of me and all my friends buying
> organic compostable biodegradable faux-plastic wrap
> made from buckwheat and coconut fibres
> while billionaires build single-use bouncy castles the size
>   of islands
> and we panic like housewives in the 80s doing bad jazzercise
> choreography in front of the television while the house
> burns down around us   Pump those arms girls
> Can you feel the burn yet

In an essay on poetry and the internet, Ash Davida Jane cites with some bemusement twentieth-century critics such as Frank Kermode who write at length about the difficulties for the lyric poet of addressing politics, when Ezra Pound's definition of poetry as 'news that stays news' seemed to rule out poetry acting *as* news, or acting in response to news that would within days be already history. Where for Pound the necessary education of a poet involved reading centuries of literature to understand the tradition the poet aspired to enter, a poet like Jane declares, '[W]e don't need more poems from the 1800s or even the 1950s. We need poems that are aware of the iPhone and climate change and millennial pink. We need poems that exist in a time where humanity has sent a spacecraft to Pluto, and Twitter is a more reliable news source than certain news broadcast programmes.' Conventional imagery can no longer work as it once did: 'How can flowers continue to evoke pure romance when bees, butterflies, and other pollinating insects that keep them alive are increasingly in danger of extinction?' How can poets continue to use the imagery of the ocean, when 'soon there will be more plastic in the ocean than fish'?

This is exactly the challenge Craig Santos Perez set himself in writing his series of love poems in a time of climate change. Their sonnet form already offers an association between romance and the natural world that is up for revisiting. With these sonnets, he takes the headily romantic imagery of Pablo Neruda's 'One Hundred Love Sonnets' and rewrites them line by line, introducing the dark notes of environmental destruction and exploitation in the context of the climate emergency. Where, for instance, Neruda's Sonnet XVII begins, 'I don't love you as if you were a rose of salt, topaz, / or arrow of carnations that propagate fire: / I love you as one loves certain obscure things, / secretly, between the shadow and the soul', Perez introduces into his first stanza notes of urgency and vulnerability, and replaces the salt and topaz with more politically charged metals and diamonds, and Neruda's somewhat obscure 'arrow of carnations' with reserves of crude oil:

> I don't love you as if you were rare earth metals, diamonds,
> or reserves of crude oil that propagate war:
> I love you as one loves most vulnerable things,
> urgently, between the habitat and its loss.
>
> I love you as the seed that doesn't sprout but carries
> the heritage of our roots, secured, within a vault,
> and thanks to your love the organic taste that ripens
> from the fruit lives sweetly on my tongue.
>
> I love you without knowing how, or when, the world will end –
> I love you naturally without pesticides or pills –
> I love you like this because we won't survive any other way,
> except in this form in which humans and nature are kin,
> so close that your emissions of carbon are mine,
> so close that your sea rises with my heat.

The urgency that Perez introduces into the first stanza returns at the end of the sonnet, where Neruda's line, 'I love you without knowing how, or when, or from where', is sharpened with the detail of the world's end. Urgency of course is hardly new in romantic poetry. Time's winged chariot was putting the pressure on in Marvell's 'To His Coy Mistress' – already there was no time for gathering all the rubies that might be found. For Perez, the particular urgency time lends to romance in an age of emergency makes it all the more precious, and yet, or because of this, the poem does somehow seem to have the cheerfulness that Ishiguro claims for *Never Let Me Go*, one of the saddest novels I have ever read. Romance, for Perez, is all the more precious too in offering values beyond the compromises and corruption of global politics and the marketplace. Like the seed carrying 'the heritage of our roots', and like the apple representing its fruition, the poem in its sonnet form carries a heritage that, like diamonds or oil reserves, has developed over time but cannot be accounted for in economic terms. This is a poem as headily romantic as Neruda's sonnets or as any Renaissance love sonnet, the new metaphors for the closeness of two lovers replenishing an endlessly urgent, endlessly secured literary tradition.

At the same time, in bringing into play the contemporary concerns of climate change, pesticide misuse, habitat loss and wars over scarce resources, the sonnet not only renews a literary tradition but also participates in broader conversations. This and other sonnets in the series circulate through their publication in online literary journals and through the Twitter links and retweets of their publication, and through shorter extracts or drafts of sonnet sections presented on Perez's Twitter feed, alongside tweets promoting or celebrating the work of fellow indigenous poets. In a blog post published in 2015, 'Are you a real literary activist? Take the quiz!', he offers thirty-two ways you can 'earn a point' towards your status as a literary activist, with quiz questions ranging from 'Do you write poetry that addresses political, cultural, environmental, and social justice issues?' to 'Do you buy other poets' books?'; from 'Do you edit publications that feature emerging and established writers?' to 'Do you write poetically inflected political speeches?' At the conclusion of the quiz, he reassures the reader that 'the point is not the points' and there is no need to add up a score. Rather, the quiz might demonstrate the ways in which a poet is already acting as a literary activist, while offering further ways they may not have thought of or included as part of their concept of the political. It is interesting to see how balanced the quiz is between acts that seem obviously political – signing petitions, joining in protest marches, contacting legislatures – and acts that seem exclusively literary, such as assigning other poets' work in classes, hosting readings and encouraging students to attend literary events. As important as conventional political activism, and as important as the literary work of writing political poems, is the work of community building.

Prolific, and often hilarious, on Twitter, New Zealand poet Tayi Tibble not only constructs and performs a politically conscious identity through her writing, but also writes *about* the politics of identity, playing with the uncertainties, locations, economics, revelry and panicking involved in contemporary identity politics. 'Ofc Bella and Gigi read BOOKS they are MODELS. Being HOT and consuming LITERATURE are correlative. I have known this since I used to walk around in plaid skirts with Kafka & Dostoevsky tucked hotly under my arm & all the fire sounds from all of the pussycatdoll songs would play,' she tweets, and @Soppho ('just like Sappho minus a few braincells') retweets this with the plea 'Pls let this tweet go viral it's the truest thing EVER haha 💅🥺👁️💚👄💅🐍😭😩🤲🤲✨🎀💜❣️.' Many of Tibble's tweets are fiercely political, protesting racism and white privilege in all its forms. Her first collection, *Poūkahangatus*, is full of the energy, character and political drive that characterises her Twitter feed. The title itself is a kind of identity politics joke, coming out of a conversation Tibble had with her friends about how Pocahontas might be spelled in te reo Māori. The collection includes the poem 'Identity Politics', which opens with an online purchase:

> I buy a Mana Party T-shirt from AliExpress.
> $9.99 free shipping via standard post.
> Estimated arrival 14–31 working days.
> Tracking unavailable via DSL. Asian size XXL.
> I wear it as a dress with thigh-high vinyl boots
> and fishnets. I post a picture to Instagram.
> Am I navigating correctly? Tell me,
> which stars were my ancestors looking at?

The question 'Am I navigating correctly?' recurs four times throughout the thirty-two line poem, and if on one level it refers to the navigation through contemporary pop culture – from shopping online, to modelling an aesthetic on the shimmering stars Rihanna and Kim Kardashian, to spending money on 'something bougie / like custom-made pounamu hoop earrings', to working out what the Waitangi Day celebrations of 6 February could mean for her – this navigation has, always, a political dimension as well, established from the start of the poem with the very first reference to the stars her ancestors were looking at. Navigation is central to Māori identity and to Oceanic identities more broadly. One of the most important poetry collections of twentieth-century New Zealand literature is Robert Sullivan's *Star Waka* (1999), a collection which magisterially, in a precisely calculated 2001 lines, charts the navigation of contemporary Māori identity from the domestic to the political, from the distant past to a sci-fi future, from the spiritual to the prosaic, invoking gods from Māori and Greek mythology, seeing 'a found poem / sent by one of the gods of the harvest' in the expiry date of the organic milk he buys from Foodtown: 6 February 1998. For Tibble, the Waitangi Day commemoration of the Treaty between Māori chiefs and the British Crown, founding New Zealand as a nation, might better be modelled on American divorce parties. If American pop culture offers a model for identity politics that is as uncomfortable as it is festive, Tibble is hardly going to allow a little discomfort to draw her from a path as sure as the terrain is vast. The poem concludes with her hungover but still steering her way:

> Steering through the storm drunk & wet-faced
>   waking up to the taste of hangover, a dry mouth,
>   a strange bed,
> shirt above my head is the flag fluttering over everything.
> What were we celebrating? The 6th of February is the
>   anniversary
> of the greatest failed marriage this nation has ever seen.
> In America, couples have divorce parties. We always arrive
> fashionably late. Tell me, am I navigating correctly? The sea
> our ancestors traversed stretches out farther than the stars.

If a community can come together over the beautiful and the funny, the combination of revelry and discomfort has its own powerful effect, and has a particular role to play in finding new audiences for poetry on the internet. Perhaps no one has taken this further than Patricia Lockwood, and no poem has more rapidly gone viral than her poem 'Rape Joke', which had received more than ten thousand Facebook likes within hours of its internet publication. The poem begins with the line, 'The rape joke is that you were 19 years old.' It continues, 'The rape joke is that he was your boyfriend.' The line 'Can rape jokes be funny at all, is the question' comes only much later in the five-page poem, after 'Rape Joke' has, disquietingly, become very funny indeed. The point the opening line makes obvious is that rape jokes can never be funny, that the rape joke is itself an assault on women. The lines 'You were 19 years old' and 'he was your boyfriend' describe a situation both unspeakably traumatic and all too common. Just as Lockwood takes the eroticism out of sexting with the absurd sexts she posts on Twitter (for example: 'Sext: I am a living male turtleneck. You are an art teacher in winter. You put your whole head through me'), so, here, she presents as a joke the self-evidently unfunny.

And yet the poem is full of the unsettling and peculiar humour that has seen her books of poetry become bestsellers and her Twitter feed currently followed by around seventy-five thousand readers. From her first collection, *Balloon Pop Outlaw Black*, she has played around with, and played up, the collapsing of distinctions between levels of reality, so a cartoon, for instance, might be forced by his mother to pull on an additional dimension like a coat. Once his coat is on, the cartoon is compelled to reach into his pockets – 'to a baby's thumb, everything looks like a mouth'. And his pockets have, of course, immeasurable depths, which comes from having no depth at all. The sequence of poems about the cartoon is called 'The Cartoon's Mother Builds a House in Hammerspace', the term hammerspace referring to the way, in cartoons, objects of any size can be pulled out of pockets, or hide behind the smallest of trees. In cartoons, as in poems, everything is made up out of lines, and so in Lockwood's poetry a fictional alphabet might have a father, a whale might end on a semi-colon, a nibble might be more appetising than a fish, the mouth of an anthill might learn to write, and, in 'Rape Joke', the rape joke might wear a goatee: 'Imagine the rape joke looking in the mirror, perfectly reflecting back itself, and grooming itself to look more like a rape joke. "Ahhhh," it thinks.

"Yes. *A goatee*."' Does a goatee make a rape joke itself a joke? But the poem moves back and forth from a personified joke to the joke of the person himself who committed the assault. 'Rape Joke' reveals – revels in? – a series of unsettling disclosures about the rapist. Who is the joke on? The victim, for not having recognised something wrong with him when he kept showing her his knife? But are we comfortable laughing at (with?) the victim? Isn't this just what the rape joke does?

> The rape joke is that you were 19 years old.
>
> The rape joke is that he was your boyfriend.
>
> The rape joke it wore a goatee. A goatee.
>
> Imagine the rape joke looking in the mirror, perfectly reflecting back itself, and grooming itself to look more like a rape joke. 'Ahhhh,' it thinks. 'Yes. *A goatee*.'
>
> No offense.
>
> The rape joke is that he was seven years older. The rape joke is that you had known him for years, since you were too young to be interesting to him. You liked that use of the word *interesting*, as if you were a piece of knowledge that someone could be desperate to acquire, to assimilate, and to spit back out in different form through his goateed mouth.
>
> Then suddenly you were older, but not very old at all.
>
> The rape joke is that you had been drinking wine coolers.

Wine coolers! Who drinks wine coolers? People who get raped, according to the rape joke.

The rape joke is he was a bouncer, and kept people out for a living.

Not you!

The rape joke is that he carried a knife, and would show it to you, and would turn it over and over in his hands as if it were a book.

He wasn't threatening you, you understood. He just really liked his knife.

About halfway through the poem are the lines, 'The rape joke is that *come on*, you should have seen it coming. This rape joke is practically writing itself.' When writing practically writes itself, it is because it is already a social script, we already *know* this. What is the politics, then, of reframing this as poetry?

The politics of rape would seem to need little in the way of reasoning or explication. We are all against rape. But what is obviously wrong can still have a place at the very centre of a society, and the same structures of power in which rape and sexual assault occur also function to maintain silence. The #MeToo movement has shown how powerful breaking that silence can be, making a real impact on actual power relations between men and women in the world, having real career implications for men (some of them) who had acted with impunity for decades. Yet these stories weren't new stories. Everyone *knew* the ways men were taking advantage of the power differences between themselves and women, everyone *knew* about these cases of serial harassment and assault, but it wasn't news. In part, it wasn't news because it wasn't new, *because* everyone knew about it already. News that stays news might be one way to think of poetry, but poetry can also make new again what has become background knowledge to the extent we hardly know what we know. By allowing what we could hardly not know to become unsettling again, by placing us in a position where we don't know how to react, or how to feel about our own reactions, Lockwood's 'Rape Joke' politicises, in the most complex way, what could seem to be beyond politics.

This chapter follows on from, and challenges, the view of poetry as a form of conversation with the poetry of the past. In particular, it challenges the idea of poetry that might be suggested by the quote from Isaiah 22.1 that Mark Ford gives as an epigraph to his poem 'Viewless Wings' – an idea of poetry as a kind of panicked retreat into partying on the rooftops, a failure to confront imminent danger. Rather, we might think of this rooftop revelry as the necessary act of community building that *allows* us to confront the dangers of our time. At the same time, the dangers that we are confronting don't always come from outside our own communities but, as Lockwood's 'Rape Joke' shows, are present in our most intimate relationships. Relationships themselves take place in conversation with the past, as each person brings to a relationship not only their own personal history but also the ways their experiences have been shaped by the histories and power structures of the society they live in (*all* history is personal history). Another poem by Tayi Tibble much shared online, 'Assimilation', looks at how even the most 'progressive' relationship can't help but be implicated in social and historical power structures. A Pākehā/Māori couple who 'take turns // giving / and receiving / oral' and who 'split the bills / evenly' are divided over his approach to laundry: 'he leaves the pegs / all over the ground' and 'she considers this to be / culturally insensitive'. Picking the pegs out of the dirt, she finds herself thinking of 'how many Māori girls / ended up on their knees / in order to erect / this modern nation / she sighs / and rolls her eyes / like a tiny haka'.

Poetry in conversation with the past can itself be a way of changing conversations in the present. The past can always be revisited. Helen Rickerby's long poem 'Notes on the Unsilent Woman' looks as far back as 350 BCE–280 BCE, the lifetime of the early feminist philosopher Hipparchia, to see what can be reclaimed of her lost work and largely forgotten presence in an age when women continue to be silenced. Rickerby's poem is made up of fifty-eight short sections, each like a short paragraph of a few sentences, that together build up a complex argument through questions, anecdotes, reframings, juxtapositions, arguments, agreements, personal response and conversations with friends. Near the start of the poem, Rickerby takes what would seem an obviously foundational quotation from classicist Mary Beard's book *Women and Power*, only to introduce complications:

3. 'When it comes to silencing women, Western culture has had thousands of years of practice.' Mary Beard, *Women and Power*. What is a woman? What is culture? What is silence?

4. Silence isn't always not speaking. Silence is sometimes an erasure. We don't know much about her, but we know she spoke. Sometimes, like today, I don't want to leave the house. I don't want to speak. I don't want to write. I don't feel like saying anything, so much, too much, has already been said. We all know what someone who speaks looks like, someone who should be taken seriously.

The poem goes on to give specific details about the ways men silenced, or tried to silence, Hipparchia, and how she answered them. An anecdote about an assault – I mean Theodorus exposing Hipparchia, pulling off her clothes, rather than Hipparchia slapping Theodorus – becomes, in Rickerby's telling of it, a scene in which Hipparchia triumphs:

> 36. Maybe my favourite part of this story is when Hipparchia went with Crates to a dinner party. There she meets her nemesis: Theodorus the atheist. 'Who is the woman who has left behind the shuttles of the loom?' he asked, affronted. Anti-Penelope. Unnatural monster. She replied, 'I, Theodorus, am that person. Does it seem wrong to you that I devote my time to philosophy rather than the loom?' And maybe that same night, or perhaps another, she said 'Whatever you do cannot be said to be wrong, and so if I do it, it can't be wrong either. For example, if you hit yourself, it wouldn't be wrong, so if I hit you, it wouldn't be wrong either.' I guess he lacked a decent comeback: he tried to pull her cloak off. Exposing her body. She stood her ground. Shameless. I see her triumphant, one woman in a room of men.

Yet, later, she reconsiders:

> 40. But probably she didn't feel so triumphant – one woman in a room of men. Maybe she feared. For her life. Maybe she went home – wherever that was – and cried. Maybe Crates said 'Don't worry, things like that happen to me all the time.' But they didn't.

The meaning of such scenes is negotiable, provisional. Hipparchia herself, it seems, was something of an expert at reframing the meaning of scenes that in the context of Athenian patriarchal culture might be expected to diminish her. Philosophy, for her, seems to have meant exactly this kind of reframing and rethinking of values, expectations and assigned social roles. But meaning can shift over time even for the person experiencing the event first-hand. Rickerby wrote this poem over several years as the #MeToo movement took hold, and as women not only told their stories, sometimes for the first time, but also came to new understandings of experiences they might not have thought of in terms of narrative, in terms of politics or even in terms of assault. Perhaps part of the power of the stories came from their dissemination online, where the women could not be interrupted while the story was being told (however much men might dominate the comments afterwards). As Rickerby writes, 'Silence might not be not speaking. It might be listening.' Too often, women have spoken and not been heard.

There might also be times when a woman chooses not to speak:

42. Some things we tell because we don't want them to have power over us. Some things we never tell because we don't want them to have power over us.

43. There are things we didn't think we could tell.

44. There are things we didn't think we needed to tell. 'Why didn't you tell anyone?' Let's pretend that everyone didn't already know.

45. I didn't want that to be what you think of when you look at me.

Silence is not necessarily erasure; it can have its own power. Writing on the borders of poetry and the essay, drawing on the possibilities each form offers for resonance, movement, juxtaposition, conversation and subjectivity, Rickerby is as alert to the power of silence as she is to the politics of women speaking. One of the loveliest sections of the poem comes when she simply quotes the lost work of Hipparchia, and offers a commentary that is a commentary on her own methods of reading and writing:

26. What we have left of what Hipparchia wrote:
    [

                                                                    ]

27. I love the way thought will leap across a space, across a silence. We sometimes won't even perceive a gap. Sometimes we will fill it.

The work of perceiving gaps, and listening to silences: this too is political work that poets are taking on. Opening up conversations with the past is another way in which we might open up conversations in the present, and another way in which we might rethink the bounds of community, even if it means also being open to grief, to a sense of what we have lost.

READING LIST

'Dear Voyage'
Brian Batchelor

'Letter to Husband'
Emily Berry

'The River Merchant's Wife: A Letter'
Ezra Pound

Ode 3.13 ['O fons Bandusiae']
Horace

'Horse'
Annaleese Jochems

'The Sick Rose'
William Blake

'Spoon Ode'
Sharon Olds

'Ode to a Blizzard'
Tom Disch

'Acorn Duly Crushed'
Heather Christle

'Lucky Orestes (Epigram 60)'
Stephanie Burt

CHAPTER NINE

Letters & odes

This chapter looks at the tradition of the ode, the rhapsodic outpouring of emotion often not even to another person but to a nightingale, a rose, a blizzard, a forest. This is a strangely private revelry, broadcast to a world that, if it is listening, is only overhearing words addressed to someone or something else and written, most likely, in solitude. These days, writers are as likely to address a 'Dear Voyage' as write 'O' to a voyage, but does it make a difference to present a poem in the form of a letter?

Letter-writing has long been important to prisoners, and poets writing from prison have often figured their poems as letters. First prize in the 2015 Pen America Prison Writing Competition went to a poem, 'Dear Voyage', written by Brian Batchelor, a prisoner serving a life sentence. Writing letters from prison offers a form of liberty, a way to be with whoever reads the letter even when you are apart: 'Stone Walls do not a Prison make, / Nor Iron bars a Cage' are lines from the seventeenth-century poem 'To Althea, from Prison', by Richard Lovelace. But while Lovelace's poem proclaims all the world a world of liberty, so that even a prisoner is free within his prison cell so long as he is free to love, Batchelor's poem proclaims life itself a prison. Instead of addressing some loved person who might read his letter, he addresses the only liberty he can call on: the final voyage out of life itself:

> Dear crusted gravestone,
> granite mortal marker,
>
>   Dear lichen
> Dear vine, Dear dirt
> ditch and spade:
>
>   Salutations.
>
> Dear death-calm waters,
> liquid-slack
>
>   Dear raft,
> anchorless and adrift,
> Dear hunched horizon,
> Dear looming dark –
>
> still air
> stale and flat –
>
>   Dear disorienting gloom,
>
> Dear cypress oar, Dear compass
> rusted and soot-stained,

>Dear farewell beacon,
>amorous star
>that breaks the black –
>
>   Hello.

It is an eerie and moving poem, and it is hardly surprising that the judges should have recognised the power of its tender address to the 'Dear crusted gravestone' and to the 'anchorless and adrift' voyage that must first be taken into the 'looming dark'. Perhaps the most surprising moment in this poem is the greeting that concludes it, a 'Hello' that might suggest an arrival. Letters, of course, are written to compensate for absence, and poems written as letters or odes resonate with the unlikeliness of response. Take, for instance, Emily Berry's 'Letter to Husband', from her second poetry collection, *Dear Boy*. 'Letter to Husband' begins not with the word 'dear' but with the word 'Dearest', and it runs through 'Beloved husband' and 'Most respected / missed and righteous husband' before shuttling back to the use of the word 'dear', intensified with further adjectives and honorifics:

>Dearest husband   Beloved husband   Most respected, missed and righteous husband   Dear treasured, absent husband   Dear unimaginable piece of husband
>Dear husband of the moon   it has been six months since I
>Dear much lamented distant husband

The poem is full of longing for a husband 'much lamented, distant' from a wife lost 'in a long undergrowth of wanting', calling, without a telephone, from 'these white corridors'. Not only the husband but also the postman, the night-time, knee bones and palms are addressed as 'dear' as the lyricism of the address spills over to fill the poem:

>   These white corridors are not
> free from longing   Dear postman   Dear night-time, dear
> dark mouth hovering over me   Dear knee bones
> dear palms, dear faithful   body   I have wants

It is a poem that poignantly evokes the vulnerability involved in letter-writing, which so often allows the writer to express themselves more intimately than they would when talking to someone present. The poem is full of gaps, spaces on the page, that seem more full of meaning, or emotion, even than the words. The broken, fragmented sentences suggest interruptions or hesitations, and the repetitions suggest false starts, revisions, a repeated attempt to find the right words that would persuade the absent husband to return, that would evoke love. What more important, impossible purpose can words have than to persuade someone to love you? Hasn't this always been the most important purpose for letters to serve; isn't this also what lyric poetry has so often been for?

'Letter to Husband' recalls, for instance, Ezra Pound's 'The River Merchant's Wife: A Letter', which in turn recalls Li Po's 'The Song of Ch'ang-kan'. Pound's poem recalls the start of the marriage and the slow coming of desire for a husband now departed, and ends on this note of longing for a hoped-for future:

You dragged your feet when you went out.
By the gate now, the moss is grown, the different mosses,
Too deep to clear them away!
The leaves fall early this autumn, in wind.
The paired butterflies are already yellow with August
Over the grass in the West garden;
They hurt me.
I grow older.
If you are coming down through the narrows of the river Kiang,
Please let me know beforehand,
And I will come out to meet you
As far as Chō-fū-Sa.

At the same time, Pound's poem, like Berry's, is very much of its time: modernist in its simplicity of language and form, and in its focus on concrete scenes and images. The absence of the husband is observed in the different mosses where he used to walk grown too deep to be cleared away, while the fallen leaves and the paired butterflies indicate the changing seasons, the passing of time. In contrast, instead of presenting images and asking the reader to supply the emotion, Berry's postmodern version presents the reader with the language of emotion, and language which is cultural and charged with social convention in a way the reader can't overlook. 'Most respected missed and righteous husband' is language that might have come out of the source material Pound worked with, while a 'serrated' husband might suggest the serrated fragments of paper we are left with: the language gets increasingly expressive, personal, particular, poetic and strange.

```
                              it is written
    over and over             that           please come.
    A scribble is the way a heartbeat is told    Dearest serrated
    husband. My heartscribbles    your name. My mouth
    scribbles
```

The source of the poem, Berry has revealed in an interview, is a series of letters that really are no more than scribbles: looping, overlapping pencil writing-like scrawls in which it is from time to time possible to make out words, 'Herzensschatzi komm' or 'komm komm komm' repeated over and over. These desperate, illegible letters were written in 1909 by Emma Hauck, a patient in a psychiatric institution, to her husband Mark. Berry's poem both expresses, and compensates for, the inarticulacy, the unreadability and the raw emotion of the original material.

Yet if Berry wasn't intentionally referencing Pound, 'Letter to Husband' does resonate with a sense of the letter in history, the place letter-writing has had as a repository for the same intense Romantic emotions that we associate also with lyric poetry. Amit Majmudar has pointed out, in his article 'Our Hidden Contemporaries', how much closer to our idea of poetry were the letters written by Victorian poets such as Matthew Arnold and Arthur Hugh Clough than their poetry now seems. Give a Matthew Arnold letter some line breaks, and the combination of his conversational description of the limestone of the Swiss Alps as 'terribly gingerbready: the pines terribly larchy' with the assertion of self in the opening lines, 'I love gossip and the small-wood of humanity generally', offers exactly the movement between self and the world, the surprising details and the associative thinking, that we find in contemporary poetry, and which seems more poetic now than the extended working out of a metaphor or argument in metred verse.

Majmudar is not alone in looking for poetry in what the subtitle to Liz Williams's *Kind Regards* refers to as *The Lost Art of Letter-Writing*. Philip Hensher's *The Missing Ink*, Ian Sansom's *Paper: An Elegy* and John O'Connell's *For the Love of Letters* are among a slew of recent books looking back on the slower, handwritten, more literary art of letter-writing that has been increasingly replaced by email, texts and other forms of messaging. The word 'dear' is rarely seen *except* in poetry these days. It has become poetic at exactly the point at which it is no longer functional, no longer a part of the vernacular.

Many of the poems that appear at first glance epistolary may be better understood as odes (including Batchelor's 'Dear Voyage'), the phrase 'Dear somebody' or 'Dear something' working much like the word 'O' in the Romantic ode. The word 'O' had, after all, its own functional origin, representing a perfectly ordinary, everyday piece of grammar, the vocative case. Even so, its use to express the address not to a person in conversation but to the subject of a poem, as when Horace writes 'O fons Bandusiae' ('O Bandusian spring', as in a spring of water), gives it a lyric strangeness even before the grammatical construction is translated into English, where the word 'O' has long been associated entirely with lyric poetry. The address to the spring allows the poem to do more than simply describe its clear waters: it turns into poetry the descriptive details that the Victorian poets were not alone, before the modernists, in seeing as insufficient in themselves as poetry. In the 1960 translation, by Joseph P. Clancy, still one of the best, the poem begins:

> O Bandusian spring more glittering than glass,
> worthy of our gifts of sweet wine and flowers,
> tomorrow a kid will be yours,
> first horns swelling his forehead . . .

LETTERS & ODES | 171

The lyric address to the fountain adds to the poetic details the drama of a relationship. The poet, in the fourth and concluding stanza, elevates the fountain – 'You will take your place among the famous springs' – just as the fountain elevates the poet, its 'clear-voiced waters' giving him a place like Orpheus in which he can write of, and as a part of, the lyric world:

> You will take your place among the famous springs:
> I celebrate the oak that stands above
>   your rocks, from your source
>   the fall of your clear-voiced waters.

Another close, and more contemporary, translation renders those last lines as 'you will become the most famous of fountains / with me singing of the wood established on hollow / stones, from which your talkative waters / jump down' – a brilliant and lively rendition that emphasises the importance of the poet to the fountain's fame. This translation retains, in the first stanza, the lyric address to the fountain, but keeps to a vocabulary of ordinary speech by replacing 'O fountain' with 'Oh fountain'. This use of the vernacular 'oh' in poetry addressing its subject can be found not only in translations but also in poetry re-introducing the very strangeness and poetic quality of the address that the shift from the now purely poetic word 'O' to the everyday 'oh' would otherwise seem a strategy to avoid. Yet the effect is equally strange, to address an object with the ordinary exclamation of surprise that a person might make as often alone as in company: 'Oh good,' we might say to ourselves, or 'Oh dear'.

The contemporary poet might say 'Oh horse' interchangeably with 'O horse'. The poem 'Horse', by Annaleese Jochems, for instance, opens 'There you are O lonely, lovely horse in moonlight', offering us in quick succession the lyrical elements of presence, address, sound echoes and moonlight, all before we learn the horse is dead:

> There you are O lonely, lovely horse in moonlight
> All flank and bone
>   suddenly but naturally
>   dead
>
>   *There the horse was*
>   *
>   *And there the horse is now*
>
> And when the moon abandons you?
>
> The stars will eat your sparkle
>
> O horse,   dead & delicious

This ode to a dead horse is also a poem about longing for the more aesthetic, more significant feelings that fill the poem itself, in contrast to the domestic scene the poet must return to, with its absence of any real intimacy, and unlike the intimacy (as much as invocation) the address to the horse gives the poem:

> I must go home for dinner,
> but I don't want to go home
>   where I play with my unrequited

LETTERS & ODES | 173

love like a banjo, knit itchy scarves and watch mediocre violence
on television

Oh Horse,
let me fit my head
in the dent of your collar bone . . .

By the end, the poem is no longer reading 'O horse' but 'Oh horse', and in fact Jochems has published different versions of the same poem which alter where 'O' and 'oh' are used. 'Oh' and 'O' in this poem seem equally to signify the same exclamation or sigh of feeling that 'oh' does in phrases like 'Oh dear', as well, perhaps, as some lingering surprise over the very address to the horse that the phrase constructs.

How interior an exclamation 'oh' can be is beautifully illustrated in Ali Smith's novel *Autumn*, when the dying Daniel Gluck dreams he is enclosed in a pine tree:

> One might imagine it'd be unpleasant, being sealed inside a tree. One might imagine, ah, pining. But the scent lightens despair. It's perhaps a little like wearing a coat of armour, except much nicer, because the armour is made of a substance through which the years themselves, formative, have run.
>
> Oh.
>
> A girl.
>
> Who's she?

Jonathan Culler, in *Theory of the Lyric*, refers to exactly this distinction between 'oh' and 'o' in discussing the significance of the lyric address in a reading of William Blake's 'The Sick Rose'. This disquieting little poem reads as follows:

> O Rose thou art sick.
> The invisible worm,
> That flies in the night
> In the howling storm:
>
> Has found out thy bed
> Of crimson joy:
> And his dark secret love
> Does thy life destroy.

Observing that 'Blake's lyric has provoked a good deal of critical discussion, especially because other texts of Blake's do *not* treat sexuality as a dark destructive secret', Culler comments on how strange it is that 'in arguments about the meaning of the poem, none of the critics ask why the speaker *addresses* the rose, rather than observing that the rose is sick: "Oh this rose is sick," or "This rose here is sick."' The difference, according to Culler, is the difference between description and ritual:

> Instead of describing with some detachment the nature of the sickness of the rose, the poem tells the rose that it is sick – poems, like prayers, often tell the addressee something the addressee presumably already knows. It thus acquires a ritual character . . . The energy of poetic address creates a surprisingly strong sense of prophetic revelation and marks this speech act as poetic discourse. If one has trouble saying what

a speaker would be doing in saying 'O Rose, thou art sick,' it is because this does not correspond to any everyday speech act, and the simplest answer to what the speaker is doing is something like 'waxing poetical.'

It is this 'waxing poetical' that contemporary odes play up, in part by the very act of writing an ode. Indeed, to write a poem at all is to wax poetical, and it no longer seems convincing to write a poem in everyday language as if writing a note on a scrap of paper, and to pass it off as both poetry and ordinary speech. Sharon Olds's 'Spoon Ode' is one of the most stringent dedications to the work of waxing poetical, an ode as much to the vocative 'O' and the letter O as to its 'spoon' that contains them. It begins (as it continues, throughout its twenty-four lines) in high flight:

> Spoon of O, spoon of nothing,
>
> spoon of ankh, spoon of <u>poonss</u>,
>
> spoon of the lady at the dressing table,
>
> spoon of ♀ , spoon of female,
>
> spoon of 𓀗 , spoon of war,
>
> spoon of the world, spoon of War of the
>
> Worlds . . .

There is a tremendous pleasure to be taken in waxing poetical, and at being waxed poetical at. But it is somewhat unsustainable. One spoon ode is enough. More intricately poised in its performance of waxing poetical is Tom Disch's 'Ode to a Blizzard'. A poem that begins not just with 'O' but with 'O!' and indeed ends every sentence, except one, with an exclamation mark, is clearly open to the charge of waxing poetical. Beginning with the presentation of the blizzard as an ideologue winning arguments by 'making the opposition disappear', by the end of the four-stanza poem a 'sponsor' has been invoked, 'whose chill is more severe / than any here . . . And every monument that you erect / belongs to him!' In the face of this dispossession, even the beautiful artifice of the ode itself is revealed as the series of snowflakes it is, with every stanza looking as if it is modelled on the same syllable count when in fact, on closer inspection, each arrangement is a little different, just as the rhymes shift about from place to place within the stanzas in almost regular but always new geometries:

> O! dear miniature of infinity with no
> End in sight and no snow-
> Flake exactly like
> Another, all
> A little different no
> Matter how many may fall,
> Just like our own DNA or the human face
> Eternal!
>
> O! still keep covering the street
> And sidewalks, cemeteries, even
> Our twice-shoveled drive,
> And all that is alive,

> With geometries that sleet
> Will freeze into Death's
> Impromptu vision of a heaven
> Wholly white!

Unlike the word 'O', the word 'Dear' doesn't offer the same echoes of Shelley, or Blake, or Horace. These days, however, it can often be used with the same purpose, as a way of playing up ironically the act of waxing poetical while, at the same time, poets continue to avail themselves of all the resources of lyric poetry. Heather Christle's 'Acorn Duly Crushed', for instance, includes a nightingale early on, though she goes straight on to tell her nightingale-filled forest to shut up. These are the opening lines:

> Dear stupid forest.
> Dear totally brain-dead forest.
> Dear beautiful ugly stupid forest
> full of nightingales
> why won't you shut up.

In the course of this lively, personable poem, the forest is addressed as a 'Dear bitchy stupendous forest', an 'Indulgent municipal forest', a 'Dear nasty pregnant forest' and a 'Dear naïve forest'. It is told it talks all the time ('You are not pithy'), that it is 'environmentally significant', and that it has 'the ancient noble terror'. It is asked to trade seats, to stop looking at the speaker and, finally, to come back to her house to bag drugs and make conversation (the conversation having, after all, been rather one-sided):

> Dear naïve forest,
> what won't you be admitting!
> Blunt international forest.
> Forest of bees and of hair.
> You should come back to my house.
> We can bag drugs all night.
> You can tell me
> about your new windows.
> How they are just now
> beginning to sprout.

Full of nightingales, 'standard old growth trees' and 'important gangs of leaves' (and with even its windows 'beginning to sprout'), it is possible to imagine this forest as a forest, but the way the forest is addressed, which is what gives the poem its energy and verve, is no way to talk to a forest, nor is it the usual address of the celebrated object of an ode, nor is it the way someone (certainly not a forest) is likely to be addressed in a letter. Like the word 'O' and not entirely unlike the way the word 'Oh' has come to be used in lyric poetry, the word 'Dear' addresses itself to the object of a poem that allows the poet to express an interiority we continue to pine for.

Is this a move backwards for poetry? Might a retreat into the ode lock poetry away from political engagement? In writing about forests or blizzards, is the poet driven back into a solitude the reader hears as loud as any address to the 'dear you' of the poem? Can this solitude itself be politically charged? Chapter Four of this book includes Allen Ginsberg's 'America', which needs no 'O' or 'Dear' to rail at America with an ode-like excess of emotion. Like a rose or a nightingale, America may not be listening – 'I am talking to myself again,' the poet realises – but this does not get in the way of the conversation the poet keeps having. 'It occurs to me I am America,' he observes, but if so, his own self is political, cultural, historical, at odds with itself, implicated in the anti-Communist paranoia, the false accusation and imprisonment of the Scottsboro boys, the atomic warfare and the underprivileged classes of America in the 1950s. More than half a century later, Terrance Hayes continues the railing against America in his *American Sonnets for My Past and Future Assassin* (discussed in Chapter Five), an intimate railing that is also a tender address and an exploration of identity. As Hayes shows, the sonnet too can contain multitudes: these are no Shakespearean sonnets fervently addressed to one obsessively loved reader. In locking up a past and future assassin, past and future readers, and past and future reading into arrangements of such beauty, Hayes unlocks the potential of intimate address to be used with political urgency and power.

The power of poetry can be frightening. So, too, can the power of the reader. In the introduction to this book, I presented Brian Blanchfield's belief that in reading poetry the reader almost becomes a writer of the poem they are reading, just as when writing poetry the poet is also reading what they are writing, almost as if it were written by someone else. Back in the third century BCE, the poet Callimachus was writing radically new poetry by looking back into the past and offering his own versions, translations, elaborations and personal takes on an eclectic collection of readings. Everything he wrote came from someone else, but everything was transformed into a poem by Callimachus. By the time he was writing the story of Orestes, among others, Callimachus was already canonical enough that he could focus in on a detail of it as a joke, putting aside the whole tragedy of murder, incest and betrayal to worry about how the friendship between Orestes and Pylades is tested by the writing of a verse drama – an act, he confesses, that has caused himself to lose his own 'many Pylades'. More than two millennia later, Stephanie Burt has transformed this, along with 120 other Callimachus pieces, into versions that read very much as Stephanie Burt poems, complete with references to synthetic hormones, email, airports and shagpile carpet, and in her version of the poem the play has become a 'book-length fictional work'. But there is always a risk for anyone inclined to pour out their soul in poetry, fiction, email or even plangent bursts of Twitter. Even fictionalisation may not be enough to protect the poet, or 'speaker' as they might like to think of the 'I' of the poem. Even if they are speaking only to a nightingale, or to a snowflake, even if they are speaking to America itself, even if they might lock up their words in a sonnet, or in a panic closet, still they cannot be said not to speak, not to have pressed send:

> Lucky Orestes.
>   If you know his story,
> you probably think that saying so makes me a jerk.
> Fair enough. But I've been losing my mind
> in my own way this week: Orestes lost his,
> but at least he didn't insist
> on asking his loyal companion to read and critique
> his own book-length original fictional work.
> That's why he kept Pylades as his friend.
> True friendship can exist.
>   As for me,
> I need to learn how not to speak,
> when not to hit send.

READING LIST

'Afterword'
Louise Glück

'Edge'
Sylvia Plath

'Jerusalem Sonnet 11'
James K. Baxter

'When I Have Fears
That I May Cease to Be'
John Keats

Sonnet 18 ['Shall I compare
thee to a summer's day?']
William Shakespeare

'The Relic' and 'The Will'
John Donne

'Bury', 'Will' and 'Will'
sam sax

'Pseudo-Martyr'
Charlie Clark

'A Touch of Death'
and 'Talking to Bede'
Alistair Elliot

'This Is My Letter
to the World'
Emily Dickinson

'O May I Join the
Choir Invisible'
George Eliot

CHAPTER TEN

Poetry &
the afterlife

> Reading what I have just written, I now believe
> I stopped precipitously, so that my story seems to have been
> slightly distorted, ending, as it did, not abruptly
> but in a kind of artificial mist of the sort
> sprayed onto stages to allow for difficult set changes.
>
> Why did I stop? Did some instinct
> discern a shape, the artist in me
> intervening to stop traffic, as it were?

To begin the last chapter of a book with a poem called 'Afterword' seems to offer a sort of double conclusion. As these opening lines from Louise Glück's poem suggest, however, to look ahead to the time of an afterword's backward glance can be an unsettling experience. A poem called 'Afterword' unsettles from the start with its reference to the imaginary work that this afterword follows, a work the reader can piece together only by the references to it in an afterword that is focused on explaining, reconsidering and perhaps revising the work the reader hasn't even read. It is the writer, not the reader, who reads what has just been written, and finds its end – which is the poem's starting point – precipitous. And in this case, the writer is troubled by an ending that seems at once precipitous and not abrupt enough, an ending, the next verse suggests, that was less of a conclusion and more of an intervention, 'to stop traffic, as it were'. You might stop traffic to save a life, but here the stopped traffic is presented as the accident itself, and the ending a failure that the approach of 'A shape. Or fate, as the poets say' might have averted.

In her 1999 essay 'Education of the Poet', Glück writes of her early desire to converse with the past, to write back to – or write her way in to – a literary tradition:

> I read early, and wanted, from a very early age, to speak in return. When, as a child, I read Shakespeare's songs, or later, Blake and Yeats and Keats and Eliot, I did not feel exiled, marginal. I felt, rather, that this was the tradition of my language: *my* tradition, as English was my language.

Yet this early confidence of her place in a tradition is, in her account, intricately linked to a displacement in terms of time and to a constant anxiety about failure. The poet is never a poet *now*, as she sees it, either as the writer working or as the canonised poet within a tradition. Writing is more a matter of 'wanting to write, being unable to write; wanting to write differently, being unable to write differently'. Essentially, she concludes, 'the only real exercise of will is negative: we have toward what we write the power of veto'. After all, while the poet is still working on a draft, 'the thing itself is wrong or unfinished: a failure', and as soon as the poem is finished, it is 'at that moment, instantly detached: it becomes what it was first perceived to be, a thing always in existence . . .

And the poet, from that point, isn't a poet anymore, simply someone who wishes to be one.' At best, the poet at that point is someone who was a poet once, when they were still writing the poem, still in the state of failure. Whether the work remains a failure, Glück sees the poet as singularly ill-equipped to judge, unlike the high-jumper who knows at once how high they have reached: 'for those of us attempting dialogue with the great dead, it isn't a matter of waiting: the judgement we wait for is made by the unborn; we can never, in our lifetimes, know it.'

The afterword, which begins by looking back on something 'just written', before very long seems to be looking back on a whole life, and the afterword might just as well be an afterword to a lifetime's work as a painter, or to a career on the stage, all of it just a way of clearing the windshield in order to keep driving:

> Chaos was what I saw.
> My brush froze – I could not paint it.
>
> Darkness, silence: that was the feeling.
>
> What did we call it then?
> A 'crisis of vision' corresponding, I believed,
> to the tree that confronted my parents,
>
> but whereas they were forced
> forward into the obstacle,
> I retreated or fled –
>
> Mist covered the stage (my life).
> Characters came and went, costumes were changed,
> my brush hand moved side to side

> far from the canvas,
> side to side, like a windshield wiper.
>
> Surely this was the desert, the dark night.
> (In reality, a crowded street in London,
> the tourists waving their colored maps.)
>
> One speaks a word: *I*.
> Out of this stream
> the great forms –
>
> I took a deep breath. And it came to me
> the person who drew that breath
> was not the person in my story, his childish hand
> confidently wielding the crayon –
>
> Had I been that person?

The stage in this poem might be explained, in parentheses, as 'my life', yet the 'I' is nothing but a spoken word, out of which stream 'the great forms'. We know that the 'I' of this poem is fictional from the start, since we first meet the 'I' as the author of the fictional text to which the poem is an afterword. When we encounter the masculine pronoun of 'the person in my story, his childish hand / confidently wielding the crayon', this may come as a further surprise, but perhaps we might still imagine Glück herself in that confident, masculine role, just as we might imagine ourselves wielding that crayon, only to retreat from what we find ourselves drawing. If the speaker is the child of parents driven onwards, driven out, by a tree that is their crisis of vision, then perhaps the speaker represents all of humanity, everyone born after

Adam and Eve. By the end of the poem, 'The empty canvases / were turned inward against the wall', and both the question the spirit asks and the answers given suggest that the poet, whether real or fictional, alive or beyond life, can never be sure of a settled place:

> *Shall I be raised from death*, the spirit asks.
> And the sun says yes.
> And the desert answers
> *your voice is sand scattered in the wind.*

In light of this shifting, dream-like landscape of misty stage sets, precipitous changes of direction, halts and revisions, frozen brushstrokes and inward-turning canvases, no wonder a poet might look to the certainty of a time beyond the provisional, a time when a final judgement can be made, a time when time itself is less troubling. Such clarity seems to be offered in Sylvia Plath's late poem 'Edge', one of the last two poems she wrote before her own suicide. The poem begins with an image of classical beauty:

> The woman is perfected.
> Her dead
>
> Body wears the smile of accomplishment,
> The illusion of a Greek necessity
>
> Flows in the scrolls of her toga,
> Her bare

> Feet seem to be saying:
> We have come so far, it is over.

The 'necessity', however, is only an 'illusion', and the second part of the poem re-introduces time. The two children are folded 'back into her body as petals / Of a rose close' at the end of the day. It is a lovely image, but the ending of the day is described as a time when 'the garden / stiffens and odors bleed', and over it all the moon watches 'from her hood of bone', the poem ending with the strangely noisy description of the moon, as I understand the image, in a sky of moving clouds looking black against the moonlight to give the line, 'Her blacks crackle and drag.' After Plath's early death, we might want to see the perfected, accomplished woman as an image for the poet herself, as she herself possibly imagined it. Yet typically in Plath's poetry visions of silent perfection – a leg's plaster cast in one poem, the peace of a hospital room in another – are displaced by the more vital demands of a messy and compelling reality, tulips insisting on their beauty, a hairy leg collecting its strength, blackberries spreading their juices, children bringing balloons into an apartment. And in 'Edge', the spare beauty of the lines imagining a completed perfection give way to the disquieting and discordant imagery of a world that, even if it is imagined continuing on after the poet's death, seems far more Plath-like than the image of the woman herself.

Like Plath's poetry, the poetry of New Zealander James K. Baxter is grounded in physical detail even as he wrestles with metaphysics, building a new form of the sonnet around this combination of the metaphysical and the everyday – fourteen unmetred, non-rhyming lines arranged in loose couplets. The 'Jerusalem Sonnets' are named after the commune he founded in 1969, Jerusalem or Hiruhārama, where he intended to live out the principles, or kaupapa, of Catholicism and

Māoritanga with whoever might turn up to live there. While many of the sonnets battle with an inscrutable and uncooperative God, Sonnet 11 battles against a Satan tempting the poet with the idea of fame, that place in the canon so yearned for by a poet such as Glück:

> One writes telling me I am her guiding light
> And my poems her bible – on this cold morning
>
> After mass I smoke one cigarette
> And hear a magpie chatter in the paddock,
>
> The image of Hatana – he bashes at the windows
> In idiot spite, shouting – 'Pakeha! You can be
>
> 'The country's leading poet' – at the church
>   I murmured, 'Tena koe',
> To the oldest woman and she replied, 'Tena koe' –
>
> Yet the red book is shut from which I should learn Maori
> And these daft English words meander on,
>
> How dark a light! Hatana, you have gripped me
> Again by the balls; you sift and riddle my mind
>
> On the rack of the middle world, and from my grave at length
> A muddy spring of poems will gush out.

Satan – transliterated into Māori as Hatana – was not wrong to state Baxter could be the country's leading poet, even if they may have been Baxter's own desires the poet was hearing in the voice of a magpie, a bird both emblematic of the New Zealand countryside (Denis Glover's ballad of settler farming has the refrain 'Quardle oodle ardle wardle doodle') and an introduced species not native to the country. For Baxter, 'these daft English words' he writes are as out of place as the magpie's song – murmuring 'Tēnā koe' at the church, he nevertheless confesses his failure to learn Māori. For a poet always wrestling with the difficulty of putting his own ego aside, fame is a temptation not to be longed for but to be resisted, and the continued publication of his writing after his death – recently, a magisterial collection of his *Complete Prose* as well as a new edition of *Letters of a Poet* have supplemented the many editions of poetry – is 'a muddy spring' he can do nothing to quench.

Who is the poet writing for? For Baxter, the reader who tells him that he is her bible, a guiding light, is another form of worldly temptation. Yet his poems seem more conversational than Glück's, even when she is presumably addressing a reader in a fictional afterword: whoever Baxter addresses, Hatana, God, a magpie, the reader feels part of a conversation, even if it is ultimately a conversation the poet is having with himself. Glück writes to take part in a conversation with the 'great dead', but it is a curiously asymmetric conversation, in which it is the 'unborn' who are the imagined readers.

This book opened with Keats's 'This Living Hand', a poem that uncannily looks ahead to the moment in which the 'warm and capable hand' writing the poem will reach out to the reader from 'the icy silence of the tomb'. The poem holds open a present tense to which the writer and reader both belong, yet the power of the poem comes from Keats's acute awareness of time passing. Into the fourteen lines of another late poem, the sonnet 'When I Have Fears That I May Cease to Be', Keats pours all the reasons why a poet might want to write, above all stirred by the visual details of the world in which he lives, the 'night's starred face', the 'huge cloudy symbols of a high romance' the sky suggests to him:

> When I have fears that I may cease to be
>   Before my pen has gleaned my teeming brain,
> Before high-pilèd books, in charactery,
>   Hold like rich garners the full ripened grain;
> When I behold, upon the night's starred face,
>   Huge cloudy symbols of a high romance,
> And think that I may never live to trace
>   Their shadows with the magic hand of chance;
> And when I feel, fair creature of an hour,
>   That I shall never look upon thee more,
> Never have relish in the faery power
>   Of unreflecting love – then on the shore
> Of the wide world I stand alone, and think
> Till love and fame to nothingness do sink.

The anxiety to 'glean' with his pen all the content of his 'teeming brain' has the urgency of a twentieth-century diarist like Virginia Woolf, who felt that to leave a day unrecorded was to allow life 'to waste like a tap left running'. Katherine Mansfield, too, frightened by the first lung haemorrhage that signalled the tuberculosis that would kill her, as it killed Keats, wrote, 'How unbearable it would be to die, leave "scraps", "bits", nothing real finished.' Like Woolf, however, she was writing in a private diary, and even as she feared leaving 'nothing real finished' for posterity, she was spending far more time writing journal entries and letters to friends than the stories that would make her famous, gleaning both her teeming brain and the riches of visual detail in the world around her out of what might look like a surfeit of attention. Keats's 'When I Have Fears That I May Cease to Be' ends with the poet alone, and thinking, 'on the shore / Of the wide world' and on the shore of mortality, which is perhaps the same thing, 'Till love and fame to nothingness do sink.' But if fame is reduced, at last, to nothing, it is a nothing set alongside the nothing that is love, and, in the moment it is given up, can be recognised as the motivating desire behind the wish to glean everything that is seen and felt, and turn it into poetry. And when we read this sonnet now, picturing the poet on the shore of mortality, left with nothing but some future in which he no longer exists, we do give the poet the fame he may once have yearned for, and perhaps it does feel like loving the poet as well as the poem.

Love and fame are sought by poets, and are offered by poets. Many poets have promised immortality in the form of lines in a poem to those whom they love. Shakespeare's Sonnet 18, declaring the beloved 'more lovely, and more temperate' than a summer's day, offers a portrait of the beloved that is a portrait of constancy, a summer without summer storms, an eternal summer that will not fade into autumn:

> Shall I compare thee to a summer's day?
> Thou art more lovely and more temperate:
> Rough winds do shake the darling buds of May,
> And summer's lease hath all too short a date;
> Sometime too hot the eye of heaven shines,
> And often is his gold complexion dimm'd;
> And every fair from fair sometime declines,
> By chance or nature's changing course untrimm'd;
> But thy eternal summer shall not fade,
> Nor lose possession of that fair thou ow'st;

> Nor shall death brag thou wander'st in his shade,
> When in eternal lines to time thou grow'st:
> So long as men can breathe or eyes can see,
> So long lives this, and this gives life to thee.

    This sonnet follows after the first seventeen sonnets, all of which presented variations on an argument to the young man they address for him to marry and pass his beauty on to the next generation. Leaving that argument behind allows the sonnet sequence a kind of blossoming into a new beauty, and a new depth of feeling, but it doesn't really give a portrait of the young man, only a promise of eternal lines. It is true that the sonnet has continued to be read so long as readers have breathed and eyes have seen, but can a sonnet really give life to the beloved person it commemorates? Keats yearned to leave behind 'high-pilèd books' that would 'in charactery / Hold like rich garners the full ripened grain' of his imagination. Shakespeare's plays could be seen as just such 'rich garners' of 'charactery', but the sonnets give little away of the characters he supposedly immortalises: the main thing we know of the young man is that he had little inclination to marry and father children; and of the woman who is the focus of the last twenty-eight sonnets, we can learn only of the poet's own passion for her, since, as we read in Sonnet 148, we cannot expect truth from 'Love's eye . . . That is so vexed with watching and with tears'. It is not the beloved but the poet's own feelings that remain warm and vital beyond the icy silence of the tomb.

    'i'm interested in death rituals', sam sax opens his poem 'Bury', then concedes, 'maybe that's a weird thing to say.' Where Louise Glück's 'Afterword' comes after an imaginary book we don't get to read, 'Bury' refers to the list sax has compiled of 'mourning practices / gathered across time & continents' that he confesses to finding 'oddly comforting' though he 'won't share it with you'. He will share his conclusion, though, that interment is a form of document, 'the body / is ink in the earth', and he will share his scepticism over the Shakespearean belief in 'two lines / that meet to make a man / alive again on paper.' At the centre of a poem about if not immortality, at least forms of memorial, he writes, with the millennially humble lower case i:

> i know i know,
> ashes to ashes & all that dust
> to irreverent dust. i know everyone
> i love who's dead didn't actually
> become the poem i wrote about them,
> their breath a caught fathered
> object thrashing in the white space
> between letters . . .

In giving up the idea that the beloved could become the poem, however, the yearning for exactly this transformation is sustained. The idea that the poet might 'father' the beloved, or a copy of the beloved, is itself a hope caught in the letters of the poem, or in the space between the letters where the word 'fathered' might suggest Emily Dickinson's feathered hope ('"Hope" is the thing with feathers – / which perches in the soul . . .'). And the poem ends with this hope for a kind of literary immortality transferred from the beloved to the poet himself:

> when i'm gone, make me again
> from my hair. carry me with you
> a small book in your pocket.

The dream of an immortality in poetry is doubly conveyed in these lines, through the images themselves and also through the act of referencing other poets kept alive through these references. The small book carried in a pocket recalls Frank O'Hara's 'A Step Away from Them', which ends with the lines, 'My heart is in my / pocket, it is Poems by Pierre Reverdy'; and the image of the resurrection of the poet made again out of hair recalls, to me at least, not so much the list of death rituals sax hasn't given us but John Donne's 'bracelet of bright hair about the bone' from 'The Relic'.

'The Relic' is one of a startling number of poems in which Donne imagines his own death; it is even one of two poems in which Donne imagines the discovery, after his death, of this bracelet of hair, this 'subtle wreath of hair, which crowns my arm', as he describes it in 'The Funeral'. It is not quite a quiet death he imagines, with the grave broken up to 'entertain' a 'second guest' – a hospitable way to think of the likelihood he recognises of a grave economically being used again for a later burial. But the poet, as always in his love poems, needs no company other than the one he loves, or loved once:

> When my grave is broke up again
>   Some second guest to entertain,
>   (For graves have learn'd that woman head,
>   To be to more than one a bed)
>   And he that digs it, spies
> A bracelet of bright hair about the bone,
>   Will he not let'us alone,
> And think that there a loving couple lies,
> Who thought that this device might be some way
> To make their souls, at the last busy day,
> Meet at this grave, and make a little stay?

In these poems it is as a lover, not as a writer, the poet imagines himself remembered, and in the second verse of this three-verse poem he imagines not only that this bracelet of bright hair might allow the grave to remain undisturbed, but that it might itself be taken as a relic, in an age of 'misdevotion', be worshipped for the miracle of the love that the two have shared. Even so, he realises:

> All measure, and all language, I should pass
> Should I tell what a miracle she was.

This is, always, the paradox of the posterity offered by poetry: the miracle is in the loving, and we might think the lines of poetry themselves miraculous, but they can never really preserve the miracle of the living person who was loved. What Donne's poems open up for the reader are miracles of space and time. For the lover, time apart from the beloved is incalculable, though in 'The Computation' the poet makes an attempt at counting up 'the first twenty years, since yesterday' when it was hardly possible to believe they had parted, an additional forty years of remembering favours, forty of harbouring hopes, a hundred of weeping, and so on, till he has, since yesterday, lived so long he must be 'by being dead, immortal; can ghosts die?' In the present tense of 'The Sun Rising', he declares that the sun's work to warm the world is done in warming the two lovers, since all the world is contracted into the 'everywhere' of their world, their bed the world's centre; the sun itself could be eclipsed with a wink, if it weren't that the lover 'would not lose her sight so long'.

If the lover's vision extends to encompass all of time and space, however, with the lover's death all is permanently eclipsed. Such is the conclusion of 'The Will', Donne's six stanzas of satiric legacies he imagines leaving the world. It begins apparently innocently, with the nicely conventional rhyme of its first couplet:

> Before I sigh my last gasp, let me breathe,
> Great Love, some legacies; here I bequeath . . .

But already with the riddle of his first bequest – his eyes to Argus, the giant with a hundred eyes whose name is synonymous with surveillance – the reader may be suspecting the satiric intent that the concluding lines of each stanza confirm and explain. Each stanza concludes with the lover having learnt a bitter lesson in love – only to give to 'such, as had too much before' or to 'such as have an incapacity' – casting a satirical light back on such bequests as ingenuity to the Jesuits and 'silence to any, who abroad hath been'. What more useless bequest than physic books to someone dying, the English language to travellers abroad?

> To him for whom the passing-bell next tolls
> I give my physic books; my written rolls
> Of moral counsels I to Bedlam give;
> My brazen medals unto them which live
> In want of bread; to them which pass among
> All foreigners, mine English tongue:
>   Thou, Love, by making me love one
>   Who thinks her friendship a fit portion
> For younger lovers, dost my gifts thus disproportion.

Love, so miraculous that 'The Relic' imagines it being worshipped in a new, idolatrous religion, here is reciprocated with an offer of friendship so disproportionate to the incommensurability of the love that there is nowhere for the poem to go but onwards to the bitter finality of its conclusion: 'I'll give no more; but I'll undo / The world by dying; because love dies too.' Yet this undoing of the world by dying is not so much the opposite as the logical extension of the lover's threat in 'The Sun Rising' to eclipse the sun with a wink if doing so would not also eclipse his vision of the woman he would rather keep gazing at. If the lover and the beloved are the whole world to each other, then the death of the lover is always going to be the world's undoing. Whereas the conventional Shakespearean sonnet promises the beloved immortal love, and immortal fame, the love that Donne elevates so sacrilegiously in his poetry is beyond even the poetry to encompass, and with the lover's death, 'all your beauties will be no more worth / Than gold in minds, where none doth draw it forth.' This is the ceasing to be that Keats feared, with the mind's gleanings lost if not drawn forth into poetry.

sam sax's collection *Bury It* both begins and ends with poems called 'Will', as well as containing a poem 'First Will and Testament'. Donne's 'The Will' paradoxically undoes the very idea of a will as a document that looks both backwards and forwards, representing a belief in a future that will continue after the individual is gone; his will refuses both past and future, preferring the world's undoing. sax, in contrast, imagines in both his 'Will' poems a drawing forth that is inexhaustible, indebted to the past and surviving into a future. The book opens with a fishing poem that seems, at least for a line, grounded in the realism of wet sneakers and waiting:

> the fisherman's sneakers trouble the water
> he baits his hooks with homophones, cartilage, pheromones
> his hooks: telephones, specula, seraphim
> he lowers his line into the dark
> > an adrenal needle plunged into the heart
> feels something bite below the river

Both bait and hooks, however, are selected not from any ordinary fisherman's tackle-box but from a storehouse of words and ideas, and to lower the line into the dark – to seek out what Glück in 'Afterword' describes as a 'crisis of vision', a 'darkness, silence', or what she describes in the essay 'Education of a Poet' as 'an ongoing experience of longing', a search for the unreachable, a restlessness almost romantic or sexual – is to plunge 'an adrenal needle . . . into the heart'. This is both mysterious and heady work, and the result both mysterious and erotic: the fisherman of sax's poem pulls up boy

> after boy,
> after boy,
> after boy,
> after boy,

and so on for line after line, making a chain down the page like a fishing line into the depths – down two pages, in fact, of the same repeated phrase, the poem ending on this line 'after boy,' comma and all.

Do these boys represent elegy or resurrection? The collection that this poem introduces contains a number of poems about the suicides of young men, some known to sax and some he knew about through the news, and some of them deaths by drowning. Emily Sernaker, reading the repetition of the phrase across the two pages as 'signifying a long line of gay youth who have committed suicide', recognises this as part of a characteristic pattern in sax's work of 'reaching out in active, sorrowful, earnest motion'. Encountering the poem at the beginning of the book, however, we might also read the calling up of these figures as a raising up of multiple selves, whether the selves of others or the poet's own selves, from the dark into the light. The concluding 'Will' of the collection begins with a question: 'how deep am i indebted to the dead?' Ranging from 'calendars & colanders & cataclysms' (beginning, always, with language and its felicities) to 'all my volumes of vonnegut & auden & baldwin', contrasting 'all my gone men' with 'all my felicific fictive children', this is a will addressed to the dead and to the living, in the understanding that the living are also dying '& i can't let this be tragic'. Indebted to the dead, the poet holds out hope for the future, trusting 'every writ letter is alive & liquid & will survive me'.

One of the strangest images of survival through alive and liquid letters comes in Charlie Clark's poem 'Pseudo-Martyr'. Like sam sax's 'Bury', Clark's 'Pseudo-Martyr' resonates with the echoes of earlier poems: it begins, for instance, with a recollection of the poet 'in the woods and lost' like Dante lost in the woods of his middle age, trying 'to track a trail of vapor home'. The title itself alludes to Donne's 1610 treatise 'Pseudo-martyr', in which Donne, who was raised Catholic, and whose own brother died in prison for confessing to harbouring a Catholic priest, argues against Catholics making martyrs of themselves by refusing to take the Oath of Allegiance to King James. By this time Donne had converted from Catholicism, but the treatise argues for the possibility of compromise in occasionally vivid, often strangely tangential prose that goes, as Clark puts it, 'from convolution into convolution'. Clark himself admits in the poem to having 'read Donne poorly' – 'He did not write of pelicans. / Yet I read him poorly. / So in reading him

I thought of pelicans.' Already strange enough in its movement from one near-death experience to another, and in its movement from a discotheque called Le Pelican to a reading of Donne that gives rise to a series of strange facts about pelicans, the poem moves into the even stranger realm of dreaming, a realm in which – as we have seen in Keats's 'Ode to a Nightingale' and Ford's 'Viewless Wings' – birds seem to take on a peculiar power. When, in the dream of this poem, a pelican fell upon the marriage bed:

> I volunteered to be the one consumed.
> I sat up inside the creature's beak beside the many dead it hauled.
> I tried to speak but its gullet swallowed every sound.
> The dead there had devised a kind of pantomime.
> I learned it soon enough.
> Its every word meant *grieve*.

The narrative of the poet departing the world of the living for the world of the dead is a familiar one, and Dante's *The Divine Comedy* has already been alluded to, but this image of the poet sitting up beside the dead in the beak of a pelican must be one of the strangest. It is no world for a poet either, with the pelican's gullet swallowing every sound, and the dead able to communicate only through a pantomime which has, in any case, only the one word. The form of Clark's poem, with every line end-stopped, and no rhyme or metre, seems antithetical to the kind of lyricism that Orpheus brought to the underworld in order to rescue his Eurydice. As it is for Orpheus, though, it is the thought of his 'sweet wife' which compels the poet to write, and the weird, visceral production of the writing is hard to forget. If the song of the poet will 'thrive inside her; humming always' even without the presence of the poet himself, this poem surely will thrive inside its readers, humming always its oddly stilted rhythms which give its deadpan narrative a dream-like resonance:

> With her in mind, I found the deadest dreadful body there.
> I tore a length of its dried flesh free.
> Upon that flesh I wrote these words.
> With some finger bones I bored a hole through the pelican's low beak.
> When we passed above our home again, I spat the message through.
> It darted, fervent as an insect, into my wife's sleeping ear.
> She woke then, not knowing what I'd done.
> My song thrived inside her; humming always, though I was gone.

Hélène Cixous, describing writing as 'a way of leaving no space for death', contrasts writing with 'turning over in bed to face a wall and drift asleep again as if nothing had happened; as if nothing could happen'. Leaving no space for death, writing leaves space for both expectation and recognition; remembering dreams is a way of staying awake to reality.

Alistair Elliot is a poet whose alertness to the strangeness of reality was kept alive through his repeated encounters with the dead as he worked over a lifetime translating poets both ancient and modern. In the first two long poems in his collection *Talking Back*, 'Talking to Horace' and 'Talking to Bede,' he imagines what kind of conversations he might have with these writers were they to find themselves awake in the twentieth century, surely surprised by some of the changes – 'you'd see ladies drinking with us; and / No slaves (none of your coupling on demand)', he warns Horace. Bede takes control of the conversation early, the first lines of the poem giving his response to what he imagines Elliot might want to recount (what Elliot imagines Bede might imagine . . .): 'You think historians must be keen to see / What followed their escape from history? / You think we can't find out?' Instead, he tells Elliot,

> 'I'd rather hear
> The Earth described. Remind us of the Wear,
> The creatures, plants and light where I began
> To look around the domicile of man,
> The home I only saw till I was seven.'

> You miss the handiworks of God, in heaven?

> 'That's what we all must go without; so when
> You die, bring news of nature, not of men.
> None of us saw enough: we lived too much

> In the small range of feelings, taste and touch.'

> What, even you?

> 'You'd think not, but I still
> Long for one walk across a field or hill.'

In 'Pseudo-Martyr', Charlie Clark found himself, while dreaming, 'alive but dead'. In 'A Touch of Death', another poem from the collection *Talking Back*, Elliot finds himself woken from sleep by the touch of his own dead arm. The poem offers an eerie reversal of Keats's

'This Living Hand', beginning with the icy touch of a hand reaching out from beyond the grave and becoming even more unnerving when nothing happens:

> Strange fingers woke me, fumbling at my brow.
> My rooms were near a roof. I thought: Somehow
> Someone's got in. The cold hand hit my nose.
> Naked between the freezing sheets, I froze.
> Then . . . nothing happened. I became aware
> Horribly slowly no one else was there . . .

The poem itself moves horribly slowly, reading, for all its rhyming couplets of iambic pentameter, like a short story, revealing uncanny detail after uncanny detail in turn: the 'foul soft way' the arm yields to the touch, the gradual realisation this dead arm is the poet's own. The arm is finally brought back to life not by the usual rubbing of muscles and pressing of veins, which may have worked if the arm had merely gone to sleep, but by the trick of matching the imaginary 'real' arm into the space of the dead arm:

> All the sensations of my arm lay there
> In order, like a well-lit thoroughfare,
> But not the arm. My soul is breaking free,
> I thought: I'll lose the arm. I might lose me!
> I grabbed the dead thing. It was powerless.
> I rubbed the muscles, stroked and tried to press
> The blood along, like air in a balloon,

> But nothing made it feel. It would die soon,
> If it weren't dead already. Then I thought:
> If I could swing it round, it might get caught
> As it goes through its image. Can you fit
> Your arm back in the space that matches it?
> The elbows fused together as they met,
> The wrists and knuckles too – a perfect set.
> And even when I moved them on, they stayed
> United as they'd been since they were made.

The uncanniness, though, is passed on to the reader, who is asked to 'keep this quiet', since 'Who'd ever shake this hand – with which I write – / Knowing it died and met its ghost one night?' This is a much more diffident approach to the reader than Keats's impassioned reaching out from the grave. The person asked to shake the hand is not even the reader, but the general public from whom the reader is asked to keep the story of the dead hand secret.

Elliot may be right to feel it is the social encounter that cannot accommodate the touch of death, while the reader is allowed to share the secret, a secret all the more unnerving for the parenthetical remark that it is with this once-dead hand (once and future dead hand) that the poet writes – and writes this *very poem*. For all the urgency of communication driving poems like 'This Living Hand' and 'Pseudo-Martyr', what is arrived at is a form of communication very far from conversation, the song thriving in someone else – you, her, the reader, myself – after the 'I' of the poem is gone. Why should a poet, wanting to write back to the dead poets they have read, imagine themselves writing for an audience who will never reply? Why should they so often imagine they are writing for an audience not yet even born? It turns out it isn't true that there are more people alive today than have ever lived in all of human history. There are a lot of us alive, but it seems the proportion is probably more like six per cent of all people who ever lived. Even so, there is no shortage of readers amongst the living to make a poet like Louise Glück need to look to the future for an audience. What is the advantage for a poet in being dead?

A younger generation of poets seems to feel this need to be dead less acutely. sam sax, for all the poems about death in *Bury It*, when asked in a Poetry Foundation interview how he might see his poems fitting 'into the lineage of people' writing after him, replied: 'I can't really presume to make a legacy for myself like that . . . I hope the poems are of use in conversations that are outside of my hands.' Later in the same interview, he explained: 'The utility and function of a poem, to me, is shifting, especially in the context of species extinction. There may not be a readership in 50 years . . . So, there's a radical refocusing on the present.' I think he is right to see the idea that there might not be a readership in fifty years as a 'radical refocusing'. The philosopher Samuel Scheffler has written about the importance not only to poets but to humanity in general, and every person in particular, of a belief that humanity will continue on beyond our own lifetime. If we lose this belief, he suggests, 'the value or purpose or meaning of what we do here and now is diminished, or perhaps lost altogether'. As a writer, if he cannot imagine himself as 'part of a larger, temporally extended practice that has endured for thousands of years and [will] endure for many more', then, he imagines, 'it's just me, sitting here, writing my measly books.'

Poetry can, and does, take part in the urgent conversations of the present, and one of the most urgent conversations to be having is about preserving a state of the world in which there *will* be a readership for poetry in fifty years, and in five hundred years. When sax hopes 'the poems are of use in conversations that are out of my hands', however, he points to the way in which the readership of all poetry is at a distance from the poet. Emily Dickinson described her poetry as a 'letter to the world':

> This is my letter to the World
> That never wrote to Me –
> The simple News that Nature told –
> With tender Majesty
>
> Her Message is committed
> To Hands I cannot see –
> For love of Her – Sweet – countrymen –
> Judge tenderly – of Me

Dickinson wrote many actual letters she sent to readers she knew, often including scraps of poetry, but the hundreds of poems she wrote and never published suggest an overflow of feeling, an excess of communication, towards a world 'that never wrote to Me' and now is represented as both hidden (holding the 'letter' in 'Hands I cannot see') and judgemental. With poetry often read today on the internet, in a way that collapses not time but distance, another way of writing into a 'larger . . . extended practice' is created, even if the *temporal* extension of the practice may be in doubt. Distance, whether of time or space, removes the poem from the usual instrumentality of a conversation (and from the immediacy of judgement). This is not the conversation that might take place on the telephone, making plans, sharing news, asking a question that needs an urgent reply. It is less like this kind of conversation and more like song.

For George Eliot, to take her place in 'the choir invisible' of poets whose words live on in the minds of readers after them is to wish not for love or fame, but for transcendence:

> O may I join the choir invisible
> Of those immortal dead who live again
> In minds made better by their presence: live
> In pulses stirr'd to generosity,
> In deeds of daring rectitude, in scorn
> For miserable aims that end with self,
> In thoughts sublime that pierce the night like stars,
> And with their mild persistence urge man's search
> To vaster issues . . .

As a novelist, Eliot's most-loved character is, if not the passionate Maggie Tulliver of *The Mill on the Floss*, Dorothea Brooke from *Middlemarch*. Yearning for some great glory, the young Dorothea imagines she must find it through supporting the ambitions of a husband, leading to a disastrously unhappy first marriage. When she marries for a second time, this time for love, her husband becomes 'an ardent public man', but her own strength 'spent itself in channels which had no great name on the earth'. Even so, Eliot assures us, 'the effect of her being on those around her was incalculably diffusive: for the growing good of the world is partly dependent on unhistoric acts; and that things are not so ill with you and me as they might have been, is half owing to the number who lived faithfully a hidden life, and rest in unvisited tombs.'

For Eliot, the role of the poet is likewise to do good in the world, and she sees poetry as a place for the distillation of the highest feelings, so that the reader might, as she writes in 'O May I Join the Choir Invisible', 'inherit that sweet purity / For which we struggled, fail'd, and agoniz'd / With widening retrospect that bred despair.' It isn't that the poet is more saintly than anyone else; rather, it is that they write out of, and towards, their best selves. Poets too struggle, fail and agonise even to see, let alone to live, what it is their poetry might mean to readers. What we read, and what the poet writes, Eliot recognises, reflects the poet's own self only insofar as it reflects the self of the poet as they were writing, or as their writing could draw forth. For her, writing is a way of drawing forth 'our rarer, better, truer self, / That sobb'd religiously in yearning song, / That watch'd to ease the burthen of the world, / Laboriously tracing what must be, / And what may yet be better.' In fact, what we most love in Eliot's writing may be less the portrayal of the rarer, better, truer characters than the portrayal of those flawed characters struggling, failing and agonising, and it may be the struggles and flaws of other poets whose work we read that move us most. Sometimes it is just a line that is needed, when you are 'pitched past pitch of grief', as Gerard Manley Hopkins writes in the sonnet 'No worst, there is none': for 'the mind, mind has mountains; cliffs of fall'. The last line of W. H. Auden's 'Funeral Blues' can be more of a relief than any more consoling line: 'For nothing now can ever come to any good.' Even on the brightest of days, though, it is possible to be caught by a line of poetry as you hear a bird 'pouring forth [its] soul abroad / In such an ecstasy'.

It is as a novelist, rather than a poet, that Eliot is mostly remembered, though a line like the opening line 'O may I join the choir invisible' lifts towards song in a way that continues to resonate when the rest of the poem is forgotten. When readers do make the pilgrimage to her grave at Highgate Cemetery in London, they will find the following two lines from the poem on the gravestone: 'Of those immortal dead who live again / In minds made better by their presence.' Remembered by readers not yet born when they were writing, poets are known so intimately we read the lines they wrote as if they were our own thoughts. At the same time, as we read the lines poets have written, the poets themselves are invisible, even when they are still alive. Would you rather be able to fly or be invisible? The viewless wings of poetry allow for both flight and invisibility, for poets and for their readers.

Writing suggestions

CHAPTER ONE: SIMPLICITY & RESONANCE

- Try borrowing the stanza form of 'Stopping by Woods' for a poem that similarly takes a single scene, perhaps a scene involving a moment of pause, trusting the resonance to arise out of the simplicity of the description and out of the form itself. Rhyme a-a-b-a, b-b-c-b, for four stanzas, with a repeated final line.

- Or borrow the form of 'Across Brooklyn' – three-line stanzas alternating with two-line stanzas, with a question making up the second stanza, and a reply (though not to the question) in the final couplet.

- From 'After Apple-Picking' you might borrow the idea of describing a physical activity in such detail that it becomes metaphysical. How far can you take it? A game of tennis that goes beyond the court, beyond childhood into adulthood, until the players are beyond the family and estranged from each other? Weeding, till you are down beyond the topsoil into the depths of the earth? You might like to write this poem in iambic metre, or you might like to keep it unmetred and with irregular-length lines.

- Dreams come with their own resonance, but the resonance that the memory of a dream retains can be hard to translate into poetry. Can you take elements from a dream and place them in a poem with the vivid detail that suggests a real situation, but holding, too, the symbolic resonance that the details held in the dream?

CHAPTER TWO: THE ORNATE & THE SUMPTUOUS

- Write a sequence of similes, as extravagant and far-fetched as you can come up with. If they are not 'lost scrolls' or 'blackouts', or, ultimately, all about love, what else could hold together a series of similes?

- Write about something you have forgotten. How can you write about something you have forgotten?

- Write a poem full of long and beautiful words. Perhaps swap word-hoards with a friend – what words do you wish they would put into a poem? What will you do with their most treasured words?

- Combine the drafts, or pieces from the drafts, of several different poems with several different subjects. Can you make something sinuous of it, connecting the different subjects so that the poem moves easily from one to the other?

- Describe your life as a mansion, as beautiful and vast as you can imagine it. Decorate it both in terms of its imaginary interior and in the language you use to describe it – how many rhymes, sound patterns, anagrams, echoes, alliterative flourishes and ornate words can you work in?

- Is the poem more, or less, interesting and effective if you make it apparent to the reader that the mansion (or the zoo, the botanical gardens, the hospital, the church, the school, the city) represents your life (or your marriage, your childhood, your faith, your illness, your anxiety, your education)?

- Describe a dream, or a dreamscape – how gorgeous, or how haunting, can you make it? Can you include in it the effect of a dream fading away as you remember it?

CHAPTER THREE: CONCISION, COMPOSITION & THE IMAGE

- Listen for repetitions, rhymes and rhythm in ordinary conversations or overheard snatches of speech. What happens if you just write the phrases down as you hear them? Can you find a way to include non-verbal parts of the conversation – 'uh' 'mmn' and sounds of laughter, emphasis or pause? Is this a poem, part of a poem, a draft you could work up?

- What do you arrange as a composition in your life? Your garden? The dinner table? A vase of flowers? The tool shed? Write a description of it, a still life.

- Look for found compositions – things that have come together in a way you find beautiful. Can you convey the beauty of the scene just by describing the placement of the objects?

- Next time someone takes a group photograph, what instructions are issued? What would it look like if you wrote them down? If it is a family photo, what does it reveal about the family? If it is a wedding, what does it reveal about the photographer, about cultural expectations, about the story the photograph is supposed to tell?

- Where do you find words that resonate with you – at a paint shop? In a fabric shop? In an instruction manual? In a knitting pattern? Put one or more of these words in the centre of a short poem.

- Look through poems you have already written for small scenes, compositional elements, a visual detail. Can these pieces stand alone?

CHAPTER FOUR: SPRAWL

- Write about your day, one day, but allowing in any associations, stray thoughts, whether you thought them at the time or think them now. Make use of parentheses. Put a full stop in the middle of a line. Let lines run over. Use couplets to make it look like poetry, and write it like an essay.

- Use anaphora like Whitman or Ginsberg – start each line with the same word or phrase, then move on to another set of repetitions.

- Imagine meeting Whitman or Ginsberg or John Donne, Ursula Bethell, Robert Frost or another poet you admire in a supermarket, on a ferry, in a library, at the dentist surgery. What will happen?

- Write a poem to your country, your school or university, your ancestors, or to poetry itself. End every line with a full stop or a question mark.

- Give a poem of yours to a friend to read and then write a new draft including their response to it as part of the poem. Reply to them in the poem.

- Give your poem room to travel. Collect up charged moments or details, and create a landscape or a journey in which they might be placed or encountered.

CHAPTER FIVE: FORM

- Try writing a villanelle, a duplex or a sestina. If it doesn't work, deconstruct it: can you use some of the repetitions, some of the images or some of the lines? Can you introduce further repetitions, a refrain?

- Invent a new form! How might form be related to identity (as the blues are related to an African-American identity)? Or how might form reflect your interests (self-described geek Gregory Pincus invented the fib, based on the Fibonacci sequence – a six-line, twenty-syllable poem with a syllable count by line of 1/1/2/3/5/8)?

- Elizabeth Bishop writes of loss as an artform. What other disasters or failures could you rethink as a form of art? What form of artistry will you bring to your argument – rhyme? A rigid verse form? Beautiful imagery?

- Terrance Hayes describes the sonnet as part prison, part panic closet. How would you describe the form you are writing your poem in?

- Describe a situation two people are caught up in from an outside perspective. Who are you, and what difference does it make to the poem what your relationship is to the people whose situation you are describing?

- How might the same story be told differently through a number of different accounts? How might you use repetition and variation to structure this poem?

CHAPTER SIX: ARGUMENT & CONVERSATION

- Make an extravagant, metaphorical argument for why you should get to do something you want to do. Work through the metaphor in detail, be scrupulous, scientific, rational . . . but also, if you like, absurd.

- Address the sun, the moon, time, death as if they were a younger sibling making trouble. Rail against reality!

- Invent a conversation between two objects – a window and the wind, a stone and a plant, the rain and the earth, a computer and a noticeboard, a bus and a road . . . Who is going to win this argument? Or what might they learn from each other?

- Write up a conversation with a friend. Use whatever you can remember of actual things you said, and the details of where you were sitting, what was happening around you, what you were drinking, what you were wearing . . .

CHAPTER SEVEN: CONVERSATIONS WITH THE PAST

- Where would you ride a dream horse to? What might stop you on the way?

- How might *you* translate the Sappho poem about jealousy and desire, about being an onlooker? Which aspects of it would you want to play up? What contemporary resonances might you find? Will you keep a version of the Sapphic form, with the three lines and then the shorter fourth?

- Write back to a canonical poem you know and love, or know and are infuriated by. How might you respond to Donne's 'The Flea' or to the Catullus poem 5 demanding kisses?

- What happens if you re-imagine the speaker of a poem: if the onlooker, in the Sappho poem, for instance, wasn't in love with the girl the god-like man was speaking to, but was trying to buy shoes while the shopkeeper was talking on the phone, or was a child waiting for his mother to stop talking to his father?

- Do you wake or sleep? What visions or reveries have you had when half asleep, or when you have drunk too much, or are otherwise drowsy and numbed? (How might these visions speak back to earlier poems?)

CHAPTER EIGHT: POETRY IN A HOUSE ON FIRE

- What secrets are you keeping from your children? And/or, how do you want to sell them the world? You might want to tackle these questions in two different poems. You could try writing one or both of them as a list poem, or as a letter to your children (real or imaginary), or you might want to borrow Maggie Smith's use of shifting repetitions ('Life is short, though . . . life is short, and . . . For every bird . . . For every loved child . . .').

- What are you panicking about? Write about that.

- What are some of the arguments people are using to avoid confronting the issues you think need to be addressed? How can you play up the absurdity of these arguments? What context might you place these conversations in (a cruise ship might work in one poem; a school, a nail salon, a television talk show or a hospital might be funnier, more heart-rending or fiercer in another).

- Try a modern take on the romantic sonnet, like Carlos Santos Perez has done, bringing in whatever incongruous political issues you would like to see given more play in poetry. Try out some unlikely similes: I love you like . . . , I love you as . . .

- How do *you* express your identity? Or, what explains *your* choice of T-shirt/latest purchase? (This might be one poem, or two.)

- If you had 58 (or 24, or 12, or 30) numbered sections in which to write, what topic or whose life might you want to think about? How widely might you be able to range, how personally might you approach the topic, how much research might you do?

CHAPTER NINE: LETTERS *&* ODES

- What happens if you turn a draft of a poem you already have into a kind of letter, using the word 'Dear' to evoke address?

- Or, what happens if you address the subject of the poem with an 'O!'? How do the effects of 'Dear' and 'O' compare? Which works better?

- Write an ode to something in the world that is really about your own interior subject state, a mood, a sensibility. It might be imaginary: imagine you have won a major award, and then write a poem to (or about) the beans growing in your garden, or the child on the trampoline next door, without mentioning the award (or mention it if you want to) – how does it colour the poem? Or, you are suffering a profound loss of confidence, despair, a break-up, grief: how will you write to – or about – the beans/child/teapot/clouds now?

- Write a letter to a vast abstraction – death, love, birth, honour, shame. What kind of intimacy can you create?

- Write a letter to a close friend. What makes it poetry? Or, use a letter you have written to a friend. How can you turn it into poetry?

- What happens if you put your poem into terza rima, or iambic verse, or into a ballad form? Or, borrow Emily Berry's use of the tab key. Space your poem out across the page, play with white space.

CHAPTER TEN: POETRY & THE AFTERLIFE

- If you were writing the afterword of an imaginary life-work, what might you want to explain, excuse or apologise for?

- If you were to imagine yourself as a work of art (a sculpture, a painting, a stage set), how might you describe yourself? You might want to describe a real work of art, with the idea that it represents yourself or your life.

- What would Satan or Hatana try and tempt you with? What animal might he take the form of?

- Can you compress this poem, or any of the poems you are drafting, into fourteen lines? How might you use fourteen lines to express an unquenchable eloquence, or an idea of endlessness?

- What weird lists might you want to compile, in the manner of sam sax's list of death rituals? Is your poem going to work better with the list as part of it, or with the list withheld?

- To what elaborate lengths might you go to communicate with someone you love? What has put you into such a situation to make communication so hard? You might want to try out Charlie Clark's way of constructing this poem with a series of end-stopped lines.

- What might you fish up from under the water? Who might you bequeath it to? What would this be telling them?

The poets

NICK ASCROFT (1973–)

Born in Oamaru, New Zealand, in 1973, Nick Ascroft is the author of four collections of poetry published by Victoria University Press. His poetry is known for its wit, formal ingenuity and extravagant vocabulary (he is also a competitive Scrabble player).

TIFFANY ATKINSON (1972–)

Tiffany Atkinson is a German-born British poet and academic. She has published three collections of poetry, *Kink and Particle* (2006), *Catulla et al.* (2011) and *So Many Moving Parts* (2014). She is currently professor of creative writing at the University of East Anglia.

W. H. AUDEN (1907–1973)

British-American poet W. H. Auden is one of the major twentieth-century poets writing in a formalist tradition. Some of his most well-known poems include 'Funeral Blues' (1936), 'Musée des Beaux Arts' (1938) and 'In Memory of W. B. Yeats' (1940).

BRIAN BATCHELOR (1983–)

Brian Batchelor is an American poet and artist who has been incarcerated since 2002, serving a life sentence without parole. During his time in prison, Batchelor has taken part in the Minnesota Prison Writing Workshop and is a member of the Stillwater Writers Collective.

JAMES K. BAXTER (1926–1972)

One of New Zealand's most well-known poets, James K. Baxter was influenced by classical mythology and British modernist poets such as Dylan Thomas and Cecil Day-Lewis, while also recognising the importance in New Zealand of Māori culture. Following an instruction given to him in a dream, he founded an inclusive community at

Jerusalem, otherwise known by its Māori name Hiruhārama, a small Māori settlement on the Whanganui River.

SAMUEL BECKETT (1906–1989)

Samuel Beckett was an Irish playwright, novelist and poet. His work is typified by tragi-comic explorations of mortality and existentialism, as in his best-known play *Waiting for Godot* (1953). He was awarded the Nobel Prize for Literature in 1969.

EMILY BERRY (1981–)

Emily Berry is an English poet and editor. She has published two collections of poetry, *Dear Boy* (2013) and *Stranger, Baby* (2017). In 2018 she was elected a Fellow of the Royal Society of Literature, and she is currently editor of the magazine *The Poetry Review*.

URSULA BETHELL (1874–1945)

Mary Ursula Bethell was a British-born New Zealand poet whose work predominantly explores themes of spirituality, time and the natural world. She is perhaps best known for her collection *From a Garden in the Antipodes* (1929), a series of poems about her garden in Christchurch that marked a distinct development in what it meant to be a New Zealand poet. Contemporary poet D'Arcy Cresswell wrote that 'New Zealand poetry wasn't truly discovered until Ursula Bethell, "very earnestly digging", raised her head to look at the mountains'.

HERA LINDSAY BIRD (1987–)

Hera Lindsay Bird is a Wellington-based New Zealand poet and a graduate of the International Institute of Modern Letters. Her self-titled debut collection, *Hera Lindsay Bird* (2016), was published to immediate critical acclaim and popularity. She is also well known for her poem 'Keats is dead so fuck me from behind' (2016), which went viral, leading to her being profiled by various outlets such as the *Guardian* and *Vice*. Former British Poet Laureate Carol Ann Duffy selected Bird's work to be published as part of the Laureate Choice series; the resulting publication, *Pamper Me to Hell & Back*, was published in 2018.

ELIZABETH BISHOP (1911–1979)

An American poet who lived in Brazil from 1951 to 1967, Bishop published few collections of poetry for a writer of such considerable reputation. Despite her commitment to craft and revision, her poems typically have a conversational, digressive, descriptive quality and are most often written in free verse, though her villanelle 'One Art' is perhaps her best-known and most anthologised poem. Her many awards and fellowships include two Guggenheim Fellowships and the 1970 Pulitzer Prize for Poetry.

WILLIAM BLAKE (1757–1827)

English poet, painter and visionary William Blake is now recognised as one of the canonical poets of the Romantic period. The illustrated collection *Songs of Innocence and Experience* was first published in 1789.

BRIAN BLANCHFIELD (1973–)

Brian Blanchfield is an American poet and essayist. He has published two collections of poetry, *Not Even Them* (2004) and *A Several World* (2014), and a collection of essays titled *Proxies* (2016). He is currently the poetry editor for *Fence* magazine and teaches at the University of Arizona.

JENNY BORNHOLDT (1960–)

Jenny Bornholdt is a Wellington-based poet whose work is grounded in familiar New Zealand domestic settings and in the close attention to ordinary everyday New Zealand speech. She served as Poet Laureate

of New Zealand from 2005 to 2007, and was made a Member of the
New Zealand Order of Merit in 2013 for services to poetry. Her most
recent collection, *Lost and Somewhere Else*, was published in 2019.

EMILY BRONTË (1818–1848)

English novelist and poet Emily Brontë is best known for her novel
Wuthering Heights (1847). Emily and her sisters Charlotte and Anne also
published a single book of poetry called *Poems by Currer, Ellis and Acton
Bell* (1846). Following Emily Brontë's death, nearly 200 other poems
were discovered and subsequently published.

JERICHO BROWN (1976–)

Jericho Brown's many awards and fellowships include the 2020 Pulitzer
Prize for Poetry. Born in Louisiana, he is currently director of the
creative writing programme at Emory University in Atlanta, Georgia.
His third collection of poetry, *The Tradition* (2019), introduces the
duplex, a sonnet form of his own invention.

STEPHANIE BURT (1971–)

As well as the collection of loose, and inspired, translations, *After
Callimachus* (2020), Stephanie Burt has published four collections
of poetry. She is also an influential poetry critic, whose books include
Close Calls with Nonsense (2009), *The Poem is You* (2016) and, most
recently, *Don't Read Poetry* (2019). She is a professor of English at
Harvard University.

ANNE CARSON (1950–)

Canadian poet, essayist and classicist Anne Carson is known not only
for her translations of classical poets such as Sappho and Euripides
but also for her own poetry that, in works such as her lyric essay

'The Glass Essay' (1995) and verse novel *An Autobiography in Red: A Novel in Verse* (1998), often plays with convention and classification. Her latest collection, *Float*, was published in 2016. As a professor of classical studies, comparative literature and English literature, she currently teaches at the University of Michigan.

CATULLUS (C.84 BCE–C.54 BCE)

Gaius Valerius Catullus wrote during the Late Era of the Roman Republic. Catullus is known for his erotic lyric poetry, breaking away from the Homeric tradition of grand narratives in favour of introspection and more personal lyricism.

JANET CHARMAN (1954–)

Janet Charman is an Auckland-based New Zealand poet whose work is stylistically inventive and psychologically astute. She has published many collections with Auckland University Press, most recently *At the White Coast* in 2012.

CHEN CHEN (1989–)

Chen Chen is a Chinese-American poet whose debut collection, *When I Grow Up I Want to Be a List of Further Possibilities*, was published in 2017. He currently teaches at Brandeis University, Boston, as the Jacob Ziskind Poet-in-Residence.

HEATHER CHRISTLE (1980–)

Heather Christle is an American poet from New Hampshire. She has published four collections of poetry and currently teaches at Emory University in Atlanta. Her most recent publication is a lyrical non-fiction work titled *The Crying Book*, published in 2019.

CHARLIE CLARK (1977–)

Charlie Clark is an American poet who graduated with a MFA from the University of Maryland and currently resides in Austin, Texas. 'Pseudo-Martyr' is among the poems included in *The Newest Employee of the Museum of Ruin*, published in 2020.

ARTHUR HUGH CLOUGH (1819–1861)

Arthur Hugh Clough was an English Victorian poet known for his explorations of melancholy, religious doubt and subjectivity. Clough's experimentation with subjectivity and introspection made him a major influence on poets of the modernist era such as T. S. Eliot.

SAMUEL TAYLOR COLERIDGE (1772–1834)

The publication of Samuel Taylor Coleridge's collaboration with William Wordsworth, *Lyrical Ballads*, in 1798, was a foundational moment for Romantic poetry, introducing the Romantic values of lyrical introspection, a more natural and unconstrained verse style, an appreciation of natural beauty, and a far-reaching imaginative speculation.

HART CRANE (1899–1932)

Hart Crane is an American modernist poet, influenced by T. S. Eliot. His long poem 'The Bridge' (1930) is his most ambitious work, combining aspects of the epic and the lyric as it explores modernity and the American metropolitan experience.

NATALIE DIAZ (1978–)

Natalie Diaz was born in the Fort Mojave Indian village in Needles, California. She is Mojave and an enrolled member of the Gila River Indian community. Her 2012 collection, *When My Brother Was an Aztec*, portrays the trauma of living with addiction in poetry that is vivid, dramatic and formally ambitious, while her 2020 collection, *Postcolonial Love Poem*, is described by *Guardian* poetry reviewer Emily Perez as 'an intellectually rigorous exploration of the postcolonial toll on land, love and people, as well as a call to fight back'. She has held many fellowships and awards, including a MacArthur Fellowship in 2018.

EMILY DICKINSON (1830–1886)

Emily Dickinson is the most important poet of America's lyric tradition. Only ten of her poems were published in her lifetime. Publication of three volumes of *Collected Poems* in the 1890s brought together the nearly 1800 poems she had written and bound in hand-sewn booklets.

TOM DISCH (1940–2008)

American poet and author Tom Disch wrote novels, speculative fiction, poems, essays and librettos.

JOHN DONNE (1572–1631)

Renaissance poet, soldier, secretary and, eventually, dean of St Paul's Cathedral, Donne is best known now as the most important of the Metaphysical poets, whose poetry is distinguished by the workings out of elaborate metaphysical conceits – extended metaphors serving logical, if sometimes absurd, philosophical arguments.

EILEEN DUGGAN (1894–1972)

Born in Blenheim, Eileen Duggan was a New Zealand poet and columnist known for her spiritual and religious poetry in a particularly New Zealand context. Her poetry appears in numerous anthologies, and she was awarded an OBE for services to the Dominion.

GEORGE ELIOT (1819–1880)

Mary Ann Evans, who published as George Eliot, was an English Victorian novelist and poet. She is perhaps best known for her novel *Middlemarch* (1872), a work that deals with politics, social identity, the status of women and idealism, all themes that permeate her work. In 1980, on the centenary of her death, Eliot was commemorated with a memorial in Poets' Corner of Westminster Abbey.

ALISTAIR ELLIOT (1932–2018)

Alistair Elliot was an English poet, librarian and translator. His work is known for its esoteric and musical qualities informed by Elliot's interest in classical literature. His final collection, *Telling the Stones*, was published in 2017.

ANNIE FINCH (1956–)

Annie Finch is an American poet, critic and playwright whose work predominantly explores feminism and spirituality. She has published numerous works of poetry and criticism concerning prosody, even publishing several verse plays and librettos. She served as director of the Stonecoast MFA programme in creative writing at the University of Southern Maine, and now continues to teach and perform. Her latest poetry chapbook, *The Poetry Witch Little Book of Spells*, was published in 2019.

MARK FORD (1962–)

Kenyan-born British poet and literary critic Mark Ford has published several collections of poetry, the most recent of which, *Enter, Fleeing*, was published in 2018. He is currently head of the department of English language and literature at University College London.

ROBERT FROST (1874–1963)

One of the most canonical of American poets, Robert Frost was a modernist less interested in experimentation than in renewing a tradition his work continued. Poems such as 'Stopping by Woods on a Snowy Evening' and 'The Road Not Taken' are still among the best-known poems in and beyond the US, widely referenced in both literary and popular culture. In the essay 'An Education in Poetry', he wrote, 'Poetry provides the one permissible way of saying one thing and meaning another.'

ALLEN GINSBERG (1926–1997)

Allen Ginsberg was one of the best-known poets of the Beat movement, which combined counter-cultural social politics with a literary practice emphasising spontaneity, loose narrative and poetic form, authenticity and self-expression.

LOUISE GLÜCK (1943–)

Louise Glück, United States Poet Laureate from 2003 to 2004, was awarded the Nobel Prize for Literature in 2020.

PAULA GREEN (1955–)

Paula Green is an Auckland-based New Zealand poet and children's author. She has published numerous collections of poetry, the latest of which, *New York Pocket Book*, was published in 2017, the same year in which she was appointed a Member of the New Zealand Order of Merit for services to poetry. Through her influential poetry blog, nzpoetryshelf.com, she does a tremendous amount to support New Zealand poets and poetry.

DIANA HARRIS (1956–)
Diana Harris is an Auckland writer now living in Sydney, where she teaches English and writes occasional but exceptional poems and literary fiction.

REBECCA HAWKES (1994–)
Rebecca Hawkes is a Wellington-based poet and painter. A graduate of the International Institute of Modern Letters, Hawkes has had work published in numerous literary journals. Her most recent appearance is in the *AUP New Poets 5* collection alongside two other emerging New Zealand writers, Sophie van Waardenberg and Carolyn DeCarlo.

TERRANCE HAYES (1971–)
Terrance Hayes is an American poet whose many award-winning collections include *Lighthead* (2010), *How to Be Drawn* (2015) and, most recently, *American Sonnets for My Past and Future Assassin* (2018). He is a professor of English at New York University.

HORACE (65 BCE–8 BCE)
Quintus Horatius Flaccus, otherwise known simply as Horace, was a Roman lyric poet most famous for his *Odes* (24 BCE–13 BCE). His poetry is noted for its confessional yet conversational tone as he explores love, politics, philosophy and even poetry itself. New Zealand poet Ian Wedde's *Commonplace Odes* (2001) offers a brilliant twentieth-century collection of odes in the Horatian tradition, celebrating the smaller details of life with a sense of their larger significance.

REBECCA GAYLE HOWELL (1975–)
Rebecca Gayle Howell is an American poet and translator. The recipient of numerous literary awards, including a United States Artists Fellowship in 2019, Howell is the poetry editor of the *Oxford*

American and is currently a senior lecturer in the Lewis Honors College at the University of Kentucky. Her collection *American Purgatory* was published in 2017.

ASH DAVIDA JANE (1997–)

Ash Davida Jane is a Wellington-based New Zealand poet whose work has been published in numerous publications and online journals. Jane is a graduate of the International Institute of Modern Letters, and her first collection *Every Dark Waning* was published in 2016, and *How to Live With Mammals* was published in 2021.

ANNALEESE JOCHEMS (1994–)

Annaleese Jochems is a New Zealand writer whose work has been published in several literary journals, such as *Sweet Mammalian* and *Turbine*. In 2016 she was awarded the Adam Prize from the International Institute of Modern Letters for her first novel, *Baby* (2017), which went on to win the Hubert Church Prize at the 2018 Ockham New Zealand Book Awards.

BEN JONSON (1572–1637)

A prolific writer of poems, plays, masques and satire, Ben Jonson was a contemporary of William Shakespeare, and the more erudite and classically influenced writer.

JOHN KEATS (1795–1821)

An English Romantic poet, John Keats is perhaps best known for his series of odes, among which are 'Ode to a Nightingale' (1819) and 'Ode on a Grecian Urn' (1819). Despite succumbing to tuberculosis at the young age of twenty-five, Keats remains one of the most-read poets of the Romantic era.

LUKE KENNARD (1981–)

Luke Kennard is a British poet and novelist known for his inventive and surreal yet deadpan style of poetry. He currently teaches English and creative writing at the University of Birmingham. His latest pamphlet of poetry, *Truffle Hound*, was published in 2018.

MICHELE LEGGOTT (1956–)

Michele Leggott is a New Zealand poet who has published numerous collections of poetry, most recently *Mezzaluna: Selected Poems* (2020). She served as New Zealand Poet Laureate from 2007 to 2009, the same year in which she was appointed a Member of the New Zealand Order of Merit for services to poetry. She is currently a professor of English at the University of Auckland.

MARK LEIDNER (1980–)

The author of several collections of poetry, short stories and screenplays, Mark Leidner is an American writer who currently teaches poetry in the School of English and Creative Writing at Emory University in Georgia.

PATRICIA LOCKWOOD (1982–)

Patricia Lockwood is an American poet and essayist. She is known for her use of irony and humour in her poetry and online presence on Twitter. In 2017 she published her memoir *Priestdaddy*, and her debut novel, *No One Is Talking About This*, was published in 2021.

RICHARD LOVELACE (1617–1657)

Cavalier poet Richard Lovelace was an English Renaissance lyricist. He is best known for his poems 'To Althea, from Prison' (1642) and 'To Lucasta, Going to the Warres' (1649), which touch upon his affiliation with the political turmoil of the English Civil War.

SARAH MANGUSO (1974–)

Sarah Manguso is an American poet and writer from Boston, with an MFA from the Iowa Writers Workshop. Her most recent work, *300 Arguments*, a series of invented aphorisms that together add up to something in between poetry, essay and memoir, was published in 2017. She currently teaches in the MFA programme at New England College.

BILL MANHIRE (1946–)

One of New Zealand's most well-known contemporary poets, Bill Manhire has published numerous collections of poetry and was the inaugural Te Mata New Zealand Poet Laureate of 1997. He founded the International Institute of Modern Letters at Victoria University of Wellington, where he is currently emeritus professor of English and creative writing. His most recent collection, *Wow*, was published in 2020.

ANDREW MARVELL (1621–1678)

Andrew Marvell was an English metaphysical poet whose lyrics are marked by their wit and complexity.

EDNA ST VINCENT MILLAY (1892–1950)

Edna St Vincent Millay, well known as a poet since the publication of her poem 'Renascence' in 1912 when she was twenty, described her life as a young writer in New York as 'very very poor and very very merry'. Her poetry was both popular and critically acclaimed in the 1920s and '30s, and she was awarded the Frost Medal for her contribution to American poetry in 1943.

CHELSEY MINNIS (1970–)

Chelsey Minnis is an American poet whose work plays with poetic conventions, pushing them to further examine their capabilities.

She has published several collections of poetry, most recently
Baby, I Don't Care (2018).

MARIANNE MOORE (1887–1972)

One of the major American modernist poets, Marianne Moore
published her first collection, *Poems*, in 1921. Many collections followed,
including several collections of *The Complete Poems* and more than
one *Selected*. Her distinctive method of writing in syllabics combined
prose-like rhythms with formal constraint. Her poem 'Poetry' begins,
'I, too, dislike it'.

FRANK O'HARA (1926–1966)

An American poet, essayist and art critic, Frank O'Hara is known
for his highly distinct style of poetry that often resembles diary entries.
As a curator at the Museum of Modern Art, O'Hara was a member of
the New York School and associated with artists of numerous disciplines
who were exploring surrealism, abstraction, action painting and jazz.

SHARON OLDS (1942–)

Sharon Olds is an American poet who is known for work that is intensely
emotional and personal. She was the recipient of the Pulitzer Prize for
Poetry in 2013 for her collection *Stag's Leap* (2012) and her most recent
collection, *Arias*, was published in 2019. She currently teaches creative
writing at New York University.

ALICE OSWALD (1966–)

Alice Oswald is an English poet and classicist, whose book-length poetry
projects include *Dart* (2002), which follows the social and ecological
history of the River Dart in her home of Devon, and *Memorial* (2011).
Oswald is also well known for her particular interest in the performative

element of poetry, recalling its oral tradition by reciting her poems from memory, describing the poem as 'passing through me'. She is currently the professor of poetry at Oxford University, and her latest collection, *Nobody*, was published in 2019.

RON PADGETT (1942–)

Ron Padgett is an American poet, editor and translator whose work has been influenced by various poets such as Frank O'Hara, Ezra Pound, Arthur Rimbaud and the Beat poets. He is the author of over twenty collections of poetry, as well as contributing poems to the Jim Jarmusch film *Paterson* (2016). Padgett also served as chancellor of the Academy of American Poets from 2008 to 2013. He currently resides in New York.

CRAIG SANTOS PEREZ (1980–)

An indigenous Chamorro from the Pacific island of Guam, Craig Santos Perez is a poet, editor, academic, essayist and critic. His work primarily explores colonial history, immigration and diaspora relating to the Pacific Islands. His most recent collection, *from unincorporated territory [lukao]*, was published in 2017. He is currently a professor in the English department at the University of Hawai'i, Mānoa, teaching creative writing, eco-poetry and Pacific literature.

SYLVIA PLATH (1932–1963)

Sylvia Plath was an American poet, novelist and fiction writer. Her collection *Ariel*, published after her death in 1963, dazzled with the intensity of its imagery and with its original approach to form, and her sole published novel, *The Bell Jar* (also 1963), vividly portrays the tensions, hypocrisies and constraints of postwar American culture.

EZRA POUND (1885–1972)

An American modernist poet, translator and literary critic, Ezra Pound is known for his contribution to the development of Imagism as a form of poetry that sought to emphasise the essence and value found in a single image, presented in a direct manner with a highly distilled economy of language. Perhaps the most famous example of this type of poetry is his 'In a Station of the Metro' (1913). Working as foreign editor in London, Pound came into contact with and assisted in the careers of writers such as T. S. Eliot, Robert Frost and Ernest Hemingway. Due to his affiliation with and open approval of fascist politics, Pound remains a highly controversial figure, yet is considered one of the most significant writers of the twentieth century.

ESSA MAY RANAPIRI (1993–)

essa may ranapiri (Ngāti Raukawa) is a takatāpui (using pronouns they/them/theirs) poet from Kirikiriroa, Aotearoa, whose first collection, *ransack*, was published by Victoria University Press in 2019.

HELEN RICKERBY (1974–)

Helen Rickerby is a poet, editor and publisher living in Wellington, New Zealand. A co-founder and former managing editor of the literary journal *JAAM*, Rickerby is currently founder and managing editor of Seraph Press. She has published four collections of poetry, the latest of which, *How to Live*, was published in 2019 and won the Mary and Peter Biggs Award for Poetry at the 2020 Ockham New Zealand Book Awards.

KAY RYAN (1945–)

Kay Ryan is an American poet whose work has been described as tightly compressed and rhythmically dense, and has been compared to the work of Marianne Moore. The recipient of a Pulitzer Prize for Poetry in

2011, and United States Poet Laureate from 2008 to 2011, Ryan is considered by critics to be one of the most significant contemporary American poets.

SAPPHO (620 BCE–550 BCE)

Little is known about her life, and her work is represented by only a handful of surviving poems, many of which were recorded by later writers, yet new poems have recently come to light including the 'Brothers' poem translated by Anne Carson and Alistair Elliot. Sappho is regarded as one of the greatest poets in antiquity – referred to as 'the Poetess', as Homer was 'the Poet'. Her importance today rests not only on her significance as the foundational poet of the lyric tradition but also on the loveliness of her verse, even in fragments, even in translation.

SAM SAX (1986–)

sam sax is an American poet whose work has been published in numerous literary journals and online publications. His most recent collection, *Bury It*, was published in 2018. He is currently the poetry editor at BOAAT Press as well as a Wallace Stegner Fellow at Stanford University.

ERIN SCUDDER (1979–)

Erin Scudder grew up in Montreal, Canada, spent some years living in Wellington, New Zealand, and now lives in Melbourne, Australia. A selection of her poetry was published in *AUP New Poets 4* in 2011.

WILLIAM SHAKESPEARE (1564–1616)

A Renaissance poet and playwright, as you would need to be told if you belonged to the alternative world of Sandra Newman's novel *The Heavens* (2019), in which Shakespeare has been largely forgotten.

MAGGIE SMITH (1977–)

Maggie Smith is an American poet whose 2016 'Good Bones' went viral worldwide, leading it to be considered the 'Official Poem of 2016' by Public Radio International. She is a freelance writer and editor, her most recent collection of poetry is *Good Bones* (2017) and her latest collection of essays, *Keep Moving*, was published in 2020.

A. E. STALLINGS (1968–)

A. E. Stallings is an American poet now living in Greece, where she is director of the Athens Poetry Centre. Her acclaimed poetry collections include *Like* (2018), *Olives* (2012), *Hapax* (2000), and *Archaic Smile* (1999), winner of the Richard Wilbur Award and finalist for both the Yale Younger Poets Series and the Walt Whitman Award. She has also published a verse translation of *The Nature of Things* by Lucretius.

C. K. STEAD (1932–)

Poet, novelist, critic and essayist Christian Karlson Stead is one of New Zealand's best-known writers. Stead was made a Member of the New Zealand Order of Merit in 1985, and served as Poet Laureate from 2015 to 2017. His latest novel, *The Necessary Angel*, was published in 2018, and the third and final volume of his memoirs, *What You Made of It: A Memoir, 1987–2020*, was published in 2021.

ARTHUR SZE (1950–)

Arthur Sze is a Chinese-American poet whose work is characterised by the juxtaposition of Eastern philosophy with American culture and industrialisation. He served as chancellor of the Academy of American Poets, and his latest collection of poetry, *Sight Lines*, was published in 2019.

WISŁAWA SZYMBORSKA (1923–2012)

Wisława Szymborska was a Polish poet and essayist whose work is known for its use of irony, paradox and contradiction to explore various philosophical themes such as war, death and love. She was the recipient of the Nobel Prize for Literature in 1996.

TAYI TIBBLE (1995–)

Wellington-based New Zealand poet Tayi Tibble (Te Whānau-ā-Apanui/Ngāti Porou) is a graduate of the International Institute of Modern Letters and recipient of the Adam Foundation Prize in 2017. Her work explores themes of identity, beauty, activism and popular culture, and her first collection, *Poūkahangatus*, was published in 2018.

HONE TUWHARE (1922–2008)

Of Ngāpuhi descent, Hone Tuwhare grew up versed in waiata and whaikōrero as well as the King James Bible. He worked as a boilermaker from 1939 and was an active member of the New Zealand Communist Party. His first collection of poetry, *No Ordinary Sun*, was published in 1964 to immediate popular and critical acclaim, and was followed by twelve further collections. His collected works, *Small Holes in the Silence: Collected Poems*, was published in 2016. He received many honours and awards throughout his life, serving as Poet Laureate from 1999 to 2001 and named as a Living Icon by the Arts Foundation in 2003.

WALT WHITMAN (1819–1892)

As important a figure in nineteenth-century American literature as Emily Dickinson and as different a poet as could be imagined, Walt Whitman developed a distinctly American form of prose-like free verse which celebrated both American democracy and the freedom of the individual self. His single work of poetry, *Leaves of Grass*, was

published in successive editions, each building on and adding
to the first edition (1855).

RICHARD WILBUR (1921–2017)

Self-described as 'a continuator of Robert Frost', Richard Wilbur was
an American poet who looked for patterns of order that could be found
in what he called the 'glorious energy' of the universe. He served as
America's second Poet Laureate, and his many honours and awards
include two Pulitzer Prizes for Poetry.

WILLIAM CARLOS WILLIAMS (1883–1963)

An American poet and physician, William Carlos Williams is well
known for his Imagist poetry, which captures American life and
language. He was particularly interested in capturing the music
and rhythm of American vernacular by utilising colloquial and regional
imagery, along with formatting his poems in specific ways to emphasise
the particular rhythms of the American speech he sought to emulate,
best exemplified in his well-known poems 'This Is Just to Say' (1934)
and 'The Red Wheelbarrow' (1923).

WILLIAM WORDSWORTH (1770–1850)

Along with Samuel Taylor Coleridge, William Wordsworth was one
of the founders of the Romantic movement in English literature,
famous for his *Lyrical Ballads* (1798) and the semi-autobiographical
poem 'The Prelude' (1850).

W. B. YEATS (1865–1939)

One of the most important modernist poets of the early twentieth
century, W. B. Yeats drew on Irish myth in poems such as 'The Song
of Wandering Aengus' (1897) and on Irish nationalism in poems such
as 'An Irish Airman Foresees His Death' (1919) and 'Easter, 1916',

and is loved too for the lyricism of poems such as 'The Lake Isle of Innesfree' (1890) and 'The Wild Swans at Coole' (1917). He was awarded the Nobel Prize in Literature in 1923.

Notes and references

INTRODUCTION: READING & WRITING POETRY

Epigraph:
'I think a poem, when it works, is an action of the mind captured on a page . . .', Anne Carson, 'The Art of Poetry. No. 88', interview with Will Aitken, *Paris Review*, issue 171, Fall 2004, www.theparisreview.org/interviews/5420/the-art-of-poetry-no-88-anne-carson

p. 1   'This living hand, now warm and capable . . .', John Keats, 'This Living Hand', in Jack Stillinger (ed.), *John Keats: Complete Poems* (Cambridge, MA: Belknap Press, 1978). This untitled poem was discovered after Keats's death as marginalia he had scribbled beside a stanza of his very long, unfinished verse narrative, 'The Cap and Bells; or, the Jealousies'. Some biographers have read it as a poem written for Fanny Brawne, to whom Keats had offered his hand in marriage; anguished letters from Keats to Fanny suggest she may have had reason to wish she could be 'conscience-calm'd' after his death. (See, for instance, Robert Gittings, *John Keats: A Biography*, 1968.) Other scholars have read it as a fragment that Keats may have intended to write up at a later date, the blank verse metre of the writing and its place beside an extended narrative perhaps suggesting it was imagined as a new piece of dramatic fiction, perhaps part of a blank verse drama he may have been intending to write. (This theory was first put forward by Walter Jackson Bate in *John Keats*, 1966.) If the demands on the reader lose their directness and intensity when we imagine them spoken by a character in a verse drama, this only makes more apparent how lyric poetry works: readers respond to lyric poetry as if they are addressed urgently, personally, by the poet, as if they were possessed by the poet's words. Most readers might not sacrifice themselves to the point of draining their own blood, but readers do, as Jonathan Culler observes, 'temporarily sacrifice their sense of reality in allowing the poem to create for them a temporality in which the hand lives and is held towards them' (Jonathan Culler, *Theory of the Lyric*, Cambridge, MA: Harvard University Press, 2015, pp. 196–97).

p. 2   '"Irreducible Sociality", a poem about not going to a party . . .', Chen Chen, 'Irreducible Sociality', in *When I Grow Up I Want To Be a List of Further Possibilities* (Rochester, NY: BOA Editions, 2017).

p. 4   'A poem is best read in the light of all the other poems ever written . . .', Mark Richardson (ed.), 'The Prerequisites', in *The Collected Prose of Robert Frost* (Cambridge, MA: Belknap Press, 1954), p. 174.

p. 5   '[T]he sensations of reading are charged with the creative feeling of writing, and vice versa . . .', Brian Blanchfield, 'On Reset', in *Proxies: Essays Near Knowing* (Brooklyn, NY: Nightboat Books, 2017), p. 124.

p. 5   'I think a poem, when it works, is an action of the mind captured on a page . . .', Anne Carson, 'The Art of Poetry. No. 88'.

CHAPTER ONE: SIMPLICITY & RESONANCE

p. 9   'Because a fire was in my head . . .', W. B. Yeats, 'The Song of Wandering Aengus', in Richard J. Finneran (ed.), *The Collected Poems of W. B. Yeats* (New York: Scribner, 1996).

p. 10   'I felt as though the words of the poem, like the storm itself, had cast a "tyrant spell" on me . . .', Edward Hirsch, *How to Read a Poem and Fall in Love with Poetry* (New York: Houghton Mifflin Harcourt, 2010), pp. 61–66. This book also includes a reading of 'This Living Hand', in which Hirsch refers to scholarly views on the poem as a fragment of a drama but prefers to read it as if Keats were addressing himself, directly, with the directness and intimacy that lyric allows. 'I have never,' Hirsch writes, 'been able to read the line "So in my veins red life might stream again" with any equanimity' (p. 49).

p. 10   'The night is darkening round me . . .', Emily Brontë, 'Spellbound', in C. W. Hatfield (ed.), *The Complete Poems of Emily Jane Brontë* (London: Hodder & Stoughton, 1923).

p. 11   'Whose woods these are I think I know . . .', Robert Frost, 'Stopping by Woods on a Snowy Evening', in *Complete Poems of Robert Frost* (New York: Holt, Rinehart & Winston, 1964).

p. 12   'As the poetry critic John Ciardi observes, this creates a particular difficulty when Frost gets to the end of the poem . . .', John Ciardi, 'How Does A Poem Mean?', in John Ciardi and Miller Williams (eds), *How Does A Poem Mean?* (New York: Houghton Mifflin, 1975), pp. 1–13.

p. 13   'I suppose people think I lie awake nights worrying . . .', Robert Frost, cited in Louis Mertins, *Robert Frost: Life and Talks-Walking* (Oklahoma: University of Oklahoma Press, 1966), p. 371.

p. 14   'He advised his friend, the literary critic and scholar Sidney Cox, not to "disillusion your admirers with the tale of your sources and processes". . .', Robert Frost, 'To Sydney Cox', in Lawrence Thompson (ed.), *Selected Letters of Robert Frost* (New York: Holt, Rinehart & Winston, 1964), http://theamericanreader.com/10-july-1913-robert-frost-to-sidney-cox/ In another letter to Cox, he wrote, 'Poetry . . . is a measured amount of all we could say and we would. We shall be judged finally by the delicacy of our feeling for when to stop short' (ibid., p. 361).

p. 14   'My long two-pointed ladder's sticking through a tree . . .', Robert Frost, 'After Apple-Picking', in *Complete Poems of Robert Frost*.

p. 17   'This is the street where they still make coffins . . .', Bill Manhire, 'Across Brooklyn', *London Review of Books*, vol. 26, no. 23 (2004).

p. 19   'Enough', Rebecca Gayle Howell, 'A Catalogue of What You Do Not Have', in *Render / An Apocalypse* (Cleveland: Cleveland State University Poetry Center, 2013).

p. 20   'Westron wynde, when wilt thou blow . . .', Anonymous (sixteenth century), 'Westron Wynde', in Hugh Benham (ed.), *Early English Church Music Vol. 35, John Taverner: IV, Four- and Five-Part Masses* (London: Stainer & Bell, 1989).

p. 21   'The tides run up the Wairau . . .', Eileen Duggan, 'The Tides Run Up the Wairau', in *Poems* (London: Allen & Unwin, 1939).

p. 22   'I went out to the hazel wood . . .', W. B. Yeats, 'The Song of Wandering Aengus'.

CHAPTER TWO: THE ORNATE & THE SUMPTUOUS

p. 25   'I have been doing a little tapirising & reading Keats, you'll be sorry to hear . . .', in Martha Dow Fehsenfeld and Lois More Overbeck (eds), *The Letters of Samuel Beckett: Volume I: 1929–1940* (Cambridge: Cambridge University Press, 2009), p. 21.

p. 26   'There is plenty of crouching and brooding going on in the work of New Zealand poet Rebecca Hawkes . . .', Rebecca Hawkes, 'softcore coldsores', in Anna Jackson (ed.), *AUP New Poets 5* (Auckland: Auckland University Press, 2019).

p. 26   '[W]ell now I must admit to painting you . . .', Rebecca Hawkes, 'Technicolour Dreamcake', in ibid.

p. 27   'Never never never never never . . .', William Shakespeare, *King Lear*, Act V, Scene 3.

p. 27   'And as imagination bodies forth . . .', William Shakespeare, *A Midsummer Night's Dream*, Act V, Scene 1.

p. 28   'The first seventeen sonnets after all make the same essential argument over and over again . . .', A new edition of the sonnets, *All the Sonnets of Shakespeare*, edited by Paul Edmondson and Stanley Wells (Cambridge University Press, 2020), replaces the original order of the sonnet sequence with a new estimation of the chronology in which they may have been written; the editors reject the customary reading of the sonnets in terms of a narrative centring on two relationships, one with a young man and one with a woman mistress, reading them instead in terms of a range of repeating themes and motifs. In a review of this edition, Shakespeare scholar (and my father) MacDonald P. Jackson defends the case for accepting the original order of the sequence, as first published in 1609, 'as reflecting Shakespeare's own division between sonnets associated with a fair young man and sonnets associated with a dark woman', and this is how I, too, like to read the sonnets. (Mac Jackson, 'Love's Labour's Found', review article on Paul Edmondson and Stanley Wells (eds), *All the Sonnets of Shakespeare*, in *New Zealand Listener*, 12 December 2020, pp. 34–37.)

For detailed commentaries on the arguments elaborated in the Shakespeare sonnets, see Helen Vendler, *The Art of Shakespeare's Sonnets* (Cambridge, MA: Harvard University Press, 1999).

p. 28 'When to the sessions of sweet silent thought . . .', William Shakespeare, Sonnet 30.

p. 30 'Coleridge's evocation of impressions "vivid beyond common sight of common things, sweet beyond sound of things heard" . . .', from a review of Coleridge's letters by Andrew Lang, 'The Letters of Coleridge', *Littell's Living Age*, vol. 206 (July, August, September) (Boston: Littell & Co., 1895). I also love the more equivocal remarks on the poem made by Coleridge's friend Charles Lamb: 'there is an observation: "never tell thy dreams," and I am almost afraid that *Kubla Khan* is an owl that won't bear daylight', quoted by Oswald Doughty in *Perturbed Spirit* (London: Associated University Presses, 1981), p. 433.

p. 30 'The effect could scarcely have been more satisfactory to the ear had every syllable been selected merely for the sake of its sound . . .', John Bowring, 'Coleridge and Poetry', in *Westminster Review*, n.d.

p. 31 'In Xanadu did Kubla Khan . . .', Samuel Taylor Coleridge, 'Kubla Khan', in Ernest Hartley Coleridge (ed.), *The Poems of Samuel Taylor Coleridge* (Oxford: Oxford University Press, 1921).

p. 32 '[I]t is worth listening to some of the memorable renditions of the poem available on YouTube.' For the YouTube renditions, best simply to go to YouTube and search the titles of poems and names of the readers, as any link I offer may be obsolete by the time of this book's publication.

p. 33   'I cannot see what flowers are at my feet . . .', John Keats, 'Ode to a Nightingale', in Jack Stillinger (ed.), *John Keats: Complete Poems* (Cambridge, MA: Belknap Press, 1978).

p. 35   '[W]hat can you give me that begins with *hinna*? . . .', Michele Leggott, 'Helix', in *As Far as I Can See* (Auckland: Auckland University Press, 1999).

p. 35   'Mark Leidner's "Blackouts" . . .', in *Sixth Finch*, http://sixthfinch.com/leidner3.html

p. 36   'Like a passive aggressive gun that fires . . . . nothing instead of bullets . . .', Hera Lindsay Bird, 'Lost Scrolls', in *Hera Lindsay Bird* (Wellington: Victoria University Press, 2016).

p. 37   'This is like crying while trying on different outfits . . .', Chelsey Minnis, 'Poemland', in *Poemland* (Seattle: Wave Books, 2009).

p. 37   'Monica / Monica / Monica / Monica . . .', Hera Lindsay Bird, 'Monica', in *Hera Lindsay Bird*.

CHAPTER THREE: CONCISION, COMPOSITION *&* THE IMAGE

p. 41   'No ideas but in things . . .', William Carlos Williams, *Paterson*, new revised edition by Christopher MacGowan (New York: New Directions, 1992).

p. 41   'Use absolutely no word that does not contribute to the presentation . . .', 'A Retrospect', in T. S. Eliot (ed.), *Literary Essays of Ezra Pound* (London: Faber, 1960), originally published 1918. Strictly speaking, he is listing the principles of the Imagist movement, rather than issuing an imperative: '"In the spring or early summer of 1912, "H.D.", Richard Addington and myself decided that we were agreed upon the three principles following

1. Direct treatment of the "thing" whether subjective or objective.
2. To use absolutely no word that does not contribute to the presentation.
3. As regarding rhythm: to compose in the sequence of the musical phrase, not in sequence of a metronome.'

p. 41   '[N]ot to follow a story but discern a pattern . . .', Stephen Spender, *The Struggle of the Modern* (Berkeley: University of California Press, 1963), p. 16.

p. 42   'The apparition of these faces in the crowd . . .', Ezra Pound, 'In a Station of the Metro', in *Lustra* (New York: Knopf, 1917).

p. 42   'Three years ago in Paris I got out of a "metro" train at La Concorde . . .', Ezra Pound, 'Vorticism', *The Fortnightly Review*, 571 (September 1914), pp. 465–67.

p. 43   '[S]o much depends . . .', William Carlos Williams, 'The Red Wheelbarrow', in Christopher MacGowan (ed.), *The Collected Poems of William Carlos Williams, Volume 1, 1909–1939* (New York: New Directions, 1991).

p. 45   'A little to the left . . .', Jenny Bornholdt, 'Photograph', in *Mrs Winter's Jump* (Auckland: Godwit, 2007).

p. 46 'Yesterday I bought / a blender . . .', Jenny Bornholdt, 'Being a Poet', in *Turbine*, 1 (Wellington: International Institute of Modern Letters, 2001).

p. 47 '[W]e planted one / Magnolia Stellata Waterlily . . .', Jenny Bornholdt, 'In Memory', in *These Days* (Wellington: Victoria University Press, 2000).

p. 48 '[G]ardening is painting with living things . . .', Gertrude Jekyll, *Wood and Garden* (London: Longmans, Green, & Co., 1899).

p. 48 'My garage is a structure of excessive plainness . . .', Ursula Bethell (pseudonym Evelyn Hayes), 'Detail', in *From a Garden in the Antipodes* (London: Sidgwick & Jackson, 1930).

p. 50 '[F]or instance, Mike Goldberg . . .', Frank O'Hara, 'Why I Am Not a Painter', *The Evergreen Review* (New York: John Oakes, 1957).

p. 51 'When you offer only three . . .', Hone Tuwhare, 'Hotere', in *Deep River Talk: Collected Poems* (Auckland: Godwit, 1993). The question mark at the end of the poem, which I love so much, appears in some but not all editions. It is in *Mihi: Collected Poems* (1987), p. 163, and in *Deep River Talk: Collected Poems* (1993), p. 51, but it is left out of a later edition, in which the poem simply ends with no punctuation at all, in both the English and in the Māori translation; that edition is Hone Tuwhare, *Small Holes in the Silence: Collected Works*, edited by Janet Hunt and Rob Tuwhare, translations by Herewini Muru, Waihoroi Shortland and Patu Hohepa (Auckland: Godwit, 2011), p. 100. (Thanks to Jack Ross for these bibliographical details!)

p. 53   '[T]he smeared blood / flat down caught . . .', essa may ranapiri, 'she cut her face shaving', in *ransack* (Wellington: Victoria University Press, 2019).

p. 53   'In an interview about the collection *ransack* . . .', essa may ranapiri, Q & A with Tayi Tibble, https://vup.victoria.ac.nz/blog1/essa-may-ranapiri-qa/. Elsewhere in the same interview, they compare writing poetry to carving, 'trying to bring up the shape that is held in the page rather than adhering to an expectation of form'.

p. 54   'There are charms / that forestall harm . . .', Kay Ryan, 'Linens', *Poetry*, May 2011, www.poetryfoundation.org/poetrymagazine/poems/54647/linens

p. 55   'Oswald confesses to a "reckless dismissal of seven-eighths of the poem" . . .', Alice Oswald, *Memorial* (London: Faber & Faber, 2012), preface.

p. 55   'And someone's face pierced like a piece of fruit . . .', in ibid.

CHAPTER FOUR: SPRAWL

p. 59   '[W]hen people talk about poetry they often mention compression . . .', Jenny Bornholdt, 'Confessional', in *Summer* (Wellington: Victoria University Press, 2003).

p. 59   'I guess I could say I don't read Whitman because I don't need Whitman's big stride . . .', Kay Ryan, 'Antagonism: Whitman', *Poetry*,

October 2004, www.poetryfoundation.org/poetrymagazine/browse?contentId=60450

p. 60   'I celebrate myself, and sing myself . . .', Walt Whitman, 'Song of Myself', in *Leaves of Grass* (self-published, 1885).

p. 60   '[A] sort of excited prose broken into lines . . .', Charles Eliot Norton, 'A Review of Leaves of Grass (1855)', September 1855, www.whitmanarchive.org/criticism/review/leaves1855/anc.00011.html

p. 61   'Flood-tide below me! I see you face to face! . . .', Walt Whitman, 'Crossing Brooklyn Ferry', in *Leaves of Grass* (expanded second edition, 1856).

p. 62   '[A] self that fits Ralph Waldo Emerson's description of an ideal writer existing like a "transparent eyeball" seeing all and being nothing . . .', quoting Ralph Waldo Emerson in *Nature* (Boston: James Munroe & Co., 1836).

p. 63   'By 1955 I wrote poetry adapted from prose seeds, journals, scratchings . . .', Allen Ginsberg, 'Notes', *Howl* [LP] (Los Angeles: Fantasy Records, 1959).

p. 63   '[H]e had something to say and I wanted him to say it . . .', Walter Sutton, 'A Visit with William Carlos Williams', *The Minnesota Review*, 1 (April 1961).

p. 63   'What thoughts I have of you tonight Walt Whitman . . .', Allen Ginsberg, 'A Supermarket in California', in *Collected Poems, 1947–1980* (New York: HarperCollins, 1984).

p. 64   'America I've given you all and now I'm nothing . . .',
Allen Ginsberg, 'America', in ibid.

p. 66   'Walt Whitman's poetry has been important to my evolution
as a poet . . .', 'Arthur Sze reads and discusses Walt Whitman's "Crossing
Brooklyn Ferry"', www.loc.gov/programs/poetry-and-literature/audio-
recordings/poetry-of-america/item/poetry-00001025/arthur-sze-
walt-whitman

p. 66   'I gaze through a telescope at the Orion Nebula . . .', Arthur
Sze, 'Before Completion', in *The Redshifting Web: Poems 1970–1998*
(Port Townsend, WA: Copper Canyon Press, 1998). Copyright © 1998
by Arthur Sze. Reprinted with the permission of The Permissions
Company, LLC on behalf of Copper Canyon Press.

p. 68   'I find that when I'm writing, I write lots of fragments and lots
of phrases . . . ', Ayleen Perry, 'Charging through the line: An interview
with Arthur Sze', *Terrain*, February 2018, www.terrain.org/2018/
interviews/arthur-sze/

p. 68   '[T]he aphorism is not a fragment, but a complete stand-alone
text . . .', Sarah Manguso, *300 Arguments* (Minneapolis: Graywolf Press,
2017). Or see 'In Short: Thirty-six ways of looking at the aphorism', *Harper's
Magazine*, September 2016, https://harpers.org/archive/2016/09/in-short

p. 68   '[T]he aphorism when memorised may not change minds but
may accelerate action . . .', John McGhee, *How Much Shall We Bet? Defining
Surreal Futures*, Doctoral dissertation, University of Birmingham, 2019,
https://etheses.bham.ac.uk/id/eprint/9024/7/Mcghee2019PhD.pdf

p. 69 'When fate sleeps, it dreams of chance . . .', Online Aphorism Generator (http://joehalliwell.com/aphorisms.html), in ibid.

p. 70 'George Zweig, a contemporary physicist, once said to me . . .', Ayleen Perry, 'Charging through the line: An interview with Arthur Sze'.

p. 70 '[T]he ex-musician, insurance salesman . . .', Arthur Sze, 'The Chance', in *The Redshifting Web: Poems 1970–1998*.

p. 71 '[T]he cook re-dresses / the abstract / any sort of building / stitching or paste . . .', Paula Green, 'freshly picked blueberries', in *Cookhouse* (Auckland: Auckland University Press, 1998).

p. 72 'After Modernism I walked to the shops . . .', Paula Green, 'After Modernism', in *Making Lists for Frances Hodgkins* (Auckland: Auckland University Press, 2007).

p. 73 'Flying above Rome in the summer heat . . .', Paula Green, 'Letter to Anne Kennedy', in ibid.

p. 74 'The poem concludes with a description of reading Anne Kennedy's own verse novel, *The Time of the Giants* . . .', Anne Kennedy is one of New Zealand's most brilliant and intriguing writers of fiction, poetry and screenplays, including the extraordinary verse novel *The Time of the Giants* (Auckland: Auckland University Press, 2005). See her website (annekennedy.co.nz) for more details of her work.

CHAPTER FIVE: FORM

p. 77   'I like to say that form is not about having control . . .',
A. E. Stallings, 'Women in Form: A E Stallings', *Tupelo Quarterly*,
14 July 2014, www.tupeloquarterly.com/women-in-form-ae-stallings

p. 78   '[T]o set American poetry on its proper tracks . . .', Linda
Welshimer Wagner (ed.), *Interviews with William Carlos Williams:
'Speaking Straight Ahead'* (New York: New Directions, 1976).

p. 78   '[T]he physical features of // ac- / cident – lack . . .', Marianne
Moore, 'The fish', from *The Egoist* (August 1918), in *New Collected Poems*
(London: Faber & Faber, 2017).

p. 82   'What lips my lips have kissed, and where, and why . . .',
Edna St Vincent Millay, 'What lips my lips have kissed, and where,
and why', *Vanity Fair* (November 1920).

p. 83   'That time of year thou mayst in me behold . . .',
William Shakespeare, Sonnet 73.

p. 83   'This Is Just to Say . . .', William Carlos Williams, 'This Is Just
to Say', in Christopher MacGowan (ed.), *The Collected Poems of William
Carlos Williams, Volume 1, 1909–1939* (New York: New Directions, 1991).

p. 84   'funny / how / spring / always / makes / me / feel . . .', sam sax,
'sonnet', (published on Twitter).

p. 85   'I lock you in an American sonnet that is part prison . . .', Terrance
Hayes, 'American Sonnet for my Past and Future Assassin', in *American
Sonnets for my Past and Future Assassin* (New York: Penguin, 2016).

p. 87 '"What does a sonnet have to do with anybody's content?" . . .', Jericho Brown, 'Invention', *Poetry*, April 2019, www.poetryfoundation.org/harriet/2020/05/invention

p. 87 'A poem is a gesture toward home . . .', Jericho Brown, 'Duplex', in *The Tradition* (Port Townsend, WA: Copper Canyon Press, 2019). Reproduced with permission of the Licensor through PLSclear.

p. 89 'The art of losing isn't hard to master . . .', Elizabeth Bishop, 'One Art', in *Poems* (New York: Farrar, Straus & Giroux, 2011) © 2011 by The Alice H. Methfessel Trust. Reprinted by permission of Farrar, Straus and Giroux.

p. 91 'When I see a young boy and his dad . . .', Nick Ascroft, 'Five Limericks on Grief', in *Back with the Human Condition* (Wellington: Victoria University Press, 2016).

p. 92 'A joke can be made of its repetitiveness, as in "Cashpoint: A Pantoum," by James Brown . . .', James Brown, 'Cashpoint: A Pantoum', *Turbine*, 5 (Wellington: International Institute of Modern Letters, 2005).

p. 92 '[I]t can offer a more serious take on the helpless submission to relentless forces, as in Donald Justice's "Pantoum of the Great Depression" . . .', Donald Justice, 'Pantoum of the Great Depression', in *Collected Poems* (New York: Alfred A. Knopf, 2004). www.poetryfoundation.org/poems/58080/pantoum-of-the-great-depression

p. 93 'He sat cross-legged, weeping on the steps . . .', Natalie Diaz, 'My Brother at 3 A.M.', in *When My Brother Was an Aztec* (Port Townsend, WA: Copper Canyon Press, 2012).

p. 95   '[T]he six words of Elizabeth Bishop's "Sestina" – house, grandmother, child, stove, almanac and tears . . .', Elizabeth Bishop, 'Sestina', in *Questions of Travel* (New York: Farrar, Straus & Giroux, 1965).

p. 95   'See Sextus slip . . .', Erin Scudder, 'Sextina', in *AUP New Poets 4* (Auckland: Auckland University Press, 2013).

p. 97   '[T]he earliest version written almost five hundred years after the events . . .', Titus Livius, *Ab Urbe Condita*, 1:57–58.

p. 99   'Now we're all "friends," there is no love but Like . . .', A. E. Stallings, 'Like, the Sestina', in *Like* (New York: Farrar, Straus & Giroux, 2018). Copyright © 2018 by A. E. Stallings. Reprinted by permission of Farrar, Straus and Giroux.

CHAPTER SIX: ARGUMENT & CONVERSATION

p. 103   '[T]he death of all literature as we know it . . .', Frank O'Hara, 'Personism: A Manifesto' (1959), in Donald Allen (ed.), *The Collected Poems of Frank O'Hara* (Berkeley: University of California Press, 1995).

p. 103   'Odi et amo . . .', Catullus, poem 85.

p. 104   'Mark but this flea . . .', John Donne, 'The Flea', in Christopher Ricks and Ilona Bell (eds), *John Donne: Collected Poetry* (London: Penguin, 2013).

p. 106   'My vegetable love should grow . . .', Andrew Marvell, 'To His Coy Mistress', in Elizabeth Donno (ed.), *Andrew Marvell: The Complete Poems* (London: Penguin, 2005).

p. 107   'Samuel Taylor Coleridge's "The Eolian Harp" is one of several odes collectively called his "conversation odes" . . .', Samuel Taylor Coleridge, 'The Eolian Harp', in Ernest Hartley Coleridge (ed.), *The Poems of Samuel Taylor Coleridge* (Oxford: Oxford University Press, 1921).

p. 108   '[T]his practice of telling the addressee what they already know being one of the stranger conventions of lyric poetry . . .', See, for instance, Jonathan Culler on the Catullus poem 'To Licinius' (Catullus 50), in Jonathan Culler, *Theory of the Lyric* (Cambridge, MA: Harvard University Press, 2017), p. 205.

p. 109   'William Blake's "The Clod and the Pebble" attributes to the clod and pebble two opposing ideas about love . . .', William Blake, 'The Clod and the Pebble', in *William Blake: The Complete Poems* (London: Penguin, 1978).

p. 109   'Adrienne Jansen's "The Rain and the Spade" is subtitled "a poem about love and ambiguity?" . . .', Adrienne Jansen, 'The Rain and the Spade', in Bill Manhire (ed.), *Mutes and Earthquakes: Bill Manhire's Writing Course at Victoria* (Wellington: Victoria University Press, 1997).

p. 109   'Think'st thou that this rope would twine . . .', Andrew Marvell, 'Ametas and Thestylis Making Hay-Ropes', in Donno (ed.), *Andrew Marvell: The Complete Poems*.

p. 110   'O who shall, from this dungeon, raise . . .', Andrew Marvell, 'A Dialogue between the Soul and the Body', in ibid.

p. 110   '"The Garden", which offers a gorgeous vision of the sensuous pleasures the garden can offer . . .', Andrew Marvell, 'The Garden', in ibid.

p. 112   'I knock at the stone's front door . . .', Wisława Szymborska, 'Conversation with a Stone', in *Poems New and Collected: 1957–1997*, translated by Stanisław Barańczak and Clare Cavanagh (San Diego: Harcourt Brace, 2012).

p. 114   'According to Phillips, the "productive shocks" such overhearing allows "are only made possible by the presence of the other person". . .', Adam Phillips, 'Bored with Sex?', *London Review of Books*, vol. 25, no. 5 (2003).

p. 114   '"There is one thing," I say, trying to stop the points of light pitching and rolling . . .', Luke Kennard, 'Wolf on the Couch', in *The Migraine Hotel* (Cromer, Norfolk: Salt Publishing, 2009). Reproduced with permission of the Licensor through PLSclear.

p. 115   'Your ancestors should have found out what was going on and seized power in a humourless coup . . .', Luke Kennard, 'Wolf Nationalist', in ibid.

p. 116   '"The frustration scene," Phillips writes, "is the scene of transformation" . . .', Phillips, 'Bored with Sex?'.

p. 116   'I trust that brief Time will unfold / our youth, before he makes us old . . .', Annie Finch, 'Coy Mistress', in *Eve* (Evansville, IN: Story Line Press, 1997).

p. 117   '[S]he describes Emily Dickinson as "[choosing] to gnaw at iambic pentameter" . . .', Annie Finch, *The Ghost of Meter: Culture and Prosody in American Free Verse* (Ann Arbor: University of Michigan Press, 1993), p. 18.

p. 118   'To write is to want to rewrite . . .', Roland Barthes, *The Preparation of the Novel*, translated by Kate Briggs (New York: Columbia University Press, 2010).

CHAPTER SEVEN: CONVERSATIONS WITH THE PAST

p. 121   'Catullus, fired up from the exchange of witticisms, one-liners and improvised versifying with his friend Licinius, went home and, unable to wait to talk again the next day, composed another poem . . .', See www.annajackson.nz/catullus-50.html

p. 121   '[A] member of the congress in the republic of letters, not debating, but discussing . . .', Richard Wilbur, 'A Great Wonder: Richard Wilbur in Conversation', https://poets.org/text/great-wonder-richard-wilbur-conversation

p. 122   'The horse beneath me seemed . . .', Richard Wilbur, 'The Ride', in *New and Collected Poems* (Boston: Mariner Books, 1989).

p. 124   'He seems to me equal to the gods that man . . .', Sappho, Fragment 31, in Anne Carson (tr.), *If Not, Winter: Fragments of Sappho* (New York: Alfred A. Knopf, 2002).

p. 125   'Carson's edition . . . "of which at least one word is legible" . . .', in ibid.

p. 126   'Leisure, Catullus, is bringing you down . . .', Catullus, poem 51, translated by Anna Jackson.

p. 128   '[Q]ui sedens adversus identidem te / spectat et audit . . .', Catullus, poem 51.

p. 128   'There is another way to know yourself . . .', Daniel Mendelsohn, *The Elusive Embrace* (New York: Vintage, 1999), p. 92.

p. 129   'There you sit man-god . . .', Diana Harris, 'Lovely   I have none', in Diana Harris and Anna Jackson (eds), *E-mailing Venus* (Auckland: Venus Press, 1998).

p. 130   '[L]ove him / if / you will / he looks / like me . . .', Janet Charman, 'After Sappho', in *Rapunzel, Rapunzel* (Auckland: Auckland University Press, 1999).

p. 131   'Kember is a minor character in Katherine Mansfield's long story "At the Bay" . . .', Katherine Mansfield, 'At the Bay', in *The Garden Party* (London: Constable & Co., 1922).

p. 132   'Let us live, my Lesbia, and let us love . . .', Catullus, poem 5, translated by Anna Jackson.

p. 133   'Come, my Celia, let us prove . . .', Ben Jonson, 'Song to Celia', in David Bevington, Martin Butler and Ian Donaldson (eds), *The Cambridge Edition of the Works of Ben Jonson, Volume 3, 1606–1611* (Cambridge: Cambridge University Press, 2012).

p. 134   'All the grass that Rumney yields . . .', Ben Jonson, 'To the Same', in ibid.

p. 134   'Clodia / do you care / does it chip at you . . .', C. K. Stead, 'The Clodian Songbook, poem 4', in *Geographies* (Auckland: Auckland University Press, 1982).

p. 135   '"Countless" as they say also of / stars / sandgrains . . .', C. K Stead, 'The Clodian Songbook, poem 5', in ibid.

p. 135   'Rufus's youngest, ASBO-boy, / whose hot-wire skills are known through / seven counties . . .', Tiffany Atkinson, 'Aurelius', in *Catulla et al.* (Hexham: Bloodaxe Books, 2011).

p. 136   'Lose count Clodia / lip and tongue tell . . .', C. K. Stead, 'The Clodian Songbook, poem 4'.

p. 136   'May you never know / how slow unlovely women burn . . .', Tiffany Atkinson, 'Catulla', in *Catulla et al.*

p. 136   'Come live with me, and be my love . . .', Christopher Marlowe, 'The Passionate Shepherd to his Love', in Stephen Orgel (ed.), *Christopher Marlowe: The Complete Poems and Translations* (London: Penguin 2011).

p. 137   'Meanwhile / kiss me in the checkout queue . . .', Tiffany Atkinson, 'Basia Mille', in *Catulla et al.*

p. 138   'I (gulp) had / to have a certain operation . . .', Mark Ford, 'Viewless Wings', in *Enter, Fleeing* (London: Faber & Faber, 2018).

p. 140   '[T]he Orpheus story, as written by Vergil and by Ovid, is a story about looking back . . .', Shane Butler, 'The Backward Glance', in *The Matter of the Page: Essays in Search of Ancient and Medieval Authors* (Madison: University of Wisconsin Press, 2011).

p. 140   'Do I wake or sleep? . . .', John Keats, 'Ode to a Nightingale', in Jack Stillinger (ed.), *John Keats: Complete Poems* (Cambridge, MA: Belknap Press, 1978).

p. 141   '[I]f thy mistress some rich anger shows . . .', John Keats, 'Ode on Melancholy', in ibid.

CHAPTER EIGHT: POETRY IN A HOUSE ON FIRE

p. 145   'According to James Baldwin, talking in 1973 from his self-imposed exile in France . . .', 'The Black Scholar Interviews: James Baldwin', *The Black Scholar*, vol. 5, no. 4 (December 1973–January 1974).

p. 146   '[W]hen my mentions start blowing up on social media, I know something bad has happened somewhere in the world . . .', Caroline Bologna, 'Behind the poem that so powerfully captures parenting in times of tragedy', *HuffPost*, www.huffpost.com/entry/behind-the-poem-that-so-powerfully-captures-parenting-in-times-of-tragedy_n_59259a01e4b0ec129d314d31?guccounter=1

p. 146   'Life is short, though I keep this from my children . . .', Maggie Smith, 'Good Bones', in *Good Bones: Poems* (North Adams, MA: Tupelo Press, 2017) © 2017 by Maggie Smith. Reprinted with the permission of The Permissions Company, LLC, on behalf of Tupelo Press, tupelopress.org.

p. 147 'To some extent at least you have to shield children from what you know . . .', Kazuo Ishiguro, 'For me, England is a mythical place', *Guardian*, 20 February 2005, www.theguardian.com/books/2005/feb/20/fiction.kazuoishiguro

p. 147 'He made these remarks after he had just published his 2005 novel *Never Let Me Go* . . .', Kazuo Ishiguro, *Never Let Me Go* (London: Faber & Faber, 2005).

p. 148 'Adults keep saying we owe it to the young people . . .', Greta Thunberg, '"Our house is on fire": Greta Thunberg, 16, urges leaders to act on climate', *Guardian*, 25 January 2019, www.theguardian.com/environment/2019/jan/25/our-house-is-on-fire-greta-thunberg16-urges-leaders-to-act-on-climate

p. 148 'She dreams "of drowning in a sea of bubble wrap and single-use plastic bags" . . .', Ash Davida Jane, 'Good People', in *How to Live with Mammals* (Wellington: Victoria University Press, 2021).

p. 149 'In an essay on poetry and the internet Ash Davida Jane cites . . .', Ash Davida Jane, in an undergraduate essay, quoted with permission from the poet.

p. 150 'I don't love you as if you were a rose of salt, topaz . . .', Pablo Neruda, 'One Hundred Love Sonnets: XVII', in Mark Eisner (ed.), *The Essential Neruda: Selected Poems* (San Francisco: City Lights Books, 2004).

p. 150   'I don't love you as if you were rare earth metals, diamonds . . .', Craig Santos Perez, 'Love Poems in a Time of Climate Change: Sonnet XVII', *The New Republic*, 4 March 2017, https://newrepublic.com/article/140282/love-poems-time-climate-change

p. 151   'Are you a real literary activist? Take the quiz! . . .', Craig Santos Perez, 'Are You a Real Literary Activist? Take the Quiz!', 2015, https://craigsantosperez.wordpress.com/2015/08/31/what-kind-of-literary-activist-are-you-take-the-quiz

p. 152   'Ofc Bella and Gigi read BOOKS they are MODELS . . .', Tayi Tibble, Twitter @paniaofthekeef, 22 March 2019, https://twitter.com/paniaofthekeef/status/1108946658635571201

p. 153   'I buy a Mana Party T-shirt from AliExpress . . .', Tayi Tibble, 'Identity Politics', in *Poūkahangatus* (Wellington: Victoria University Press, 2018).

p. 154   '[A] found poem / sent by one of the gods of the harvest . . .', Robert Sullivan, 'Waka 58 Waitangi Day', in *Star Waka* (Auckland: Auckland University Press, 1999).

p. 154   'The rape joke is that you were 19 . . .', Patricia Lockwood, 'Rape Joke', *The Awl*, July 2013, www.theawl.com/2013/07/patricia-lockwood-rape-joke

p. 155   'Sext: I am a living male turtleneck. You are an art teacher in winter . . .', Patricia Lockwood, Twitter @TriciaLockwood, 9 August 2011.

p. 155   '[T]o a baby's thumb, everything looks like a mouth . . .', Patricia Lockwood, 'The Cartoon's Mother Builds a House in Hammerspace', in *Balloon Pop Outlaw Black* (Ottawa: Octopus Books, 2012).

p. 158   '[T]ake turns // giving / and receiving / oral . . .', Tayi Tibble, 'Assimilation', in *Poūkahangatus*.

p. 159   'Helen Rickerby's long poem, "Notes on the Unsilent Woman," looks as far back as 350 BCE–280 BCE . . .', Helen Rickerby, 'Notes on the Unsilent Woman', in *How to Live* (Auckland: Auckland University Press, 2019).

CHAPTER NINE: LETTERS & ODES

An earlier version of this chapter was published as 'Dear Epistle', *PN Review* 235, vol. 43, no. 5 (May–June 2017).

p. 165   'Stone Walls do not a Prison make . . .', Richard Lovelace, 'To Althea, from Prison', www.poetryfoundation.org.poems/44657/to-althea-from-prison

p. 166   'Dear crusted gravestone . . .', Brian Batchelor, 'Dear Voyage', *PEN America*, December 2015, https://pen.org/dear-voyage

p. 167   'Dearest husband Beloved husband Most respected . . .', Emily Berry, 'Letter to Husband', in *Dear Boy* (London: Faber & Faber, 2013).

p. 169   'You dragged your feet when you went out . . .', Ezra Pound, 'The River Merchant's Wife: A Letter', in *Cathay* (London: Elkin Mathews, 1915).

p. 170 'The source of the poem, Berry has revealed in an interview . . .', 'Restraint, Dear Boy: Emily Berry Interviewed by Sam Riviere', *Quietus*, 5 May 2013, https://thequietus.com/articles/12182-emily-berry-dear-boy-interview-sam-riviere

p. 170 '"Herzensschatzi komm" . . .', Emma Hauck, 'Letter to Husband', www.lettersofnote.com/2011/08/sweetheart-come.html

p. 170 'Amit Majmudar has pointed out, in an article "Our Hidden Contemporaries" . . .', Amit Majmudar, 'Our Hidden Contemporaries', *The Dark Horse*, 30 (Spring/Summer 2013).

p. 170 '[T]erribly gingerbready: the pines terribly larchy . . .', Matthew Arnold, in Clinton Machann and Forrest D. Burt (eds), *Selected Letters of Matthew Arnold* (London: Palgrave Macmillan, 1993), p. 47.

p. 171 'O fons Bandusiae . . .', Horace, *Odes* 3.13.

p. 171 'O Bandusian spring more glittering than glass . . .', Joseph P. Clancy, 'Odes 3.13', in *Horace: Odes and Epodes* (Chicago: University of Chicago Press, 1960).

p. 172 '[Y]ou will become the most famous of fountains . . .', This translation is given on the *Lost in Translation* website: http://nonnumadanda.blogspot.com/2011/02/horace-ode-313.html

p. 173 'There you are O lonely, lovely horse in moonlight . . .', Annaleese Jochems, 'Horse', *Ika*, 4, 2016.

p. 174 'One might imagine it'd be unpleasant, being sealed inside a tree . . .', Ali Smith, *Autumn* (London: Hamish Hamilton, 2017).

p. 175   'O Rose thou art sick ...', William Blake, 'The Sick Rose', in *William Blake: The Complete Poems* (London: Penguin, 1978).

p. 175   'Blake's lyric has provoked a good deal of critical discussion ...', Jonathan Culler, *Theory of the Lyric* (Cambridge, MA: Harvard University Press, 2017), pp. 221–23.

p. 176   'Spoon of O, spoon of nothing ...', Sharon Olds, 'Spoon Ode', in *Odes* (London: Jonathan Cape, 2016).

p. 177   'O! dear miniature of infinity with no ...', Tom Disch, 'Ode to a Blizzard', *Poetry*, December 2004, www.poetryfoundation.org/poetrymagazine/poems/41335/ode-to-a-blizzard

p. 178   'Dear stupid forest ...', Heather Christle, 'Acorn Duly Crushed', in *The Difficult Farm* (Portland, OR: Octopus Books, 2009).

p. 180   'It occurs to me I am America ...', Allen Ginsberg, 'America', in *Collected Poems, 1947–1980* (New York: HarperCollins, 1984).

p. 181   'Lucky Orestes. / If you know his story ...', Stephanie Burt, 'Lucky Orestes (Epigram 60)', in *After Callimachus* (Princeton: Princeton University Press, 2020). © 2020 by Stephanie Burt. Reprinted by permission of Princeton University Press. In the 1921 translation by A. W. Mair, the poem reads: 'Orestes of old was happy, Leucarus, because though mad in all else, he was not seized by the greatest madness, nor tried the Phocian by the one test which proves the friend; nay, had he produced but one drama, soon would he by so doing have lost his comrade – even as I have no more my many Pyladae.' *In Callimachus: Hymns and Epigrams*, translated by A. W. Mair (Cambridge, MA: Harvard University Press, 1921).

CHAPTER TEN: POETRY & THE AFTERLIFE

p. 183   'Reading what I have just written, I now believe . . .', Louise Glück, 'Afterword', *Poetry*, January 2012, www.poetryfoundation.org/poetrymagazine/poems/55238/afterword-56d23699928fe

p. 184   'I read early, and wanted, from a very early age, to speak in return . . .', Louise Glück, 'Education of the Poet', in *Proofs and Theories: Essays on Poetry* (Manchester: Carcanet, 1999). This essay was first delivered as a lecture in 1989.

p. 187   'The woman is perfected . . .', Sylvia Plath, 'Edge', in Ted Hughes (ed.), *Sylvia Plath: The Collected Poems* (London: Faber & Faber, 2002).

p. 189   'One writes telling me I am her guiding light . . .', James K. Baxter, 'Jerusalem Sonnet 11', in J. E. Weir (ed.), *Collected Poems* (Auckland: Oxford University Press, 1995), p. 460.

p. 190   'Quardle oodle ardle wardle doodle . . .', Denis Glover, 'The Magpies', in *Enter Without Knocking* (Christchurch: Pegasus Press, 1964).

p. 190   'When I have fears that I may cease to be . . .', John Keats, 'When I Have Fears That I May Cease to Be', in Jack Stillinger (ed.), *John Keats: Complete Poems* (Cambridge, MA: Belknap Press, 1978).

p. 191   '[T]o leave a day unrecorded was to allow life "to waste like a tap left running" . . .', Virginia Woolf, *The Diary of Virginia Woolf*, vol. 1, 1915–1919 (Boston: Mariner Books, 1979).

p. 191   'How unbearable it would be to die, leave "scraps", "bits", nothing real finished . . .', in J. Middleton Murry (ed.), *Journal of Katherine Mansfield: 1914–1922* (London: Constable, 1927), p. 75.

p. 192   'Shall I compare thee to a summer's day? . . .', William Shakespeare, Sonnet 18.

p. 193   'Love's eye . . . That is so vexed with watching and with tears . . .', William Shakespeare, Sonnet 148.

p. 193   'i'm interested in death rituals . . .', sam sax, 'Bury', in *Bury It* (Middletown, CT: Wesleyan University Press, 2018).

p. 194   '"Hope" is the thing with feathers – / which perches in the soul . . .', Emily Dickinson, '"Hope" Is the Thing with Feathers', in *Emily Dickinson: The Complete Poems* (London: Faber & Faber, 2016).

p. 195   'My heart is in my / pocket, it is Poems by Pierre Reverdy . . .', Frank O'Hara, 'A Step Away from Them', in *Lunch Poems* (San Francisco: City Lights Books, 1964).

p. 195   '[B]racelet of bright hair about the bone . . .', John Donne, 'The Relic', in Christopher Ricks and Ilona Bell (eds), *John Donne: Collected Poems* (London: Penguin, 2013).

p. 195   '[S]ubtle wreath of hair, which crowns my arm . . .', John Donne, 'The Funeral', in ibid.

p. 196   '[T]he first twenty years, since yesterday . . .', John Donne, 'The Computation', in ibid.

p. 196   '[W]ould not lose her sight so long . . .', John Donne, 'The Sun Rising', in ibid.

p. 197   'Before I sigh my last gasp, let me breathe . . .', John Donne, 'The Will', in ibid.

p. 199   'the fisherman's sneakers trouble the water . . .', sam sax, 'Will', in *Bury It*.

p. 200   '[S]ignifying a long line of gay youth who have committed suicide . . .', Emily Sernaker, 'Grief, Ritual, and Estrangement: An Interview with sam sax', *Los Angeles Review of Books*, 23 January 2019, https://lareviewofbooks.org/article/grief-ritual-and-estrangement-an-interview-with-sam-sax

p. 200   '[I]n the woods and lost . . .', Charlie Clark, 'Pseudo-Martyr', from *The Newest Employee of the Museum of Ruin*. Originally in *Kenyon Review* (July / August 2017) © 2017, 2020 by Charlie Clark. Reprinted with the permission of The Permissions Company, LLC on behalf of Four Way Books, fourwaybooks.com.

p. 202   '[A] way of leaving no space for death . . .', Hélène Cixous, in Deborah Jenson (ed./tr.), *'Coming to Writing' and Other Essays* (Cambridge, MA: Harvard University Press, 1992).

p. 202   '[Y]ou'd see ladies drinking with us . . .', Alistair Elliot, 'Talking to Horace', in *Talking Back* (London: Martin Secker & Warburg, 1982).

p. 203   'You think historians must be keen to see . . .', Alistair Elliot, 'Talking to Bede', in ibid. This poem makes me think of David Eagleman's collection of forty short stories, *Sum*. Each of the stories imagines a different kind of afterlife, and while these scenarios are always interesting, the most powerful effect of the book is how each one of the imagined afterlives wakes us up to what is extraordinary about *this* life, and what you might already be missing out on. His story 'Circle of Friends', for instance, begins with the afterlife appearing almost the same as the life alive, with everyone familiar to you, until you realise this afterlife is made up *only* of people you've met before and have remembered – a tiny fraction of the world's population. The world comes to feel increasingly limited, you feel increasingly lonely and forlorn, but no one sympathises with you 'because this is precisely what you chose when you were alive'. *Sum: Forty Tales from the Afterlives* (Edinburgh: Canongate, 2009).

p. 204 'Strange fingers woke me, fumbling at my brow . . .', Alistair Elliot, 'A Touch of Death', in *Talking Back*.

p. 206 'I can't really presume to make a legacy for myself like that . . .', Tina Kelley, 'Boys and Bridges: sam sax's new collection, *Bury It*, is a queer coming-of-age story', Poetry Foundation, October 2018, www.poetryfoundation.org/articles/148003/boys-and-bridges

p. 206 '[T]he value or purpose or meaning of what we do here and now is diminished . . .', 'A Philosopher's "Afterlife": We May Die, But Others Live On', National Public Radio, October 2013, www.wbur.org/npr/230756192/a-philosophers-afterlife-we-may-die-but-others-live-on

p. 207 'To Hands I cannot see . . .', Emily Dickinson, 'This Is My Letter to the World', in *Emily Dickinson: The Complete Poems*.

p. 208 'O may I join the choir invisible . . .', George Eliot, 'O May I Join The Choir Invisible', in *The Works of George Eliot: Volume 10* (London and Edinburgh: Blackwood, 1901).

p. 208   '[A]n ardent public man . . .', George Eliot, *Middlemarch* (Oxford: Oxford University Press, 1998), p. 782.

p. 209   '[P]itched past pitch of grief . . .', Gerard Manley Hopkins, 'No Worst, There Is None', in *The Poems of Gerard Manley Hopkins* (Oxford: Oxford University Press, 1976).

p. 209   'For nothing now can come to any good . . .', W. H. Auden, 'Funeral Blues', in Denys Kilham Roberts and Geoffrey Grigson (eds), *The Year's Poetry* (London: Lane, 1938).

p. 209   '[P]ouring forth [its] soul abroad / In such an ecstasy . . .', John Keats, 'Ode to a Nightingale', in *John Keats: Complete Poems*.

THE POETS

p. 224   'D'Arcy Creswell wrote that "New Zealand poetry wasn't truly discovered until Ursula Bethell" . . .', D'Arcy Cresswell, 'Ursula Bethell: Some Personal Memories', *Landfall*, vol. 2, no. 4 (1948), p. 283. Cresswell himself was alluding to lines from a Bethell poem, 'Pause': 'When I am very earnestly digging / I lift my head sometimes, and look at the mountains', in Vincent O'Sullivan (ed.), *Ursula Bethell, Collected Poems* (Wellington: Victoria University Press, 2014).

p. 229   '"[A]n intellectually rigorous exploration of the postcolonial toll on land, love and people" . . .', 'Postcolonial Love Poem by Natalie Diaz Review – intimate, electric and defiant', *Guardian*, 18 August 2020.

p. 231 '"Poetry provides the one permissible way of saying one thing and meaning another" . . .', in *Robert Frost: Collected Poems, Prose and Plays* (New York: Library of America, 1995).

p. 236 'Her "Poetry" begins, 'I, too, dislike it . . .', complete text here: https//poets.org/poem/poetry

p. 237 'Oswald . . . described the poem as "passing through me" . . .', Max Porter, 'Interview with Alice Oswald', *White Review*, August 2014, www.thewhitereview.org/feature/interview-eith-alice-oswald

p. 242 'Self-described as a "continuator of Robert Frost", Richard Wilbur was an American poet who looked for patterns of order that could be found in . . . the "glorious energy of the universe" . . .', https://poets.org/text/great-wonder-richard-wilbur conversation

ACKNOWLEDGEMENTS

I would like to thank Sam Elworthy, Katharina Bauer, Sophia Broom and Lauren Donald at Auckland University Press for all they have done to support the publication of this book; particular thanks to Sam for his early belief in the possibility of a book coming together out of my notes on a lot of poems. Many of these notes on poems were initially presented to students of my poetry courses at Te Herenga Waka–Victoria University of Wellington, and I would like to thank those students for their interest, enthusiasm and contributions to my understandings of the poems. Thanks also to my colleague Nikki Hessell, whose early ideas for the course were inspiring and have in part shaped the arrangement of this book, and to my colleague Heidi Thomson and father MacDonald P. Jackson, who have both contributed to my understanding of the Keats poems discussed in this book. I am very grateful to the first readers of the manuscript, especially Paula Green, whose encouragement as well as her detailed and excellent advice were so important to me; Stephanie Burt and Michael Hulse both also offered early suggestions which did much to shape the form the book has taken. I am grateful, too, to the anonymous readers for Auckland University Press whose reports on the manuscript were extremely helpful. I would like to thank Jane Parkin for her brilliant and attentive editing, Hugh Williams for his remarkably efficient assistance with permissions and references, Charles Broughton for his very helpful assistance in compiling the notes on the poets, Matt Turner for his eagle-eyed proofread, Katie Kerr for the beautiful book design, and Simon Edmonds for applying the Anti-Flamme as the book neared completion.

Index

A

'Acorn Duly Crushed' 178–79, 271
'Across Brooklyn' 2–3, 14–18, 248
'After Apple-Picking' 14–16, 123, 248
'After Modernism' 72–73, 257
'After Sappho' 130–31, 133, 264
'Afterword' 183–87, 193, 199, 272
Aitken, Will 245
'all' 34
'America' 64–65, 179–80, 256, 271
'American Sonnet' 85
'American Sonnet for my Past and Future Assassin' 85–86, 258
American Sonnets for my Past and Future Assassin 85–86, 180, 258
'Ametas and Thestylis Making Hay-Ropes' 109, 261
aphorisms 68–69, 256–57
apples 14–16, 123, 248
'Are You a Real Literary Activist? Take the Quiz!' (blog post) 151–52, 268
arguments, in poetry 103–18
Arnold, Matthew 170, 270
'The Art of Poetry. No. 88' (interview) v, 245, 246
As Far as I Can See 34
Ascroft, Nick 90–92, 223
　'Five Limericks on Grief' 259
'Assimilation' 158–59, 269

'At the Bay' 131, 264
Atkinson, Tiffany 223
　'Aurelius' 265
　'Basia Mille' 136–37, 265
　'Catulla' 136, 265
　Catulla et al. 135–36, 265
Auden, W. H. 223
　'Funeral Blues' 209, 276
AUP New Poets 5 26, 249
'Aurelius' 265
Autumn 174, 270

B

'The Backward Glance' 266
Baldwin, James 145, 266
Balloon Pop Outlaw Black 155, 269
Barthes, Roland 118, 263
'Basia Mille' 136–37, 265
Batchelor, Brian 223
   'Dear Voyage' 165–67, 171, 269
Baxter, James K. 4, 188–90, 223–24
   Complete Prose (ed. J. E. Weir) 190
   'Jerusalem Sonnet 11' 188–90, 272
   'Jerusalem Sonnets' 188–89
   Letters of a Poet 190
Beard, Mary, *Women and Power* 159
Beckett, Samuel 25, 27, 224
   Waiting for Godot 25
Bede 202–3, 274
'Before Completion' 66–68, 256
'Being a Poet' 46–47, 253
Berry, Emily 224
   Dear Boy 167
   'Letter to Husband' 167–70, 269, 270
Bethell, Ursula 224, 276
   'Detail' 48–49, 253
   From a Garden in the Antipodes 48
Bird, Hera Lindsay 224–25
   Hera Lindsay Bird 35, 37–38, 251
   'Lost Scrolls' 35–37, 251
   'Monica' 4, 37–38, 251
   'Pain Imperatives' 37–38

birds, in poetry 138–40, 189–90, 201–2
Bishop, Elizabeth 88–90, 225
   'One Art' 89–90, 259
   'Sestina' 95, 260
'Blackouts' 35–36, 251
Blake, William 225
   'The Clod and the Pebble' 109, 261
   'The Sick Rose' 175–76, 271
Blanchfield, Brian 4–5, 180, 225
   'On Reset' (essay) 246
Bologna, Caroline 266
'Bored with Sex?' 262
Bornholdt, Jenny 225–26
   'Being a Poet' 46–47, 253
   'Confessional' 59, 254
   'In Memory' 47–48, 253
   'Photograph' 44–46, 252
Bowring, John 30–31
   'Coleridge and Poetry' 250
Brawne, Fanny 245
bridges 14–18, 228
Brontë, Emily 226
   'Spellbound' 9–11, 13, 21, 247
   Wuthering Heights 11
Brown, James, 'Cashpoint: A Pantoum' 92, 259
Brown, Jericho 226
   'Duplex' 86–88, 259

C

'Invention' 259
The Tradition 86–87
Burt, Stephanie 180–81, 226
   'Lucky Orestes (Epigram 60)' 181, 271
'Bury' 193–95, 273
Bury It 198, 206
Butler, Shane 140
   'The Backward Glance' 266

Callimachus 180–81
'The Cap and Bells; or, the Jealousies' 245
Carson, Anne 69, 226–27, 264
   'The Art of Poetry. No. 88' (interview) v, 5–6, 245, 246
   If Not, Winter 124–25
'The Cartoon's Mother Builds a House in Hammerspace' 155, 269
'Cashpoint: A Pantoum' 92, 259
'A Catalogue of What You Do Not Have' 19–20, 248
'Catulla' 136, 265
Catulla et al. 135–36, 265
Catullus 121, 125–29, 134–36, 145, 227
   'Odi et amo' 103
   poem 5 132, 264
   poem 7 132
   poem 51 125–29, 264
   poem 85 260
   'To Licinius' 261, 263
'The Chance' 70–71, 257
Charman, Janet 227
   'After Sappho' 130–31, 133, 264
   'Mrs Harry Kember, Remember' 130–31
   Rapunzel, Rapunzel 130–31

Chen Chen 2, 227
  'Irreducible Sociality' 2, 246
Christle, Heather 227
  'Acorn Duly Crushed' 178–79, 271
Ciardi, John 11–13
  How Does A Poem Mean? 247
Cixous, Hélène 202, 274
Clancy, Joseph P. 171–72
Clark, Charlie 228
  'Pseudo-Martyr' 200–201, 203, 205, 274
climate change, in poetry 148–52
'The Clod and the Pebble' 109, 261
'The Clodian Songbook' 134–36, 265
Clough, Arthur Hugh 170, 228
Coleman, Wanda, 'American Sonnet' 85
Coleridge, Samuel Taylor 38, 228, 250
  'The Eolian Harp' 107–9, 111, 261
  'Kubla Khan; or, a Vision in a Dream: A Fragment' 2, 30–33, 138, 250
'Coleridge and Poetry' 250
The Collected Prose of Robert Frost (ed. Mark Richardson) 4, 246
'The Computation' 196, 273
concision
  see simplicity
'Confessional' 59, 254

'Conversation with a Stone' 111–14, 262
conversations, in poetry 2, 27, 44–46, 50–52, 103–18, 121–43, 190, 206–7
Cookhouse 71–72
couplets 18, 73, 77, 204
  see also sonnets
Covid-19 19–20
Cox, Jo 146
Cox, Sidney 14, 247
'Coy Mistress' 3, 116–18, 121, 262
Crane, Hart 228
  'To Brooklyn Bridge' 17–18
Creswell, D'Arcy 276
'Crossing Brooklyn Ferry' 17–18, 61–62, 255, 256
Culler, Jonathan 261, 271
  Theory of the Lyric 175–76, 245–46
Cumberbatch, Benedict 33

D

Dante 200
  The Divine Comedy 201
dear, in poetry 165–68, 171, 178–79
Dear Boy 167
'Dear Voyage' 165–67, 171, 269
death & grief 1–2, 9–16, 14–19,
  90–92, 183–209, 274–75
  see also loss; sleep
Democoon 55–56
'Detail' 48–49, 253
'A Dialogue between the Soul
  and the Body' 109–10, 111, 261
Diaz, Natalie 228–29
  'My Brother at 3 A.M.' 93–95, 259
  Postcolonial Love Poem 276
Dickinson, Emily 5, 117, 121,
  229, 263
  '"Hope" Is the Thing with Feathers'
    194, 273
  'This is My Letter to the World'
    207, 275
Disch, Tom 229
  'Ode to a Blizzard' 177–78, 271
The Divine Comedy 201
Donne, John 229
  'The Computation' 196, 273
  'The Flea' 2, 104–5, 109, 260
  'The Funeral' 195, 273
  'Pseudo-Martyr' 200–201
  'The Relic' 195–96, 198, 273
  'The Sun Rising' 196, 198, 273
  'The Will' 196–98, 273
Dr Seuss 47
Duggan, Eileen 229
  'The Tides Run Up the Wairau'
    20–21, 248
duplexes 86–88
'Duplex' 86–88, 259

E

Eageleman, David, *Sum* 274–75
'Edge' 187–88, 272
'Education of the Poet'
    (essay) 184–85, 199, 272
Eliot, George 230
    Middlemarch 208, 276
    The Mill on the Floss 208
    'O May I Join the Choir Invisible'
        207–9, 275
Elliot, Alistair 230
    Talking Back 202–5
    'Talking to Bede' 202–3, 274–75
    'Talking to Horace' 202–3, 274
    'A Touch of Death' 203–5, 275
Emerson, Ralph Waldo 62, 255
    'The Eolian Harp' 107–9, 111, 261

F

Finch, Annie 230, 263
    'Coy Mistress' 3, 116–18, 121, 262
'First Will and Testament' 198
'The fish' 78–81, 258
'Five Limericks on Grief' 259
'The Flea' 104–5, 109, 260
For the Love of Letters 171
Ford, Mark 230
    'Viewless Wings' 138–42, 158,
        201, 265
form, in poetry 77–101
Fragment 31 124–25, 263
'freshly picked blueberries' 71, 257
From a Garden in the Antipodes 48
Frost, Robert 231, 247, 277
    'After Apple-Picking' 14–16,
        123, 248
    The Collected Prose of Robert Frost
        (ed. Mark Richardson) 4, 246
    'The Prerequisites' 4, 246
    'Stopping by Woods on a Snowy
        Evening' 3, 11–14, 21, 122–23, 247
    'To Sydney Cox' 247
'The Funeral' 195, 273
'Funeral Blues' 209, 276

G

'The Garden' 110–11, 262

gardens & gardening 30–33, 47–48, 110–11

gender 52–53, 99, 135

   see also identity politics

Ginsberg, Allen 63–65, 69, 231

   'America' 64–65, 179–80, 256, 271

   Howl (LP) 255

   'Howl' 63

   'A Supermarket in California' 63–64, 255

Glover, Denis 190

   'The Magpies' 272

Glück, Louise 190, 206, 231

   'Afterword' 183–87, 193, 199, 272

   'Education of the Poet' (essay) 184–85, 199, 272

God

   see religion, in poetry

Goldberg, Mike 49–50

'Good Bones' 146–47, 266–67

'Good People' 148–49, 267

Green, Paula 231

   'After Modernism' 72–73, 257

   Cookhouse 71–72

   'freshly picked blueberries' 257

   'Letter to Anne Kennedy' 71–74, 257

   Making Lists for Frances Hodgkins 72

Gu Cheng 70

H

Harris, Diana 232, 264

   'Lovely   I have none' 129–30

Hauck, Emma & Mark 170, 270

Hawkes, Rebecca 2, 4, 232

   'softcore coldsores' (poetry selection) 26, 249

   'Technicolour Dreamcake' 26–27, 249

Hayes, Terrance 3, 232

   'American Sonnet for my Past and Future Assassin' 85–86, 258

   American Sonnets for my Past and Future Assassin 85–86, 180, 258

'Helix' 34–35, 251

Hensher, Philip, *The Missing Ink* 171

Hera Lindsay Bird 35, 37–38, 251

Hipparchia 159–62

Hirsch, Edward, *How to Read a Poem and Fall in Love with Poetry* 9–11, 246–47

His Dark Materials 59

Homer 227, 239

   Iliad 55–56, 59

'"Hope" Is the Thing with Feathers' 194, 273

Hopkins, Gerard Manley, 'No worst, there is none' 209, 276

Horace 202–3, 232, 270, 274

   'O fons Bandusiae' 171–72

'Horse' 172–74, 270

I

horses, in poetry 3, 11–14, 172–74, 270
Hotere, Ralph 50–52
'Hotere' 50–52
How Does A Poem Mean? 247
'How to Cook the Head' 19
'How to Kill a Hen' 19
How to Read a Poem and Fall in Love with Poetry 9–11, 246–47
Howell, Rebecca Gayle 232–33
    'A Catalogue of What You Do Not Have' 19–20, 248
'Howl' 63

iambic metres 12, 31–32, 42, 77, 81–82, 90, 99, 107, 204
    see also metre
identity politics 152–53
    see also gender
'Identity Politics' 153, 268
'The Idylls of the King' 14
If Not, Winter 124–25
Iliad 55–56, 59
imagery 2, 13, 20, 35, 38, 55, 69, 72, 81, 86, 116–17, 138–39, 141–43, 149–50, 188, 216, 237, 242
'In a Station of the Metro' 42–43, 49, 72–73, 252
'In Memory' 47–48, 253
internet
    see social media
'Invention' 259
'Irreducible Sociality' 2, 246
Isaiah 22.1 142, 158
Ishiguro, Kazuo
    'For me, England is a mythical place' (*Guardian* article) 267
    Never Let Me Go 147–48, 151, 267

J

Jackson, Anna 5, 249, 264
Jackson, MacDonald P., *All the Sonnets of Shakespeare* 249
James K. Baxter: Complete Prose (ed. J. E. Weir) 190
Jane, Ash Davida 3, 233
   'Good People' 148–49, 267
Jansen, Adrienne
   'The Rain and the Spade' 109, 261
Jarmusch, Jim, *Paterson* (film) 5
Jekyll, Gertrude 48, 253
'Jerusalem Sonnet 11' 188–90, 272
Jochems, Annaleese 233
   'Horse' 172–74, 270
Jonson, Ben 136, 233
   'Song to Celia' 132–34, 264
   'To the Same' 133–34, 265
Justice, Donald, 'Pantoum of the Great Depression' 92–93

K

Kaur, Rupi 145
Keats, John 1–2, 25, 38–39, 191, 193, 233, 248
   'The Cap and Bells; or, the Jealousies' 245
   'Ode on Melancholy' 141, 266
   'Ode to a Nightingale' 2, 33–34, 138, 140–42, 201, 251, 266, 276
   'This Living Hand' 1, 190, 203–5, 245, 246–47
   'When I Have Fears That I May Cease to Be' 190–91, 192, 272
Kelley, Tina 275
Kennard, Luke 234
   'Wolf Nationalist' 2, 115–16, 262
   'Wolf on the Couch' 2, 114–15, 262
Kennedy, Anne, *The Time of the Giants* 74–75, 257
Kermode, Frank 149
Kind Regards, The Lost Art of Letter-Writing 171
King Lear 27
'Kubla Khan; or, a Vision in a Dream: A Fragment' 2, 30–33, 138, 250

L

Lamb, Charles 250
Leaves of Grass 60
'Lebh' 34
Leggott, Michele 234
   'all' 34
   As Far as I Can See 34
   'Helix' 34–35, 251
   'Lebh' 34
   'Snake and Jewel' 34
Leidner, Mark 234
   'Blackouts' 35–36, 251
'Letter to Anne Kennedy' 71–74, 257
'Letter to Husband' 167–70, 269, 270
letters & letter writing 165–81, 207
Letters of a Poet 190
Leukos 55–56
Li Po, 'The Song of Ch'ang-kan' 168–69
Licinius 121
'Like, the Sestina' 99–100
limericks 90–92
   'Five Limericks on Grief' 259
'Linens' 54–55, 254
listening, to poetry 32–33
Lockwood, Patricia 234, 268
   Balloon Pop Outlaw Black 155, 269
   'The Cartoon's Mother Builds a House in Hammerspace' 155, 269
   'Rape Joke' 154–58, 268
loss 19, 29, 34, 48, 54, 70, 87–90
   see also death & grief
'Lost Scrolls' 35–37, 251
love, in poetry 20, 26–29, 82–83, 85–86, 99–100, 104–7, 116–18, 124–38, 149–52, 167–70, 195–98
'Love Poems in a Time of Climate Change: Sonnet XVII' 150–51, 268
Lovelace, Richard 234
   'To Althea, from Prison' 165–66, 269
'Lovely   I have none' 129–30
'Lucky Orestes (Epigram 60)' 271
Lucretia 95–99
lyric address 19, 107, 126, 164–80
lyric poetry 18, 25–39, 108, 171–72, 175, 178, 245–46

M

'The Magpies' 272
Majmudar, Amit 170–71
 'Our Hidden Contemporaries'
  (*The Dark Horse* article) 270
Making Lists for Frances Hodgkins 72
Manguso, Sarah 68, 235, 256
Manhire, Bill 4, 235
 'Across Brooklyn' 2–3, 14–18, 248
Mansfield, Katherine 191–92, 273
 'At the Bay' 264
Marlowe, Christopher
 'The Passionate Shepherd to
  his Love' 136–37, 265
Marvell, Andrew 235
 'Ametas and Thestylis Making
  Hay-Ropes' 109, 261
 'A Dialogue between the Soul and
  the Body' 109–10, 111, 261
 'The Garden' 110–11, 262
 'To His Coy Mistress' 3, 106–7,
  109, 110, 116, 118, 151, 261
McGhee, John 68, 256
Memorial 55–56
Mendelsohn, Daniel 128, 264
Mertins, Louis 13
 Robert Frost: Life and Talks-Walking
  247
metaphor 14, 19, 21, 42, 55, 75, 86,
 140, 151, 170, 216, 229

#MeToo 157, 161
metre 2, 31–32, 44, 46, 48, 81, 105,
 117, 131, 134, 170, 201
 see also rhymes & rhyming
Middlemarch 208, 276
A Midsummer Night's Dream 27
The Mill on the Floss 208
Millay, Edna St Vincent 84, 235–36
 'What lips my lips have kissed, and
  where, and why' 81–85, 258
Milton, John, *Paradise Lost* 59
Minnis, Chelsey 235–36
 Poemland 37, 251
The Missing Ink 171
'Monica' 4, 37–38, 251
Moore, Marianne 78–81, 236
 'Poetry' 236, 277
 'The fish' 78–81, 258
mortality
 see death & grief
'Mrs Harry Kember, Remember'
 130–31
'My Brother at 3 A.M.' 93–95, 259

N

narrative, in poetry 11, 41, 49, 55–56, 68, 77, 93, 95–98, 112, 130–31, 140, 160–61, 180–81, 201–2
Neruda, Pablo
  'One Hundred Love Sonnets' 150–51
  'One Hundred Love Sonnets: XVII' 150–51, 267
Never Let Me Go 147–48, 151, 267
New Zealand Listener 71
'No worst, there is none' 209, 276
'Notes on the Unsilent Woman' 159–62, 269

O

'O fons Bandusiae' 171–72
'O May I Join the Choir Invisible' 207–9, 275
O & Oh, in poetry 171–79
O'Connell, John, *For the Love of Letters* 171
odes 107–9, 165–81, 261
  'Dear Voyage' 165–67, 171, 269
  'The Eolian Harp' 107–9, 111
  'Horse' 172–74, 270
  'Ode on Melancholy' 141, 266
  'Ode to a Blizzard' 177–78, 271
  'Ode to a Nightingale' 2, 33–34, 138, 140–42, 201, 251, 266, 276
  'Spoon Ode' 176, 271
'Odi et amo' 103
'Ofc Bella and Gigi read BOOKS they are MODELS . . .' (tweet) 152, 268
O'Hara, Frank 145, 236
  'Oranges' 50
  'Personism: A Manifesto' 103, 260
  'A Step Away from Them' 195, 273
  'Why I Am Not a Painter' 49–50, 253
Olds, Sharon 236
  'Spoon Ode' 176, 271
'On Reset' (essay) 246
'One Art' 259
'One Hundred Love Sonnets' 150–51

'One Hundred Love Sonnets: XVII' 150–51, 267
'Oranges' 50
Orestes 180, 271
Orpheus 139–40, 201–2
Oswald, Alice 3, 236–37, 277
 Memorial 55–56, 254
'Our Hidden Contemporaries' (*The Dark Horse* article) 270
Ovid 140, 266

P

Padgett, Ron 237
'Pain Imperatives' 37–38
pantoums 88, 92–95, 259
 'Cashpoint: A Pantoum' 92, 259
 'Pantoum of the Great Depression' 92–93
Paper: An Elegy 171
Paradise Lost 59
Paris Review 5–6
'The Passionate Shepherd to his Love' 136–37, 265
Paterson 63, 251
Paterson (film) 5, 237
Pen America Prison Writing Competition 165
Perez, Craig Santos 149–52, 237
 'Are You a Real Literary Activist? Take the Quiz!' (blog post) 151–52, 268
 'Love Poems in a Time of Climate Change: Sonnet XVII' 150–51, 268
Perry, Ayleen 68, 70, 256, 257
'Personism: A Manifesto' 103, 260
Phillips, Adam 114, 116
 'Bored with Sex?' 262
'Photograph' 252
Plath, Sylvia 237
 'Edge' 187–88, 272
poem 5 264

R

poem 7 132
poem 51 264
poem 85 260
Poemland 37, 251
Postcolonial Love Poem 229, 276
Poūkahangatus 152–54, 241
Pound, Ezra 41, 68, 71, 149, 238, 252
  'In a Station of the Metro' 42–43, 49, 72–73, 252
  'The River Merchant's Wife: A Letter' 168–70, 269
  'Vorticism' 252
'Pseudo-Martyr' 200–201, 203, 205, 274
Public Radio International 146
Pullman, Philip, *His Dark Materials* 59
Pylades 180

'The Rain and the Spade' 109, 261
ranapiri, essa may 238
  ransack 53, 254
  'she cut her face shaving' 52–53, 254
ransack 53, 254
'Rape Joke' 154–58, 268
Rapunzel, Rapunzel 130–31
reading, poetry 4–5, 9–10, 9–12, 74–75
reciting, poetry 32–33
'The Red Wheelbarrow' 5, 43–44, 49, 252
'The Relic' 195–96, 198, 273
religion, in poetry 62, 93–94, 108, 142, 188–90
Render: An Apocalypse 19
resonance, in poetry 9–23
rhymes & rhyming 12–13, 21–23, 54–55, 60–61, 107, 204, 263
  see also metre
Richardson, Mark, *The Collected Prose of Robert Frost* 4, 246
Richardson, Ralph 33
Rickerby, Helen 3–4, 238
  'Notes on the Unsilent Woman' 159–62, 269
'The Ride' 3, 121–24, 138, 263
'The River Merchant's Wife: A Letter' 168–70, 269

romance
see love, in poetry
Ryan, Kay 59–60, 238–39
 'Confessional' 254
 'Linens' 54–55, 254

S

Samuel Beckett 25
 Waiting for Godot 25
Sansom, Ian, *Paper: An Elegy* 171
Sappho 124–33, 239
 Fragment 31 124–25, 263
sax, sam 198–200, 206–7, 239, 274
 'Bury' 193–95, 273
 Bury It 198, 206
 'First Will and Testament' 198
 'sonnet' 83–85, 258
 'Will' 198, 200, 274
Scheffler, Samuel 206
Scudder, Erin 239
 'Sextina' 95–99, 260
Sernaker, Emily 200, 274
sestinas 77, 88, 95–100, 260
 'Like, the Sestina' 99–100, 260
 'Sestina' 95, 260
'Sextina' 95–99, 260
Sextus Tarquinius 95–99
sexual harassment & rape 95–99, 154–58, 161
Shakespeare, William 194, 198, 239, 249–50
 King Lear 27
 A Midsummer Night's Dream 27
 Sonnet 18 192–93, 273
 Sonnet 73 82–93
 Sonnet 148 193, 273

sonnets 27–29, 38, 82–84
'she cut her face shaving' 52–53, 254
'The Sick Rose' 175–76, 271
simile 35–37, 56, 72, 202, 219
simplicity 9–23, 41–56
sleep 14–16
   see also death & grief
Smith, Ali, *Autumn* 174, 270
Smith, Maggie 240
   'Good Bones' 146–47, 266–67
'Snake and Jewel' 34
social media 100, 145–63, 207, 250
'softcore coldsores' (poetry selection) 26, 249
'The Song of Ch'ang-kan' 168–69
'Song of Myself' 255
'The Song of Wandering Aengus' 3, 9, 22–23, 246, 248
'Song to Celia' 132–34, 264
Sonnet 18 192–93, 273
Sonnet 73 82–93
Sonnet 148 193, 273
'sonnet' 83–85, 258
sonnets 27–29, 38, 77–78, 81–87, 149–52, 180, 188–90, 192–93, 249–50, 258–59
   see also couplets
   'American Sonnet' 85

'American Sonnet for my Past and Future Assassin' 85–86, 258
American Sonnets for my Past and Future Assassin 85–86, 180, 258
'Jerusalem Sonnet 11' 188–90, 272
'Jerusalem Sonnets' 188–89
'Love Poems in a Time of Climate Change: Sonnet XVII' 150–51, 268
'No worst, there is none' 209
'One Hundred Love Sonnets' 150–51, 267
'One Hundred Love Sonnets: XVII' 150–51, 267
Sonnet 18 192–93, 273
Sonnet 73 82–93
Sonnet 148 193, 273
'sonnet' 83–85, 258
'What lips my lips have kissed, and where, and why' 81–85, 258
'Spellbound' 9–11, 13, 21, 247
Spender, Stephen 41
'Spoon Ode' 176, 271
Stallings, A. E. 77, 81, 240
   'Like, the Sestina' 99–100, 260
   'Women in Form: A E Stallings' (interview) 258
Star Waka 153–54
Stead, C. K. 240
   'The Clodian Songbook' 134–36, 265

T

'A Step Away from Them' 195, 273
'Stopping by Woods on a Snowy Evening' 3, 11–14, 21, 122–23, 247
stories
   see narrative, in poetry
Sullivan, Robert 153
   Star Waka 153–54
   'Waka 58 Waitangi Day' 268
Sum 274–75
'The Sun Rising' 196, 198, 273
'A Supermarket in California' 63–64, 255
Sze, Arthur 66–68, 69, 240, 256, 257
   'Before Completion' 66–71, 256
   'The Chance' 70–71, 257
Szymborska, Wisława 241
   'Conversation with a Stone' 111–14, 262

Talking Back 202–5
'Talking to Bede' 202–3, 274–75
'Talking to Horace' 202–3, 274
'Technicolour Dreamcake' 26–27, 249
Tennyson, Alfred, 'The Idylls of the King' 14
Terrain 68, 70
Theodorus 160
Theory of the Lyric 175–76, 245–46
These Days 253
'This Is Just to Say' 83, 258
'This is My Letter to the World' 207
'This Living Hand' 1, 190, 203–5, 245, 246–47
Thunberg, Greta 148
   'Our house is on fire' (*Guardian* article) 267
Tibble, Tayi 4, 152–54, 241, 254
   'Assimilation' 158–59, 269
   'Identity Politics' 153, 268
   'Ofc Bella and Gigi read BOOKS they are MODELS . . .' (tweet) 152, 268
   Poūkahangatus 152–54, 241
'The Tides Run Up the Wairau' 20–21, 248
The Time of the Giants 74–75, 257
'To Althea, from Prison' 165–66, 269
'To Brooklyn Bridge' 17–18

V

'To His Coy Mistress' 3, 106–7, 109, 110, 116, 118, 151, 261
'To Licinius' 261, 263
'To Sydney Cox' 247
'To the Same' 133–34, 265
'A Touch of Death' 203–5, 275
tourism 17–18
The Tradition 86–87
translating & translations 55, 124–32, 137–38, 140, 171–72, 180, 202
Tuwhare, Hone 241
   'Hotere' 50–52, 253

Vanity Fair 83
Vergil 140
'Viewless Wings' 138–42, 158, 201, 265
villanelles 77, 88–90, 92, 95, 255
   'One Art' 77
'Vorticism' 252

W

Waitangi Day & the Treaty 153–54
Waiting for Godot 25
'Waka 58 Waitangi Day' 268
Waxwing 146
'Westron Wynde' 20, 248
'What lips my lips have kissed, and where, and why' 81–85, 258
'When I Have Fears That I May Cease to Be' 190–91, 192, 272
Whitman, Walt 59–63, 63–64, 66, 69, 241–42, 254–55
   'Crossing Brooklyn Ferry' 17–18, 61–62, 255, 256
   Leaves of Grass 60
   'Song of Myself' 255
'Why I Am Not a Painter' 49–50, 253
Wilbur, Richard 242, 263, 277
   'The Ride' 3, 121–24, 138, 263
'Will' 198, 200, 274
'The Will' 196–98, 273
Williams, Liz, *Kind Regards, The Lost Art of Letter-Writing* 171
Williams, Miller, *How Does A Poem Mean?* 247
Williams, William Carlos 5, 41, 46, 47, 63, 68, 78, 242, 255, 258
   Paterson 63, 251
   'The Red Wheelbarrow' 5, 43–44, 49, 252
   'This Is Just to Say' 83, 258
'Wolf Nationalist' 2, 115–16, 262
'Wolf on the Couch' 2, 114–15, 262
women, silenced 159–62
Women and Power 159
'Women in Form: A E Stallings' (interview) 258
Woolf, Virginia 191
   The Diary of Virginia Woolf 272
Wordsworth, William 242
Wuthering Heights 11

Y

Yeats, William Butler 242–43
'The Song of Wandering Aengus'
3, 9, 22–23, 246, 248

Z

Zweig, George 70

Anna Jackson is a New Zealand poet who grew up in Auckland and now lives in Island Bay, Wellington. She has a DPhil from Oxford and is an associate professor in English literature at Victoria University of Wellington.

Anna made her poetry debut in *AUP New Poets 1* before publishing six collections with Auckland University Press. Her most recent book, *Pasture and Flock: New and Selected Poems*, gathers work from her previous collections as well as twenty-five new poems. The book includes poems from *Catullus for Children* and *I, Clodia*, the two collections that engage with the work of Catullus, as well as poems about badminton, billiards, salty hair, takahē, head lice, indexing, proof-reading, hens, truth and beauty.

As a scholar, Anna Jackson is the author of *Diary Poetics: Form and Style in Writers' Diaries 1915–1962* (Routledge, 2010) and, with Charles Ferrall, *Juvenile Literature and British Society, 1850–1950: The Age of Adolescence* (Routledge, 2009).